What Audrey Did Next

All About Audrey
II

What Audrey Did Next

by George Logan

What Audrey Did Next

All about Audrey II
by
George Logan

ISBN: 9798692950208

All Rights Reserved
Copyright © George Logan 2020

This book is sold subject to the condition that it shall not, by way of trade or otherwise, be resold or otherwise circulated without the publisher's prior consent in any form or binding other than that in which it is published.

No part of this book may be replicated without the publisher's prior permission.

Big Aud Books

39 Avenue de Verdun
87210 Le Dorat
France

Dedication

For Tommy

'Hold your hat, hang onto your soul
Something's coming to eat the world whole
Look out! Here comes Audrey Two
Look out! Here I come for you'
Little Shop of Horrors
© Howard Ashman 1982

Contents

1. Dream Lover — 1
2. And Then He Kissed Me — 24
3. Teenager in Love — 49
4. A House is Not a Home — 72
5. Jail-house Rock — 97
6. Standing on the Corner — 119
7. It's My Party — 133
8. Marry Me — 157
9. Hats Off to Larry — 180
10. Down the Aisle — 207
11. We Gotta Get Out of This Place — 234
12. The Carnival is Over — 256

Preface to the Second Edition

September 2020

I was highly delighted to find that such a large number of people who read the original version of '**A Boy Called Audrey**' seemed to have enjoyed the experience. I wrote it for myself essentially, but did anticipate that it might possibly provide amusement to some others. This, it appears, has been the case. More, I gather from some of the reactions I have received that, as well as diversion, it has provided a degree of instruction here and there; which is more than I had hoped for.

One negative point that was made now and then was a technical one. Since it appears, unsurprisingly, that a fair proportion of my readers are of my own generation, with eyesight that is, to put it kindly, not that of a teenager, I did receive a few complaints that the type size was on the small side.

This I endeavoured to correct; to discover that increasing the font size by one point made the total length of the book over five hundred pages. Now, I enjoy immersing myself in a long tome as much as anyone else, but for what is essentially a light read I felt the length was excessive. In addition, I wanted to add to the book here and there - there were a few incidents and stories I had left out in the interests of concision. But I realised that if I were to split the book in two, I would be able to be even more self-indulgent then previously. It would also allow me to correct a few errors that had crept into the original; and to re-work the cover art which I had come to dislike.

Then there was the question of a sequel. I had originally planned one, then decided that it was unnecessary. But a fair number of my readers indicated that they definitely wanted one.

And somehow it got written anyway. Well, rather, it is nearly finished.

Then I decided that the series title I didn't like; there were health issues; musical matters took up a lot of my time; I got married to my partner of twenty years; the other series of books I have been working on - '**Evadne's Odyssey**' - demanded a sequel too.

And as a result, Audrey got left on the back burner.

But now I have decided that if it is ever to see completion, I need to take it up again and formulate it better. So, for those interested enough to read this far, this is how matters currently stand:

'All About Audrey' I - 'I, Audrey'
The first half of the original book with revisions and additional material

'All About Audrey' II - 'What Audrey Did Next'
The second half of the original book with revisions and additional material

'All About Audrey III' - 'Turn Again, Audrey'

'All About Audrey IV' - 'Forever Audrey'

If you have already read the original 2015 '**A Boy Called Audrey**', there is really no need to read the first two above - although they do contain a fair bit of new material, some of it, I venture to think, likely to entertain,

I will be removing the original 2015 book from sale, as the 'new' volumes represent my definite and final thoughts on the strange creature I became/invented.

I really need to finish this!

For anyone curious about the progress of '**Evadne's Odyssey**', the second book - '**The Doctor Up The Front**' - is well on its way and will appear… Sometime soon.

George Logan
Le Dorat
France

1. Dream Lover

> Ev'ry night I hope and pray
> A dream lover will come my way
> That's the only thing to do
> Till all my lovin' dreams come true.
> *Bobby Darin, 1959*

Is there? Something wrong with me, that is? It certainly looks that way. But it's not as if I have been heretofore unsuccessful in the Courts of Love. Indeed, far from it.

So what's going on here? Come on, it's about due. Where is love? Indeed, *what* is love? Have I ever experienced it?

I consider my past *liaisons*.

There was the first, Andy. Andy the Unknown. Andy X. Was it cruel just to abandon him as I did? I suppose it was. I remember feeling a huge surge of pity when he finally told me about his tragic past, his history of incarceration and 'aversion therapy'. Pity, nothing more. And pity is not, I instinctively understand, a healthy foundation for love. In any case, Andy and I had hardly got to that stage. The truth is, I barely knew him.

Then Bobby Savage. '*He was nice, Bobby*', I think to myself. Nice, yes; but God, he was dull. I fancied him, and liked him at first. Indeed, I continued to like him even after I ceased to fancy him. He was irresistibly likeable, Bobby. I *still* like him. I see him regularly, always with his current *inamorata*, Vera Ellen. Vera certainly seems to love him, and he her.

Nice for them.

The Three Stooges. Big George - well, that was a sudden infatuation, and a fleeting one. When harsh reality kicked in, I found that not only did I not love him, I didn't even like him.

Red-haired Billy, on the other hand, I liked immensely. And I can't deny that the fact that he was, at the time of our involvement, 'on the run', lent an exciting edge, a piquancy, to our fling. And Bill liked me, I know. But our intimacy was no more than a pleasant way of passing a few days. No deeper feelings on either side. An almost ideal interlude.

The third of the trio, Brian, when I consider it, meant more than that. It wasn't a serious affair - indeed, it was so brief I'm not sure it should even count as an affair at all. But there was something there, something more. Love? I don't think so. It never got that far. But maybe it could have been the beginning of love.

There remains the question of Nicky. If I have ever loved anyone, surely it was he? I was mad about him. I thought of him constantly, yearned for him, fantasised over him. I am still able, now and then, to re-evoke these feelings, that passionate hungry longing, like a phantom of the past, when I am in his company. But the fact that this conjuration now takes an increasingly more conscious effort reveals the fundamental shallowness of my attachment. That was an obsession, it wasn't love.

So, gather the facts. Analyse, collate, and organise them into a pattern. Consider the results of these calculations.

The conclusion is irrefutable. I have never yet known love. QED.

But I want to. To love, to *be* loved. I want that more than anything.

Dream Lover, where are you?

August 1963.

It's Friday the ninth. But it feels more like Friday the thirteenth. Angie is still cloistered in Drumchapel, mourning her faithless lover, so I am on my own.

Nine o' clock, and I'm in *Guy's*. I would rather be in the *Strand*, which is my favourite pub, but I'm currently *persona non grata* there. There is no particular reason for this. Robert the Bastard, head barman, has a habit of barring someone or other now and then for no discernible reason. It just happens to be my turn. I didn't do anything particular to merit it. You don't have to. It's true that for some reason he doesn't like me, but then he doesn't really like anybody. I'm not sure what this ill-natured and presumably straight man is doing running a gay bar, anyone less appropriate would be hard to find. He is permanently disgruntled, hates his customers, and this is his petty revenge, his little show of power. In a week or two I will go back there and nothing will be said. Just got to wait it out.

Guy's is dead. It's holiday time, so a lot of the regulars are away, only a few familiar faces are clustered round the bar. No-one I particularly want to talk to. I am nursing my first lager and lime, wondering if I should just go home. I wave, and mouth a *hello* to Judy Garland, who is standing at the other end of the bar with her sister Bridie Gallacher.

The door bangs open and in comes Kay Starr, in the inevitable brown Crombie, and with the inevitable miserable expression on her face. She stands next to me at the bar.

"Awright, Audrey? Hot night, isn't it."

"Yes, isn't it? How are you, Kay?" I don't point out that she would be cooler without that heavy coat.

She orders a pint of beer. She sighs.

"A bit down, Audrey, tae tell ye the truth. Ma birthday the day, the big one."

"Oh?"

"Aye, thirty." Kay is at least forty. "Terrible, isn't it?"

"Oh well, many happy returns, anyway. I must say, you don't look thirty."

That is certainly true.

She brightens up momentarily. "Thanks, Audrey, that's cheered me up a bit. Drink?"

"No thanks, Kay, I'm fine. Enjoy your evening."

"Aye, Ah'll try. Vivien should be in later."

She moves off, once more sunk in gloom.

Nine thirty. The place has filled up a bit. I am aware of someone standing behind me.

"Can Ah get ye a drink?"

I turn round. It's no-one I know. A rough-looking man in his late twenties, not tall, greasy hair, pot-belly, in a cheap double-breasted suit that might have fitted him when he was eighteen. Now the waistcoat buttons are straining round his gut.

Oh hell, why not?

"Thanks. I'll have a gin and orange."

I'm getting sick of the taste of lager and lime.

"Sure, doll."

My drink arrives.

"Cheers, thanks," I say.

"Nae problem, doll."

We drink in silence for a moment or two. Suddenly, he leans close to me.

"Huv ye goat a place tae go? Jist you an' me?"

He caresses his crotch. "Ah'd love tae pit this here right up your shiter."

Among the many gross remarks I have heard in the last year or two, this has to be the grossest. Indeed, it is so hideously vulgar it is ridiculous. I all but collapse in slightly hysterical laughter.

The idiot smiles, thinking he has delivered some devastating witticism.

He leans closer, breathing whiskey fumes over me. "So, whit dae ye say, doll, eh?"

I pull myself together. "I say, *'Why don't you get lost?'* "

His jaw drops.

I start to turn away. "Go on, fuck off."

He grabs my shoulder. "Whit? Here, you, Ah've jist bought ye a drink. What makes ye think ye can talk tae me like that?"

I am all of a sudden furiously angry. I put my glass down and turn back to face him.

"Listen, you, if you know what's good for you, you'll disappear right now, do you hear me?"

Now, I am no battler, that's understood. But in this place I have support. And right on cue back-up arrives behind me.

"Aye, that's right, you heard. Fuck off, pal, OK?"

My white knight to the rescue. Alec McGowan. I haven't seen him in a while.

Shiter-man shuffles off, muttering to himself.

"Ignorant bastard, speakin' tae a lady like that," says Alec, indignant, pulling out the stool next to mine. "Ah don't know whit this toon's comin' tae."

I notice my would-be suitor move further down the bar to exercise his charms on Judy Garland.

Good luck, I think. I know Judy well, and I like her, but she is a devious character. And she makes no secret of her bedroom preferences. If Mr Cheap Suit ends up with her, he'd better look out for his own shiter.

"Thanks, Alec," I say.

"Nae problem, nae problem," says Alec. "Get us a drink, gawn—Ah'm skint."

"Sure, Alec—a pint?"

"Aye, thanks, hen."

I order his drink.

"So how are you, Alec? Not seen you in a while. Everything OK?"

He sighs, puts his elbows on the bar, and sinks his chin in his hands.

"No' really, Audrey. Helluva week. Wan thing an' another."

God, why is everybody so down this evening?

I try to lighten the atmosphere.

"Don't tell me you've finally got Big Olivia pregnant, Alec? God knows, you've been trying long enough, and I've always thought of you two as natural parents."

But he refuses to be diverted.

"Naw, naw, Olivia's fine. It's Connie that's the problem."

"Oh?"

"Aye, Connie. Connie Stevens."

He heaves himself onto the stool.

"Ye know her and Wilma huv goat this flat, in the toon?"

I nod.

"Well, like an eedjit, Ah said Ah wid help Connie move in, gie her a hand wi' her stuff. Maybe dae a wee bit of decorating jist tae help oot. Yon place is a tip."

Of course, I already know all this. But Alec doesn't know I know.

"Oh? That was nice of you, Alec."

He shakes his head and looks away, pensive. "Aye, well, Ah wish Ah'd kept ma big mooth shut."

He turns back, picking up his story. "So Ah gets there, right? Ah've borrowed a van tae move her gear. Wilma's oot. So Ah gets up the stairs, in the door, laden doon wi' claes an' junk. A couple of trips, and Ah finally get aw' her stuff unloaded. An' she says—Connie— dae Ah want a drink."

I smile to myself. '*Ah, yes, good so far.*'

"So Ah says '*Aye, OK, Connie, thanks.*' So Ah sits doon, an' she pours me a wee whisky."

"Very hospitable, Connie," I say.

"Aye. So we're chattin' away aboot this an' that. Ah finish ma drink, she gets me a top-up. An' Ah'm thinkin' '*Ah shouldnae really be drinkin', wi' the van an' that.*' But ye know how it is, a bevy's a bevy."

Yes, I know how it is.

"She's no' drinkin', Connie. Well, Ah've jist picked up the bottle an' ma glass tae pour masel' another… An' suddenly, she's oan me like a vampire! Undoin' ma belt, kissin' me, unbuttonin' ma shirt. An' Ah cannae dae a thing, ma hauns are full."

He puts his head on one side, shrugs, and gives me a '*what's-a-guy-to-do?*' face.

"An'—well, ye know how it is, Audrey, Ah'm a gentleman. Ah mean, she's been after me for months."

No. For years.

'*Well, three cheers for Connie,*' I think. '*Sounds like she finally got Alec's trousers off.*'

"An' now it's every bloody day. She cannae get enough. She's…"

He hesitates, lost for the word. "She's in…"

"Insatiable?"

"Naw, in bed, usually."

He heaves an enormous sigh. "Ah'm worn out, so Ah am."

I have to smile at Alec's self-pitying distress.

"Well—why don't you just stay out of her way?"

"Aye, Ah could, Ah suppose. But, thing is, I kind of like Connie, Audrey. An' Ah don't want tae ruin ma reputation. Like Ah said, Ah'm a gentleman."

He smiles.

"An' it's *good* wi' her, really good. She's very—very lively, Connie."

I love the unexpected delicacy of his speech.

"But, honest, Audrey, it's getting beyond a joke. Whit, between her oan the wan hand, and Big Olivia oan the other, Ah'm red raw doon there."

He indicates his crotch region, which gives me much more information than I really want to have.

"Shame. So does that mean you're not going to be able to fit me in?"

He takes this quite seriously. Alec thinks every queen longs for his caresses.

"Aw, love tae, Audrey, Ah wid. But the way things are…"

"No problem, Alec, I'll just have to wait till your dance card is less full."

Just at that moment Mr Cheap Suit and Miss Judy Garland pass on their way to the door, arm in arm.

"G'night, Audrey," carols Judy.

"Cunt," growls Cheap Suit says as he passes me.

"Get fucked," I respond pleasantly. And knowing Judy as I do, that's exactly what he's going to get.

Alec gets down from his stool. "Sorry Audrey, need tae go fer a piss. Ah'm dreadin' it, wi' the state of ma—"

"OK, Alec, no problem. Good luck."

He wanders off in the direction of the toilets.

I'm not allowed to be alone for long. Next through the door is a completely unexpected face. Al. Al Fraser. Angie's *Ell*.

He comes straight over, wreathed in smiles.

'*It should be lilies,*' I think.

"Good evening, Audrey. Nice to see you. Drink?"

I am stunned at his coolness, his nerve. After the way he treated Angie. To just walk in here, walk up to me, her best friend, as if nothing has happened. Angie hasn't been in town for ages. She's not back at work till Monday, and I have no way to contact her at home.

And here he stands, this grinning bastard, not a care in the world, it appears.

Right. The simmering anger that has been building up in me all night can now find a legitimate outlet.

"How dare you talk to me, you shit. How can you even show your face? How could you treat someone you're supposed to care about like that? Two hours Angie waited at the airport, till the plane had gone. Where *were* you? What reason..."

He looks genuinely baffled, and takes a step or two back.

"Whoa, hold on there, Audrey, hold on. What do you mean? I *was* there. It was Gordon who didn't show up. Tickets in my hand, luggage at my feet, bunch of flowers, magazines—*Country Life, Vogue,* all his favourites..."

This stops me in my tracks. Eh? Al was *there*?

"Hang on, Al; this was Prestwick Airport, yes?"

"Yes, Prestwick. Only place you can fly directly to Canada from. I was *there*, Audrey, I swear it. Can you imagine how I felt? I'd arranged time off from work, which wasn't easy. Had to call the folks and let them know there had been a hitch. And they had been dying to meet Gordon. I was *angry*, understand?"

He plonks himself on Alec's stool. "May I? Thanks. Get you a drink?"

Now it's his turn to do the sighing thing.

"And now he's lying low." He nods. "Yeah, poor thing, just too embarrassed to face me, I guess."

He orders some drinks, and then turns to me again. "I suppose he got cold feet, that's all I can think."

Is this possible? Surely not.

But—Angie can be unpredictable. Just maybe, as he says, just *maybe*, she had second thoughts and didn't want to deal with the consequences.

No, surely she would have confided in me? I remember her distress. No, that couldn't have been put on.

Or could it? I remember other occasions... Oh, the hell with it, I can't even be bothered thinking about it right now. Angie will be back at work next week. I'll deal with it then, when I see her.

"OK, OK, Al, leave it for now, I'm sorry for going off at you. I'll speak to him when I see him, find out what went wrong."

"Thanks, I'd be grateful, Audrey, if you would. I thought this was the real thing, but it seems I was wrong."

His distress appears so genuine that I am convinced.

"Don't worry, Al, I'll find out. Thanks for the drink. Cheers."

Just then the bell for last orders sounds, it's nearly ten o' clock.

"Another, Audrey? Keep me company? I'm a bit down, as you can imagine."

"No, sorry, I have to go, I'm afraid," I say.

I can't wait for this horrible evening to end. Everyone, it seems, is in a mood, depressed, aggressive, miserable. Time to draw a line under it.

He plays the courteous gentleman. "Aw, please, say you will. Just one more. Help a guy out?"

He smiles, putting on the appeal.

"Oh, OK, Al. Just the one."

"A double? Go on."

Why argue?

At closing time, we stand and chat for a moment or two outside the bar. Just before we part, he says, "Look, I'm going through to Edinburgh tomorrow, around lunchtime, business thing. If you fancy the trip… why don't you come with me?"

He backs away and raises his hands with a disarming grin. "No strings, I promise. Please—I could do with some friendly company."

I consider it. Why not? I have absolutely no designs on Mr Fraser, but he's generous, agreeable, and—well—I have no other plans. I can phone the record shop and play the sick card. Edinburgh might turn up something, someone. Who knows?

"OK, Al. What time tomorrow?"

"Oh, say twelve, noon? At the Shell, in the station?"

"OK. I'll be there."

"Great, great. It'll be fun, just a couple of friends on a jaunt. It'll make a change. I love Edinburgh. Good—see you the morra."

"Ye'll see me the morra?" I mimic.

I snigger. "You want to be careful, Al. You're starting to pick up a Glasgow accent."

He heads off in the direction of Sauchiehall Street. I am going the other way, towards the bus station.

I stop outside the *Strand*, which is emptying out. I see one or two familiar faces. I say *hello* to Dora Doll and Maggie Wilde, who stop to chat for a moment.

I don't actually recognise Miss Wilde immediately, as she is, for a miracle, not wearing the famous white trench coat. Instead she is attired in a very smart grey tweed number which I haven't seen before.

"Wow, like the coat, Maggie," I say as I pass her the inevitable cigarette. "New, is it?"

She laughs. "Well, it's new tae me, Audrey. The Queen Mother pinched it from the Crown Salerooms yesterday. Then when she got it home, she found out it didnae fit her, so she passed it on. Nice, no?"

She does a twirl.

Maggie, I know, rents a room from the legendary and very elderly Queen Mother.

"Very nice, Maggie. But are you telling me she *stole* it?"

The Crown Salerooms is a large auction house in the city centre where you can buy just about anything.

"Oh aye," says Maggie, drawing on her cigarette as though her life depended on it, "talk aboot sticky fingers? She's a right thief, that auld bastard, never out of the place, seeing whit she can help herself to. She wis *very* pissed off the other day—not only wis the coat too small, but she nicked a pair of shoes too. Got them hame and found out their were baith left feet."

We share a laugh at this, and then the two of them wave goodbye as they trot off down the road.

Pat Calhoun and Susan Strasberg wish me goodnight as they follow suit.

Damn, I can't even connect with a friend this evening, it seems.

"Hello," comes a voice from behind me.

I nearly jump out of my skin. I turn round.

'*Oh shit,*' I think. '*Another freak.*'

He's shorter than me, mid-twenties maybe, cropped, jet-black hair. Jeans in a camouflage pattern, checked shirt, boots.

And a beard.

People are still piling out of the bar. Faces I know, faces I don't.

"Hello," I say.

What does he want? He has had a few, I can tell, but he's not drunk. I've had a few myself, if it comes to that.

"What's your name?" he asks.

"It's George."

Not Audrey. I don't think this guy's One of Us. He doesn't look it. He looks strange, wild, maybe dangerous. Who knows what he's after?

He puts out his hand, and I take it. What else can I do?

"Ah'm Tommy. Tommy Molony. Nice tae meet you, George."

He shakes my hand firmly.

"Er—you too," I say.

He takes out a tin and starts rolling a cigarette, leaning against the wall. "Were you in the bar, there? Ah didn't see you. Ah would have noticed, I'm sure."

"No, I was up the road. In *Guy's*."

"Oh, *Guy's*, aye. Is that your regular place, then?"

"No—well—yes, one of them. But I'm barred from here at the moment."

He raises his eyebrows. "Oh? Barred? Did you do something you shouldnae have done? Are you a bad boy, then, George?"

OK, it's actually quite funny.

"No, no, it's just—well, it doesn't matter, really."

I look back up the road in the direction of *Guy's*, and see old Ken, The Queen Mother herself, shuffling down the street, headed in our direction, in her usual tatty Astrakhan coat and 'Mr Kruschev' fur hat. Ken's about a thousand, and doesn't go into the bars, ever. Just pops up outside at closing time to see if there are any stray pickings around.

Rather like myself, tonight.

As she approaches, I try to see if she is wearing two left shoes, but can't actually tell.

This Tommy finishes rolling his cigarette and lights up. "Want one?"

"Er—no, thanks. Look, I'm sorry, but I'd better be going."

"Oh? OK. Shame, that."

The last few come out of the bar.

"Evening, girls." It's Shirley Temple and Julie London. I catch the expression of mild contempt on my companion's face, and don't respond.

"Dirty low gutters an' nancies," mutters the Queen Mother, looking at them and grumbling to herself, as she finds a position tucked in by the door of the bar.

"Well, suit yourselves," says Shirley, and she and her sister trot off down the road.

I turn to my new acquaintance. "Well—good-night, then."

Maybe I can catch Shirley and Julie up, go for a coffee or something.

He hesitates.

"Ah was wondering… Can Ah see you home? Would that be alright?"

God, why is everyone mad tonight?

"But I don't know you."

Yes, that's the best I can come up with.

"Well," he says, logically, "if you let me see you home, you'll get to know me, won't you?"

Oh-oh. This guy is a weirdo, definitely. Maybe a psycho, a Norman Bates. And it's only a few years since mass murderer Peter Manuel prowled the Glasgow suburbs and left bodies scattered hither and yon.

Time to fold your tent, Audrey.

"No, I'm sorry, I can't. Rutherglen, it's miles away. Anyway, I live at home with my family, it's tricky."

I tail off. I'd be hard-pressed to say why I am being so honest with this strange character, who may be an escaped lunatic for all I know. I usually keep my own counsel as far as personal things go.

He puffs on his cigarette. "You live at home?... Yeah, me too. And you're right, it's difficult sometimes."

"Yes. Anyway, I'd better go and get my bus."

And I turn and start to walk away.

"Ah'll walk you down the road then, if that's OK." He catches up with me. "Make sure you're alright. Friday night, pubs just out. Do you mind?"

God knows why, but I don't. "OK, if you like."

And we head off together towards Waterloo Street.

As we walk along, he chats away. He looks a bit scary, but his manner is unobjectionable.

"What do you do? What do you work at, I mean?" he asks me.

"I'm a student. At the University."

I am beginning to relax. He's quite agreeable. Harmless, anyway. Just a bit of a nutter.

"Oh, a student? Studying what?"

"Music, basically. And English." I smile. "When I can be bothered."

He smiles back as he dogs out his cigarette. I take my pack from my pocket and offer him one.

"No, no, it's OK," he says. "You've only got a couple left."

I light up in my turn, and we continue together.

"Music, eh?" he says. "I enjoy a bit of music. Do you like Country and Western?"

I am not entirely sure what that is. I stall.

"Er—some. Is that what *you* like?"

"Oh, aye. Hank Williams is the man. You know Hank Williams?"

The name is vaguely familiar.

" '*Your cheating heart*'—that's one of his songs, isn't it?"

"It is. One of many."

He starts to sing.

> '*If you loved me half as much as I love you*
> *You wouldn't worry me half as much as you do.*
> *You're nice to me when there's no-one else around.*
> *You only build me up to let me down.*'

He has a pleasant and mellow voice. One or two heads turn in our direction. I don't quite know whether to be embarrassed or not by this serenade. I decide not to be. This has turned out to be one of those strange evenings that happen now and then. I will just go along with it.

I smile when he finishes. "Nice. So what do *you* do? A folk singer, or something."

Yes, he could be that type, with the beard and all. Though he's clean-looking, and not at all scruffy, as most of the few I've known tend to be.

He laughs heartily, "Och, if only. Naw, I'm a painter and decorator. Work up at the Odeon Cinema in Renfield Street, maintenance. No' a bad job, work's easy, nice people. Been there a couple of years."

We round the corner into Waterloo Street, the bus station just a step away.

"Ah'll see you to your bus, OK?"

"Yes, that's fine."

We turn into the station, but the stand is empty.

"Oh—the bus is not here yet. Every fifteen minutes, shouldn't be long. Thanks for walking with me. I'll say goodnight."

I put out my hand.

"Och, no problem, I'll wait till your bus arrives, make sure nobody bothers you. Glasgow on a Friday night, you know how it is."

There can't be many people who know better than I do.

He takes out his tin, and I agree to let him roll me a cigarette. It nearly chokes me.

We chat some more, about nothing in particular. He lives, he tells me, in Maryhill. With his parents and his brother, Charlie.

Eventually my bus pulls in to the terminus.

"Right," I say, turning. "Here it is. Thanks again. May see you around some time."

He grabs my arm. "Wait, hang on a wee minute."

He seems a bit flustered. "Look—Ah'd like tae see you again. For a drink, maybe? Get to know each other a bit better? How about it?"

"But…"

He speaks in a rush, as if a bit embarrassed. "Look, if you don't want to, if Ah'm botherin' you, just tell me tae piss off, it's nae problem."

Well, I've been complaining about getting no attention recently. And there is something genuine about this peculiar man. I decide not to probe the possibilities too deeply.

"Yes, alright. Tomorrow night? *Guy's*?"

He frowns. "Aw, dammit, Ah can't make it tomorrow. Got a T.A. meeting."

'*T.A.? What's that?*' I wonder. '*Something like Alcoholics Anonymous?*'
A crazy notion comes into my head; appropriate for this crazy evening.
"What are you doing tomorrow? Daytime, I mean?"
"Nothing special. Want to meet up tomorrow?"
"Maybe… You see, I'm going through to Edinburgh tomorrow lunchtime, with a friend, he's driving. Just for the afternoon, we'll be back by six, maybe seven."

I don't actually know if we will, but hey, that's this guy's problem. And if he turns out to be a lunatic, at least Al will be with me.

His face lights up. "Yeah, sounds good. What time? Where?"

I hear the bus driver slamming his door and the engine revving up. I rush for the mounting platform.

"Twelve o' clock, at the Shell, Central Station," I call over my shoulder.
I jump on the platform as the bus starts to move.
I turn round. He waves.
"OK, got that—twelve, at the Shell. Ah'll be there."
The bus gathers speed, and I find a seat.

'*Yes, of course you will. And pigs will fly. And how are things in Glocca Morra, Mr Molony? Bloody loony…*'

I get into town early the next day. It is beautiful, sunny and warm. I have phoned Caldwell's and made an excuse, a murderous toothache. As I pass by McLaren's, I am amazed to see Angie in the window, doing something dazzling with a selection of ties. I knock, nearly causing her to have a seizure. I beckon, indicating that she should come outside for a moment.

She hurries out of the shop. "What is it, Audrey? I'm really busy."
"Oh? And good morning to you, too. Thought you were off work still. Not back till Monday."
"Got bored at home, thought I might as well come in."
"Right. And how are you feeling now? About…"
"Oh well—a little better, I suppose. After—"
I can't wait to tell her. "That's what I wanted to talk to you about. I saw him last night."

She lights a cigarette. Obviously, despite her protests, she's not *that* busy.

"Saw who?"
"Him. Al—*your* Al. He was in *Guy's*. Bought me a drink."
Angie blows out some smoke. "*That* bastard? Well, good luck to you, Audrey. I never want to see him again."

I wait a moment. "Angie—look—truth time."

I don't want to offend her, but...

"Did you really go to meet him at the airport? Honestly? 'Cos he says he was there and you just didn't show up."

She just stares at me.

"What? You think I would lie about something like that? You don't believe me? You?"

She looks up, seeking support from the heavens.

"Of course I was there. I put calls out for him, everything. Do you really think I would pass up that kind of chance? A free holiday in Canada? Really, come on, you know me better than that!"

And of course, I do.

Right. So it is Mr Fraser who's lying. Unless they just somehow managed to miss each other. Or one of them got there at the wrong time. But no, that's impossible—Prestwick Airport is tiny, there are no more than half a dozen flights a day, it just couldn't happen.

Angie treads out her cigarette. "Anyway, I need to get back to work. Have him if you like. With my blessing."

"Wait a minute. No, no, Angie, I'm not even slightly interested in him, honestly. But—the thing is, he asked me if I wanted to go through to Edinburgh today. I'm supposed to be meeting him in the station shortly."

"Oh?"

Suddenly, I have her full attention.

"Yes—and I thought—if you were there too, waiting—you'd have to hide somewhere, he'll probably run a mile if he sees you—you could confront him. Force him to explain."

Her eyes gleam. "What time?"

"Twelve. At the Shell."

She glances at her watch.

"Right. I'll take an early lunch, twelve to one, leave here about ten to. Where could I hide? What do you think?"

Reanimated, Angie is immediately business-like. Which makes a nice change from the wilting, abandoned-at-the-altar act she has been featuring recently.

I know exactly how to do this.

"In the booking office—you can see the whole station from there, through the big windows. When he arrives I'll stall him for a minute or two—say I have to get cigarettes or something. Then you jump out, come over. He won't be able to get away."

I hug myself with glee at the prospect of a drama, and a justified revenge for my jilted sister. As far as Edinburgh is concerned, I couldn't care less. This promises to be a much more entertaining scenario.

"Right, right, that's good. What time is it now?"

I look at my own watch in turn. "It's half eleven, got half an hour. You up for it? You sure?"

Angie smiles grimly.

"Oh yes, I'm up for it alright. We'll show that bastard, eh?"

It's about five to twelve, and I am waiting by the Shell. Angie is inside the booking office. I can't see her, but I know she can see me. I gaze round hoping to spot Al. There's no sign of him yet, but I'm a little early.

I light up a cigarette and look over towards the Gordon Street entrance. Oh no!

It's Blackbeard the Pirate. Mr Molony. Tommy, I remember. I have completely forgotten about him with all this excitement. Never really expected to see him again, anyway, last night seems weeks ago.

But it's him. And today he's featuring a hat. Camouflage pattern again, he obviously favours that look. A soft hat with a brim—don't know what you call it, Angie's the fashion expert, not me. A fishing hat, maybe? A few flies stuck round the edge would certainly not look out of place.

A safari hat, that's it.

He heads towards me. Big smile.

"Well, there's a surprise. Didn't think you'd show up—thought Ah might have scared you off. Sorry, was a bit tanked up last night, hope Ah didn't say anything to offend you."

"No, no, not at all."

Indeed, he didn't. He was kind and polite.

I look at him. This is the first time I have really seen him properly. And I register first that he has warm, dark brown eyes. Neat ears under the hat. Nose slightly twisted to one side.

That's it. The rest is hair. He could be Italian, or maybe Spanish.

But no—Molony—Irish, obviously. What they call Black Irish—as the legend has it, the descendants of a few shipwrecked Spanish Armada sailors who had their wicked continental way with the local colleens.

Irish origins notwithstanding, accent-wise he is pure Glasgow, if a cut above the usual common type.

I stare at him. And realise that, in spite of the weird attire and the beard, he is a nice-looking man. Compact physique, trim build, no belly. Shame he's not taller. But with a shave and some proper clothes, he might be considered handsome. Even hairy and eccentrically dressed, he's attractive.

He is a little uncomfortable under my scrutiny.

"What's the matter? Have Ah got food in my teeth? Or a bogey?"

I laugh. "No, not at all."

Indeed, his teeth are white and even, under the slightly overhanging moustache.

"I was just thinking what a fine-looking fellow you are."

I can be bold, and say things like that now. We are on my territory today.

He blushes. You can only see a hint of it, but I know that underneath that beard his face is burning.

He tries to hide his embarrassment, shuffling his feet. He looks away. "Oh aye, God's gift, me."

His beard is black, jet black, like the little I can see of his hair under that terrible hat.

"But Ah'm no' as good-looking as you," he smiles, as he turns back.

Now it is my turn to blush, and I do, unmistakably.

"You're gorgeous."

Oh dear, I was right first time. This guy is not right in the head. On a good day I'm presentable. Luckily, today is a good day.

"Well," he goes on, "Now we've told each other how fanciable we both are, where's this friend of yours?"

My head is all over the place. Having earlier entirely overlooked my arrangement with Mr Molony, I have now completely forgotten about Mr Al Fraser, not to mention 'Olga Pulloffski, The Beautiful Spy', hiding in the booking office.

"Oh, he'll be along any minute. It's only just twelve."

It crosses my mind to wonder what this Tommy will make of the upcoming confrontation—a *sherricking*, as we call it in Glasgow. It consists of a lot of shouting, insults, verbal abuse and general character assassination. Preferably conducted in front of as large a number of people as possible. It's designed to embarrass the victim, rather than to actually resolve a difference. It's the revenge of the weak against the strong.

"Cigarette?" he asks me, proffering a packet. "Thought I'd get tailor-mades the day. Ah noticed that the roll-up I gave you didn't go down too well last night."

"Thanks," I say, taking one. My own brand, too, Embassy.

I remark on the coincidence.

"It's not a coincidence," he says, smiling, offering his lighter. "I noticed what fags you were smoking last night."

Ah. Not that pissed then. That was a kindly thought.

We chat away like old friends. He is very easy to talk to. He tells me he plays the guitar—'*Not great, but I like strumming away.*' I learn that the mysterious T.A. is in fact the Territorial Army, of which he is a member, and that the bent nose is the result of boxing—'*Just amateur stuff, at the local sports club. But I've copped a few whacks in ma time.*'

He smiles. It's a nice smile.

"Dished out a few as well." He's twenty-seven, apparently.

It is nearly ten past twelve when I suddenly remember Angie, still trapped in the ticket office—she hasn't even had any lunch. And it certainly looks by now as though Mr Al Fraser is not going to appear. He must have a sixth sense, that one. I suppose that helps, if you are a liar and a manipulator. I make a mental note that, at some point in the future, Mr Fraser will need to be dealt with.

I interrupt Tommy.

"Sorry, look… I've just remembered my friend—not the one who was supposed to meet us, another one. Watching us, in the ticket office, over there."

"Really? Got them posted all over, have you? Is that in case Ah kidnap you?"

"No—I'll explain later, but I really must go and release her."

Angie must have spotted us coming over, because she achieves her own escape, somewhat flustered, from her temporary prison.

She is not happy.

"Hmph. Well, there you are—didn't turn up, did he? I'm not surprised, I didn't think he would. The bastard!"

Obviously the word of the day.

"You see now what a total *bastard* he is?"

"Yes, I suspect you're right. He's a bastard."

Tommy looks at me enquiringly.

"Well, there's a surprise. When you said you needed to release her, Ah was expecting a lady."

Angie sniffs. "I *am* a lady, *ekchewly*."

"Oh? OK, if you say so."

Angie pats her hair into place carefully.

"And who is this bit of rough you've just picked up, you? I must say, Audrey, whatever people say about you, you do have a remarkable knack. It only took you five minutes."

I feel the need to explain. "No, no, this is another friend of mine. We had already arranged to meet up here."

She sniffs again. "Oh, I see. A kind of insurance policy? Very smart, Audrey."

"Who is Audrey?" Tommy asks.

'*What is she?*' I mentally add. I sense that this is not going to end well.

Angie turns on the full flood, performing for her new audience.

"My dear man, *she* is; Audrey Hepburn. Didn't you know that? And, since she hasn't had the politeness to introduce us, allow me. Angie—Angie Dickinson."

She shakes his hand, which he proffers somewhat reluctantly.

"Oh, yes," she goes on, apparently unstoppable. "Everybody knows Audrey and me—sorry, Audrey and *I*."

"No, Audrey and *me*," I contribute, just for something to say.

"Audrey and me are the toast of Glasgow."

"Audrey and *I* are the –"

She rounds on me. "Well I wish you'd make your mind up."

She turns back to Tommy. "We're sisters, her and me—her and I—both of us."

I grit my teeth.

'*Oh, my dear Angie,*' I think, '*one of these dark nights I will quietly strangle you, and close that big mouth for good.*'

This Tommy is looking increasingly uncomfortable. But Angie seems completely unaware of this. She sails on regardless. She links my arm.

"Now, I've still got half an hour for lunch—I'll grab a sandwich in *Ferguson's*. Come down to *Woolies* with me, they've got some new foundation in—it's only *Outdoor Girl*, but lovely new *today* shades. *Pale Face* is the one I've got my eye on. I thought I might try a wee change in my make-up."

As I look at her, I wonder if *Red Skin* is another shade Outdoor Girl might be promoting?

She drags me off down the stairs towards Union Street. Tommy follows us, glowering. He walks four or five steps behind.

There follows a very trying half-hour. I realise that my new friend finds my sister intimidating, or embarrassing, or maybe just plain annoying. Whichever it is, he continues to keep a few steps behind all the way to *Woolworth's*, and when we get there, says he will wait outside for us.

'*Yes. And he will be gone when we get back, I know it. And I don't blame him.*'

It could not be clearer that he finds Angie's behaviour not at all to his taste. And she is not featuring discretion. On the contrary, the volume control is set to maximum. I can see on the man's face that he is embarrassed by the display. That he is cringing inside, and longing to be somewhere else, anywhere else.

What a shame. And he and I were getting on so well, earlier. He's interesting and different.

'*But,*' I philosophise, '*if he can't deal with a little high camp on a low light, he's hardly the man for me.*'

This is, after all, my life, and this is the way I live it.

It's a bit of a shame, nonetheless.

Angie finds what she was after in *Woolworths*, and I too make a small purchase.

'*Just in case,*' I think.

For a wonder, Tommy is still waiting outside when we leave.

I look at my watch. "You'd better get back to work, Gordon. It's nearly one o' clock."

She looks at hers in turn.

"Oh, I see—desperate to get rid of me are you? Are you, *George*?"

"Yes, I am."

She smiles sweetly.

"Don't worry, I'm off. Got the Burberry rep in this afternoon—he's a fine boy, and I *know* he wants me. Bye-bye Tommy, it was a pleasure. Have fun, you two."

And she saunters off in the direction of her shop.

Still standing in the middle of Union Street, we are silent for a moment or two, Tommy and I. The sun has gone in.

He sighs and shakes his head.

"What was *that* all about? Angie and Audrey? All that posing and carrying on like girls?"

I don't know quite what to say. I know he has found the last half-hour awkward to say the least, but I am not prepared to accept his reaction meekly, without some kind of defence.

"Well—it's just a bit of a laugh. No harm in it, just to amuse ourselves. Why not? Why do you care? It's our business how we behave, who we are."

He looks at me.

"But that's *not* who you are. At least, it's not who you were last night. It's not who you were earlier, when we met up. It only started when this—this *sister* of yours turned up. What's his name, anyway? His real name, I mean. I don't suppose he was christened Angie Dickinson?"

"It's Gordon. Gordon Curran."

"OK—so you're Gordon and George. What's wrong with that? Ah hate all that phoney behaviour—she *this*, Audrey *that*... Really, Ah can't stand it."

I don't know what to say.

Eventually I have to speak, since he is obviously not going to.

"Right. I didn't know you felt like that. Sorry to have embarrassed you, OK?"

He doesn't say anything at all.

"And—well, I'd better be on my way. Sorry the Edinburgh thing didn't work out."

I turn to leave. But he stops me, his hand on my arm.

"Where are you going?"

Anywhere where I can have a bit of a laugh and not be criticised for enjoying myself in the way I choose to.

'*Smug little sod. Trying to tell me how I should behave, what I should call myself. What gives him the right? He doesn't even know me. Running down my best friend who, God knows, is sometimes a pain in the arse, but has a good heart.*'

But I don't say any of that. I just say, "I really don't know."

Just brilliant, Audrey. Oops, George, rather.

I remove his hand from my arm and turn to walk away. He follows, and stops me again.

"Look, don't go, please."

He hesitates for a second. "Ah'm sorry for what Ah said. It's none of my business what you do, what you call yourself, how your friends behave. Really, Ah'm sorry. It just threw me a bit. Can we forget it?"

I look at him, undecided.

"Go on, please—Ah'll call you Audrey, if that's what you want."

He looks up at me, just a hint of a cheeky grin on what I can see of his face.

"No, don't do that."

I consider the situation. Angie *was* a bit over the top. And the sun has come out again.

I come to a decision. "All right, Thomas, we'll forget it. It never happened, OK?"

His face breaks into the widest of smiles.

"Good, that's good. Again, Ah'm sorry. And I really prefer Tommy."

We walk up Union Street together. After a few steps, he stops.

"So—what are we going to do now? Got the day ahead of us, after all."

I know exactly what I want to do. And there's no question it's what he wants to do.

Problem is—where are we going to do it?

He explains he has just about enough money to pay for a cheap room, but Morrison's hotel, the only place I know of within his budget, has too many memories for me. Memories of the occasional commercial venture with *signori incogniti*; not the kind of ambiance I am after. I don't explain my reasons, just tell him Morrison's is scruffy and dirty.

"OK then," he says, "I get it. Any other ideas? Ah'd take you back tae my place, but... you know, family, all that."

So, an outdoor job, then. But it's high summer, won't be dark till God knows what time. And anyway, I don't want that kind of encounter with him, though I couldn't say exactly why.

He understands.

"It's no problem—we'll just spend a bit of time together, then. Maybe we can sort something out for another day."

The look in his eyes is unmistakeable. Mingled disappointment and lust.

"Shame, though..."

Shame is not the word. I rack my brains. I am just as keen as he is for this encounter to go somewhere, and as soon as possible. I know quite well what 'another day' leads to. Nothing at all.

Carpe diem. This iron is hot, and I want to strike it.

I wonder if by any chance Elaine could be hanging around in the station? She might be able to suggest something. We head up the stairs together.

Elaine is not there. But I spot Barry Nelson lounging casually against a wall.

"Wait here a minute, Tommy. Maybe..."

"OK, no problem," he says.

I stroll over to where Barry is standing. He sees me.

"Afternoon, George, how's it goin' with you?"

"Fine, Barry, fine."

I cut to the chase.

"Look—you remember you said I could use your flat if I needed to?"

"Yes."

"Well—I need to."

"Now? OK—that's fine."

He digs in his pocket. "Here's the keys. You know where it is, don't you?"

"Oh, yes."

"Punter, is it?" He laughs and holds a hand up. "Never mind—I don't want to know the details. Your business. Oh—you can do the washing up, if you can be bothered, I didn't have time this morning. There's not much."

He passes me the keys.

"Lock the door when you leave and put the keys through the letter-box."

"Wow, thank you," I breathe.

"It's fine, any time. Have fun."

I smile. "Well, I hope so. Thanks again. Maybe I can do something for you one of these days."

He raises his eyebrows.

"Well—there's an offer I can't refuse, I must say. No, really, you're welcome."

I head back towards Tommy, and jingle the keys alluringly.

"Hey," he says, looking surprised. "Well done! How did you manage that?"

"Ah," I reply, "it's not *what* you know…"

We are alone. Alone at last, as they say.

I don't like my body. Really, I don't. The one thing in my favour is that I am tall and have broad, straight shoulders. I look OK in clothes. Features-wise I'm not hideous. But as for the rest, no. I am skinny. I wear glasses. My arms and legs are thin, I have a twenty-eight inch waist and no backside to speak of. I am bony. I generally avoid getting undressed in front of anyone at all.

I am in an agony of apprehension. I wait.

But he doesn't, not for a second. And, to make the situation worse, when out of his clothes, he is beautiful. He is in perfect proportion. His chest is broad, his legs strong, his belly flat, and his bottom perfect. He is not over-muscled at all, he just stands there naked, looking completely unselfconscious and—beautiful. It's the only possible word.

How I wish it was night-time! But it is bright daylight, and Barry's curtains don't really do the job. I feel embarrassed by my puny physique. I don't want him to look at me.

But he seems completely at ease, and happy with what he sees.

We move to the bed. I'm a little concerned about that beard, thick and black as it is. But, no, it is soft and smooth, and tickles just a little. But it doesn't scrape or scratch.

I remember something. I try to sit up.

"Oh—hang on a minute. I said we'd do the washing up."

He laughs. "Did you, now? Well, OK, but later, later…"

He pulls me back down.

Matters progress as matters do. At the appropriate point, I reach for my recent purchase. It's high time, I've just turned nineteen.

I look down. And I am relieved to note that, now his pump is well primed, the prospect doesn't look too alarming.

A few moments later, virginity *adieu*. The Deed is finally done.

2. And Then He Kissed Me

> I didn't know just what to do.
> So I whispered, "I love you"
> And he said that he loved me too,
> And then he kissed me
> *The Crystals, 1963*

Oh dear. I've got it bad, and that ain't good. No, that ain't good at all.
It's one week later, Friday night.
We have a date. And he doesn't show up.
Did I do or say something wrong?
'*Yes,*' I think. '*Typical. Hit and run. One of those guys who likes a bit of something different on the side now and again, then scuttles back home to his safe straight life.*'
I am sitting in *Guy's*, where we have arranged to meet. I kick idly at the legs of my bar-stool. I would rather like to be kicking him.
'*Probably married, like whatshisname.*'
I can't even bring the name of George Cooper to mind for a moment, then am amazed to discover I have nearly forgotten him.
'*Ah, lest we forget.*'
Well, it's only just, I suppose. I've forgotten George, and Tommy has forgotten me.
I am thoroughly depressed. Not just disappointed, I am sad. I felt something, something indefinable for him. And I thought it was the same for him. We seemed to—oh, I don't know—*like* each other, beyond the physical.
And the virgin sacrifice—what a waste.
Still, I hadn't mentioned it at the time, so he was probably completely unaware of having received that priceless gift.
'*Pearls before swine,*' I think vindictively.
I while away an hour or two, chatting to this one or that one, then head for home. I have a vague hope that he might be waiting for me outside the *Strand*, or even at the bus station. But he isn't.
'*If you only loved me half as much as I love you…*' I hum to myself on the bus home, like an utter, daft idiot.

Saturday night starts rather better. There are a lot of people in the bar, and the atmosphere is lively and fun. Gradually my mood lifts. I have a few drinks—it's gin for me now, no more lager, that just makes me pee all the time.

I try to call his face to mind.

'*Fuck you,*' I think, '*Who needs you? I am with my friends, and we are having fun. So bye-bye, Mr Molony, take your perfect body, your stupid beard, and your utterly average cock, and shove all three of them.*'

My already mellow mood improves even further when I notice Nicky coming through the door. I've not seen him for a week or two, and I always have fun with Nicky. Just behind him, Connie and Alec arrive—very obviously 'together', and, to my experienced eye, behaving like an established couple. They share little smiles and nudges, he pats her arm, she gazes at him adoringly.

I wonder how Big Olivia is dealing with this alienation of Alec's affections? Is she preparing a poisoned wedding gown for the unfortunate Connie, like the sorceress Medea? Or is she just biding her time, still living up to her famous dictum? '*Oh aye, if you have a license for a dog you can let it run wild.*'

Who knows? Alec is certainly running wild. But experience tells me this will not be the end of the story.

The four of us greet each other delightedly, and find places together. Away from the stools that fringe the bar, the seating in *Guy's* is arranged as a line of horseshoe booths, each with a table in the centre. I sit at one end, Nicky next to me.

"Drink, Audrey?" he says.

"Oh, yes, please—I'll have a gin and orange, Nicky, thanks."

"Got it, gin and orange."

"Oh—the hell with it, make it a double."

"A *double*?" He laughs. "Well, well, look out, Glasgow, Audrey means business. God help the guy she gets a hold of the night."

The drinks keep coming, and I keep drinking them. We chat about this and that. Connie and Alec are sat opposite us. She is rapturous that she has finally snared her man. And, God knows, if anyone deserves an 'A' for effort, it is Connie. I decide not to mention Olivia. I don't want any bad moods or arguments tonight. I am out to enjoy myself.

I'll forget that Tommy. Maybe this will be the night I finally manage to ensnare my first love.

The man in question taps me on the arm.

"Oh, meant tae tell ye—had a great night out last night. We went through tae Edinburgh, me and Conrad, tae a party. Didnae get back till four in the morning—God, what a night. We were plastered, out of it. Ah don't know how Conrad could see straight enough tae drive hame."

The name means nothing to me.

"Shame you weren't there, right up your street it was. No' too rowdy, but a wee bit rough roon the edges, if ye know what Ah mean. An' Ah know you enjoy a bit of rough round yer edges now and then."

And he nudges me roguishly.

"Aw, sorry I missed that, Nicky, it sounds fun."

It does. I could have been there, instead of wasting my evening sitting in here waiting for The Return of the Missing Link.

"So who is this Conrad? Do I know him?"

"Oh, Conrad? Well—not sure if ye do. Manager of the Odeon, Renfield Street. Ma latest. Been seein' him for a month or so now."

His latest? Typical. He's with someone new. My timing stinks.

I ask what this Conrad is like.

"Nice guy, really nice. Treats me well. He'll be at hame recoverin' the night." He grins. "He cannae stand the pace like us youngsters."

"Oh? How old is he?"

"No' sure. He'll be about thirty, Ah suppose."

"Thirty?" I say, with a calculated smile. "Doesn't sound like *your* style at all, Nicky. I thought you liked them young?"

"Oh, Ah dae, ah dae," he laughs. "But Conrad's more of a—well, put it this way, Audrey, he's got plenty of money an' disnae mind spendin' it."

He has the grace to blush slightly. "It's more of a—well—an arrangement, if ye follow me."

I do. Nicky has found a sugar daddy.

I make for the bar to get Nicky and the other two a drink. When I bring it back I see that Pat Calhoun and Susan Strasberg have arrived and joined our table.

"Hi Pat, Susan," I say. "Get you a drink?"

"Naw, it's OK," says Pat, getting up, "I'll get a round in. Gin is it, Audrey?"

"Yes, thanks. Gin and orange."

"A double, mind, Pat," says Nicky, as I sit back down next to him.

Pat nods and heads off towards the bar. I turn back to Nicky.

"So—how is life on the buses these days? Still driving the passengers wild?"

"Oh, Ah'm no' drivin' for the Corporation any more. Got made redundant aboot two months ago. On the dole these days. Well, for now, anyway."

"That must be a bit tough, Nicky. How are you managing for money without a job?"

He has always worked since I have known him, and always had money in his pocket. Never short of a few quid, Nicky.

He smiles slightly self-consciously. "Well, let me put it this way—Conrad looks after me pretty well, so I'm doin' OK. He's well paid, so between that and the dole money…"

I understand, and am confirmed in my earlier reading of the situation. Something else tugs at my memory.

"Oh yes. The Odeon, Renfield Street, you said? Manager?"

"Aye, that's right. He's been there aboot two years. Likes it, easy work, nice staff, he says. He brought one of them along last night. Tommy something. Nice guy. Beard."

I nearly drop my drink.

What? Oh, you utter, you despicable bastard! So—while I was bleeding my heart out here, waiting for you, you were running wild in Edinburgh, never giving me a thought.

I could nearly burst with anger and hurt. And with sadness and disappointment. On one level I would truly like to have him hung, drawn and quartered for treating me like a person of no account. But on the other hand, I desperately want to see him again, alive and kicking. Maybe just to have the chance to treat him the way he treated me.

'*And especially after me giving him…*'

No, stop, Audrey, stop, that way madness lies.

Nicky must not know any of this. I adopt a carefully casual tone.

"Oh," I say, "rings a bell. Tommy. Yes, I think I might have met him. A beard, like you said."

Nicky looks at me, his brow furrowed. "Oh—know him, do you?"

"Yes, I think so—if it's the same one. Not a lot of beards in Glasgow."

I should stop there, change the subject. But it's no good, I have to know.

"So—how did he get on last night? Get off with anyone, did he?"

Nicky is as smart as a whip, and I worry that something in my words may have alerted him. But his tone remains neutral.

"No, no, he didn't. He was as drunk as Ah wis, and he was with me an' Conrad aw night. We dropped him off in the early hours, in Maryhill somewhere."

He turns a speculative glance in my direction. He grins. "Why? Fancy him, do you?"

I scoff. "Oh come on! A *beard*? As if! No, of course I don't. I just wondered."

♦

It's about nine o' clock, and I am by now unquestionably more than a little drunk. But bright, happy drunk, not sick, vomiting drunk. We are having a great laugh, and there is talk of a party afterwards, at the flat Connie and Wilma now share. I press closer to Nicky—yet another couple have joined our table, and it's a bit of a squeeze—and he appears to have no problem with that arrangement. Vera Ellen and her boyfriend Bobby Savage are sitting next to Connie and Alec. I have kept my place on the end of the horseshoe, and Nicky's arm is round my shoulder.

"Hey, Nicky," someone says behind me. I half turn.

My God, it's Bluebeard himself. What's *he* doing here?

I turn back, resolved to ignore him.

"Recovered, have you?" he goes on, still addressing Nicky.

Nicky looks up. "Oh aye, Tommy, nae bother. Bit of a heid this morning, but good now. You?"

"Aye, fine. Just been to a T.A. thing, that helped tae sort me out."

But I just can't hold it in. I glance again over my shoulder.

"Oh? A *Territorial Army* meeting? Christ, that must have been fuckin' riveting!"

I am angry. And I am loud.

Suddenly our table is silent. He puts his hands on my shoulders, dislodging Nicky's arm, and twists me half-round to face him.

Recognition dawns.

"Oh, it's you. Hello again, didnae see you there. What's the matter? Not in a very happy mood the night? Something wrong?"

Seated, I turn fully round. He is still standing, now in front of me. His crotch is in my face. A snap of my teeth, and I could do him a serious injury if I chose to.

But I don't. Instead I look up and smile.

"No, nothing important, nothing at all. Just waiting for my date. He's a wee bit late. About twenty-four hours late."

He looks puzzled. I refuse to take my eyes off his. And gradually, it appears, comprehension dawns.

"Oh shit. Sorry, so sorry."

He hits his forehead with the heel of his palm.

"Ah got a bit drunk last night, an' Ah'm afraid Ah forgot. Ended up in Edinburgh, and…"

He *forgot*?

I do an Angie on him.

"Please, Mr Molony," I interrupt, "don't give it another thought. Really, no problem at all. Don't apologise, it's completely unnecessary."

Is it my imagination, or does he look at a bit of a loss? He is, I think, about to expand on his explanation, but I don't wait to hear it. I turn back to my friends and burst into a flurry of girlish giggles at something nobody has said.

"Here, find a seat, Tommy," says Nicky. "Squeeze in on the other end. Somebody can move up. A drink?"

"Ah'll have a Coke, thanks, Nicky, not drinking the night. Ah had mair than enough last night."

As the babble of conversation resumes, he manages to perch himself at the end of the crowded table next to Vera Ellen and her Bobby, who move round to make room for him.

'*If that Vera looks at him sideways,*' I think, '*I will hit her with something.*'

"Some problem, Audrey? Wi' you an' him?" whispers Nicky, when he comes back from the bar with Tommy's Coke.

As I stand up to let him into his place, I mutter, "No, no, it's nothing, Nicky. Tell you about it later, but it's nothing serious."

Tonight Tommy is dressed rather more conservatively. No camouflage, no hat. Jeans and a black zip-up jacket. And he sits there and stares at me for the rest of the night.

So naturally I start carrying on outrageously, in just the way I know he hates.

'*Fuck him, who does he think he is?*' I say to myself.

I behave truly appallingly; girly names fly across the table, shrieks and giggles shoot back and forth, and I spur on Connie and Vera to be more and more outrageous. Not that they need much encouragement.

And all the time he just sits there and stares. He talks to nobody.

I bend my head slightly, and whisper in Nicky's ear, giving him an artificial languishing glance.

"Nicky, OK, just go along with this, please."

He turns in my direction. "Eh?"

I wrap my arms around him and plant my lips on his. Good boy scout, and quick on the uptake as Nicky always is, he goes for it, and we are locked in an embrace for a full ten seconds. Tongues, the lot.

'*Yeah, Mr Molony, have a good look. See how desirable I am? See what you're missing?*'

When we finally disengage, Nicky says, "Wow!", very convincingly.

Rasputin is still staring at me, frowning.

So I bring out the big guns.

"Girls, girls, listen, have I ever told you how I lost my virginity?

Believe it or not, it was just last week. Well, that's quite a story. Ran into this guy outside the *Strand*…"

He stands up.

"OK, that's enough, George. You're making a fool of yourself."

He gets to his feet and stands in front of me.

"Who's George?" I hear Vera whisper to Connie.

Connie nudges her, "Ssh, you."

"Making a fool of myself?" I say, looking up at him. "No doubt you'd prefer it if I left it to *you* to make a fool of me? You've already done it once."

"C'mon, home time for you."

He reaches down, grabs me under the arms and hoists me unceremoniously to my feet.

"Ah'll see you to your bus, George. You're drunk."

"Oh, he means Audrey," Vera titters nervously.

I try to shake him off, unsuccessfully.

"OK, I'm drunk. And you're ugly. But in the morning I'll be sober."

He sighs and shakes his head, as if I'm a badly behaved child.

"No, you won't—in the morning you'll be ill."

"Ugly? He's no' *that* bad," I hear Susan mutter.

"Anyway, I'm going nowhere," I protest. "You can't *make* me."

"Actually, Ah can. But I'd prefer not to have to."

Our group have been reduced to silence once more. The whole bar is, in fact, deathly quiet. We have become the focus of universal attention.

Nicky stands up. He will defend me, he always does. Then there's Pat Calhoun and Alec. Bobby too. They all like me, they are my friends. They will sort this idiot out.

But no. Instead, Nicky claps me on the shoulder.

"Aye, Tommy's right, ye should go home. Yiv had a bit too much tae drink. Happens tae us all."

He is absolutely correct.

"Here, Ah'll help ye wi' yer jacket."

As he does so, he whispers in my ear. "OK, Ah get the picture. Don't worry, you'll be fine. Ah'm tellin' you, he's *mad* for you, that Tommy."

Mad *at* me, more like.

Throughout this, the man in question has simply stood by, waiting. When I am ready, he takes me by the arm and leads me towards the door.

I pull back and address the company.

"G'night, ladies and gents." I giggle. "Sorry, everyone, looks like I'm being kidnapped."

I address my captor imperiously. "OK, Valentino, carry me off to the Kasbah."

When I trip over my feet and nearly stretch my length on the floor, he helps me up carefully.

The fresh air hits me, and I feel at first as if I have started to sober up. I also start to worry a bit.

'God, he might kill me,' I think. I remember how strong he is.

But at first he does nothing, says nothing. He just stares at me for a moment. Then starts to frog-march me down the road, his hand gripping my arm above the elbow.

"Hey," I protest, "stop *pushing* me. You'll make me fall over."

"Just be quiet, you."

But he does ease the pace a little.

It's about now I realise that I haven't sobered up at all, I am actually *very* drunk. Maybe I can vomit over him; that would be satisfying.

Opposite the *Strand*, I pull back. "Aw, Thomas, let's have a wee drink in the *Strand*. What do you say?"

"You're barred."

"I most certainly am *not*. Who told you that?"

"You did."

Oh yes, so I did. And so I am.

He is still hustling me along.

"Don't hold me so *tight*, please."

He ignores that.

How can I get a reaction?

"I'll scream for help."

"Scream away."

A little further on, I sneak a look at him from the corner of my eye. His face is grim.

I try wheedling.

"Oh, c'mon, give me a wee smile, Thomas. You've got a lovely smile, you know. Did I ever tell you that?"

"Shut up. And call me Tommy, not *Thomas*."

Well, I can hardly do both.

OK. I'm not allowed to speak. Well in that case I'll sing.

> *'If you missed me half as much as I miss you*
> *You wouldn't stay away half as much as you do...'*

I sneak another look. He's trying very hard not to laugh.

"Aw, Thomas, that's better," I say.

"You're a fuckin' nightmare, you," he says.

But he is smiling, a little. And this is, I think, the very first time I have heard him say A Really Bad Word.

"A nightmare?" I shrug. "Don't worry, Thomas, you'll have forgotten me by the time you wake up. Just like you did last week."

He says nothing.

I am starting to feel a little better. And I just have to keep pushing his buttons.

"You know your problem, Thomas, don't you?"

"Yeah, *you're* ma problem, George."

"No, your other problem?"

"OK, you tell me."

I decide to do just that.

"You're ashamed of what you are. You hide away with your dirty little secret. You're gay, but you'd die if anyone found out."

"Ah'm *not* ashamed –"

"Oh yes, you are. And when you're with people like me or Angie, people who don't give a damn what anyone thinks, it scares the shit out of you. '*Oh dear, what if somebody sees me? What if someone suspects that big, butch, boxing, Territorial Army Mr Thomas Molony is a poof?*' That's right, isn't it?"

"Will you *shut up*?" His jaw is clenched. He is furiously angry.

I have touched a nerve. "OK. Just thought I'd share that with you."

I am dicing with death here, but what the hell, it feels good.

He is silent for a moment.

Then he growls, "You know nothing about me".

"OK, tell me, then. Confession's good for the soul. So tell me everything, Thomas."

"No."

Moments go by. One or two people stare at us as they pass.

"You know you're abducting a minor, don't you?"

He suddenly laughs; but bitterly, not in amusement.

"You're nineteen. Don't you remember telling me? Don't you remember anything we talked about last time?"

I remember every word.

"No, I don't. How come you do? Do you take notes or something?"

He doesn't reply.

We have reached the bus station, and he propels me onto the platform. There is a bus waiting.

"OK, George, there's your bus. Get on it."

I don't think I will. No, no, this game's not over.

"No."

His teeth clench.

"Go on, for Christ's sake, before Ah lose ma rag. Or Ah'll *put* you on it."

"If you do, I'll get off at the first stop and come back."

He has let go of my arm. I move up the platform, away from him, in the direction of the rear of the bus. He follows me. I raise the volume a notch.

"And I'll keep doing that until there are no buses left. Well, till the last one's gone, I mean."

I look around to see if there is any possibility of a rescue. There isn't. Anyway, I'm not entirely sure I want to be rescued.

"And there's a party at Wilma's place later. I might go there, she and Connie are very anxious for me to attend. And you can't stop me. Who do you think you are anyway, telling me what I can do and what I can't do?"

With an enormous effort, he manages a calm, reasonable tone. Just as well, as there are three or four people on the platform, and another half-dozen already on the bus, and I am putting on quite a show.

He takes me by the shoulders.

"Look, George, listen tae me, please. You're pissed. You need to go home. I can't leave you here on your own. What if something happened to you?"

"Why would you care?"

I look away.

I wait a beat—good dialogue is like music, timing is everything.

I look back.

"Is it because you love me?"

"What?"

"I said, '*Do you love me?'* Do you, Thomas?"

"Are you mental? No, of course Ah don't. And keep your voice down, *please*."

It's way too late for discretion. Every eye is on us.

He moves a few paces away from me.

I call after him. "Aw, go on, tell me you love me, Thomas. I love *you*, you know."

Yes, I know, my behaviour is simply inexcusable.

"Aw, for Christ's sake…"

He is close to losing it, but I just can't stop. I've found out how to really niggle him and I am helpless to resist the temptation.

A old lady is passing me. I stop her.

"He doesn't love me, you know."

She looks at him then back at me. "Aw, that's a shame, dear. Ah bet he does, deep down. Yer brother, is he?"

"No, he's my lover, not my brother."

I see his jaw tighten and his fists clench. Now, what else can I come up with?

I've got it. This will finish him. It did before.

The little lady is now behind me, looking at the destination board on the back of the bus. I turn and tap her on the shoulder.

"If you've got a moment, dear, would you like to know how I lost my virginity?"

BANG!!

For a daft split second I think he has hit me on the back of the head, the noise is so loud. But I feel nothing.

I turn back. No, he has crashed his fist into the solid metal wall that separates this platform from the neighbouring one. It rings like a bell. Then, silly bugger, he yelps in pain, and, bent over, cradles his bruised knuckles in his crotch.

This evening I have been, so far, a happy drunk, a loud drunk, and a cheeky drunk. Now I become a weepy drunk. I truly can't help it, it's the tension and the booze. I burst into tears.

He looks at me in disgust, shaking his injured hand, and comes back towards me.

"Aw, stop that crying, for God's sake. Stop it, come on. OK, Ah'm *sorry*."

"But your h-h-hand," I sob.

He turns away slightly. "It's nothing. You just wound me up, that's all. Now, stop crying, right now."

But I can't. Try as I may, I just can't halt the flood of tears. They run down my face and drip off my chin.

"L-l-leave me alone, go away, I *hate* you."

He simply doesn't know what to do.

"Aw, *please*, George, stop. You're embarrassing me."

That is the last straw. With a huge effort, I manage to stem the torrent. I am utterly incredulous. Did he actually say what I thought he said?

In a flash I am furiously angry.

"What?" I screech. "*I'm* embarrassing *you?* It's not *me* who's making an exhibition of myself, punching a bloody metal wall. It's *you*, you fuckin' lunatic."

I sniff back some snot. "I'm not bothering anybody. I'm just slightly upset."

He is finally lost for words.

But I've not done yet. I know the button to push. I force my voice down to a normal level.

"You know what, Tommy, you're a really sad case. OK, you're embarrassed to be seen with me, that's fine, I couldn't care less what you think. But worse, you're ashamed of *yourself*. Really, you're just pathetic."

I turn away to board the bus.

He pulls me back and turns me round. He is right in my face. His voice is suddenly calm and quiet.

"Ah told you before. I'm not ashamed. Not of you, and not of me."

And he kisses me, there, in front of the world. Well, in front of the bus queue. It's not like Nicky's calculated kiss, deep, and made for display. But it's not a peck, either.

I have a moment of panic when it starts, remembering the last time someone kissed me when I was drunk. But there's not a gurgle.

I kiss him back. There is a little ironic applause.

As the elderly lady boards the bus, she says, "There you are dear, see, he *does* love you. Ah'm sure he's a nice boy, really. Families, eh?"

And, shaking her head in despair at the follies of humankind, she heads off to find a seat.

Tommy puts his arm round me. I can see one of my tears glistening in his beard,

"Come on, let's go and get a coffee, George, OK?"

"Really, honest, Ah'm *not* ashamed. You don't understand how it is."

We are in the *Gondola*, drinking tea in a quiet snack bar that few people I know use.

"Tell me how it is then, Tommy."

I feel completely sober. I examine his poor hand. The knuckles are blue and swollen.

He sips his tea and looks up at me. "Oh? Nae mair *Thomas*, then? Glad you've dropped that."

"Why? Don't you like it?"

He grins. "It makes me feel like a naughty wee boy."

I smile back at him. "And that's what you are."

We have both calmed down.

"But I like 'Thomas'. Anyway, it's my middle name, too."

"Eh? Naw, yer kiddin' me?"

"No. I'm George Thomas Wallace."

"Yeah? How about that?"

He seems to come to a decision. "OK then, you can call me *Thomas*. But only in private; and only if I'm being out of order; and just now and then. OK?"

I'm happy with that arrangement. We're going to be *in private* at some point, apparently.

"OK. Anyway, go on. You were saying?"

He looks down. I realise this is difficult for him.

"Aye—well, it's true, I *am* gay, like you said. But I come from a bit of a rough area, it wouldnae do if anyone round there found out. My maw an' ma da', ma brother… they would have to put up with all sorts. Ah wouldn't put them through that, Ah couldn't. Do you understand?"

Oh yes. I've been there.

"Yes. I understand."

"There you are then."

I hesitate for a moment.

"But—what I *don't* understand is—when you're out here, in the town, away from home—what's the problem? No-one's going to see you, what does it matter?"

What am I saying? Have I completely forgotten Jake Quinn and his whistle-blowing telephone call?

"No, you're wrong." He pauses. "Look—you live in Rutherglen, right? A good way from the city?"

"Mm."

"Ah live in Maryhill. It's just fifteen minutes up the road from here. Half the guys Ah know drink in the town pubs now and then. I could run into one o' them at any time. So Ah have to keep a low profile. Do you see what Ah mean?"

With my own experience, that should have occurred to me.

"Yes, I see, now. I just hadn't thought. I'm sorry."

He puts his cup down. "Why would you? You barely know me. Why would it even cross your mind?"

He lights two cigarettes and passes me one. We are Paul Henreid and Bette Davis in *Now, Voyager*.

"Your poor hand…"

I take it and raise it to my lips. We're the only customers.

"Aye, it's bad." He examines it. "Ah'm a fool. Ah've done that quite a few times. Knuckles are shot on that hand."

He leans back in his chair and sighs. "It's just that I sometimes get that angry and frustrated, and it's better that than hitting someone. Ah never do that. Hit people, I mean. Well, unless they throw a punch at me first."

I pick up his hand again. His left hand. He has already told me he is something called a *southpaw*. Then he had to explain to me that that meant left-handed, a boxing term apparently. I kiss it again, and look up at him under my eyelashes. Very sultry and come-hither, I imagine.

"Another thing," he goes on, quickly looking round to check that we are unobserved. "You know I don't like all that stuff, the screaming and bitching, the female names, all yon lot, acting like girls. Your friend Angie, a prime example. Well, it's not only because there's the chance that somebody I know might see me. It just—well—it puts me off.

"You maybe don't realise it, but you become a different person when you're with them. You're unrecognisable. It's put on, it's phony."

He takes a draw of his cigarette.

"I liked the person I met, when was it? Just a week ago. Quiet, a bit shy. A wee bit wary of me, Ah think, at first? But with that town crowd, it's like Jekyll and Hyde—suddenly you're loud, mouthy, aggressive. Ah just don't believe that's the real you."

'Maybe,' I think, *'he's right. Who, then, is the real me?'*

This is perhaps dangerous territory to investigate too closely. For now anyway. We've been through a lot tonight. Best to leave it.

"OK," I say. "I understand. I'm not saying I agree. And please—Angie—Gordon—is my best friend, and no worse than anyone else. But I'll think about what you've said."

"OK. I don't ask for more than that."

I look at my watch.

"Oh—are you worried about the time?"

He is staring at me intently.

"Yes—I need to be going. Bus."

He puts on a sad face. "Pity, that. This is nice here, just you and me. You sure? Could you no' stay a wee while?"

And to think that half an hour ago he couldn't get rid of me quick enough. Though I'm tempted, I indicate *'No'*. Some instinct tells me that this is the right time to play a little hard to get. Anyway, it's past eleven.

I make to get up, but he stops me.

"Just one more thing. It's been on ma mind. What's all this stuff about 'my virginity'? You're joking, right, it's a joke? That wasn't really your first time?"

"Actually, it was. Well, for that, anyway. The Deed."

He raises his eyebrows, looking genuinely shocked. "Really?"

He is obviously not sure what reaction I am expecting.

"Well, I'm honoured, Ah suppose. And Ah'm sorry, Ah thought you were just saying it tae get a rise out of me."

"Well, I was. But it's still true. But it doesn't matter. It was about due. And…"

I hesitate—is this a step too far?

"…I'm glad it was with you."

Then I add hurriedly, all innocence, "Anyway, since we'll probably never see each other again, you really don't have to worry about it. It's unlikely I'm pregnant."

He knows that I am trying it on. He was meant to know.

He smiles. "Oh—is that right? Well, I'll be in *Guy's* next week. Friday, eight o' clock. Be there or not, it's up to you."

He stares at me. "But I hope you will."

My face must be registering 'dubious'.

He smiles. "Oh, don't worry, George, Ah'll be there. Ah can't wait, tae tell you the truth. An' who knows, maybe you'll be able tae lay your hands on the keys tae that guy's flat again?"

His voice drops to a whisper. He grins.

"An' then later, if we're lucky, maybe Ah can try tae fuck a wee bit of sense into you, eh?"

Eh?

Then I catch the twinkle in his eye and realise that it was meant to be funny; and that, under the beard, he is bright red.

I must be looking a little shocked.

He hangs his head. "Aw, shit, sorry, Ah'm sorry… Christ, me an' ma big gob. It was just a joke, sorry."

I wonder idly how many times tonight each of us has said *sorry*? I think he's ahead by a good bit.

"It's OK," I say, ruffling his hair. "Just as long as you realise that that might take a long time."

He laughs as he stands up.

"Och, fine. We're young yet, there's nae rush, is there?"

He sees me, once again, to my bus.

He stays with me until the bus leaves.

All the way home I hug myself with delight. Have I hooked him? I think I have.

He's certainly hooked me.

And he's there, bang on time. And, oh Lord, he's wearing a *suit*. Navy blue. And the beard has been trimmed. It's now neat and tidy. It's hard to convey how different he looks.

Oh, no question, he looks good—handsome, smart.

But does he look better? I would have expected him to, certainly. Whether he actually does is a more difficult question to answer. I was expecting one of his Jungle Jim get-ups, and for a tiny moment I don't recognise him.

The trouble is that, beard apart, he now looks not unlike a dozen other young men of my acquaintance. He doesn't look like *my Tommy*.

Yes, I have already begun to think of him in those terms, I'm afraid.

"Like it?" he asks me, meaning the suit. "Thought Ah'd smarten myself up a bit. Ah got the idea you were not that keen on ma usual style."

"You look great," I say. "Just one problem."

He looks up. "Oh? What's that?"

"Well—I like you in jeans. In that jacket I can't enjoy the sight of your gorgeous bottom."

He blushes. He is incredibly easy to embarrass.

"Ma bottom, eh?"

He casts a glance over his shoulder, as if there might be a chance of catching a glimpse of it.

"Gorgeous? Is that what you think?"

"Certainly do," I say.

"OK."

He does a deliberate double-take. "Hang on—should Ah be getting a wee bit worried here, George?" he says with a quizzical little smile.

I'm flustered. "No, no, I didn't mean *that*."

Hm. *Did* I mean that? No, surely I didn't?

To cover my embarrassment, I ask him if he wants a drink.

"No, no, my treat tonight. Got paid the day, Ah'm loaded. What'll you have?"

"Oh—I don't know. Beer has me peeing all the time, and that gin and orange is so *sweet*…"

"Right. I know what you need."

He orders a pint for himself, and a vodka with ice plus an orange juice for me.

"Try that. Tip the orange juice into the vodka. Yon orange mixer is awful."

He's right. This is a new drink experience, delicious, sophisticated, and not sugary.

On the whole, the evening goes well. There are just one or two sticky moments when this one or that one comes up to say *hello*.

'Hello, Audrey,' inevitably.

I note a hint of the familiar tensing of the jaw muscle when that happens.

"Look," I say, after the third or fourth time of this. "I know, I know. But you need to deal with this. It's not going to change. Can't you just accept it, or ignore it? If we're going to drink in here, or in the *Strand*, or any gay bar, it's going to happen. I'm too well known. I can't change that, it's too late."

He's not angry. He's just uncomfortable.

"Who says we have to drink in a gay bar? We can drink anywhere—the town's full of pubs."

I find this a bizarre suggestion.

"Oh? And what are we supposed to do in some straight bar, you and me? What are we supposed to be? Pals? Workmates? Am I your apprentice, maybe? No, I don't think so."

He purses his lips and gives a little smile. "Well, yes, now I think about it…"

Is he finally beginning to relax a little?

"You get my point?"

"Oh aye, Ah do—an' you'll be getting' mine later on, if you're a good boy."

I snort into my drink.

He gives a little sigh.

"Oh aye, sure, George, I know what you're saying. Hard to find the answer, isn't it? But don't worry." He squares his shoulders, as if he had just agreed to take part in a suicide mission. "Ah'll behave myself. I suppose I'll just have to get used to it in time. If you see me getting a bit pissed off, just *Thomas* me, an' Ah'll pull myself together."

He smiles lecherously. "Though Ah'd rather we pulled each other together."

"Oh, enough, Thomas, stop it!"

It is near closing time when he pops the question I have been anticipating. We've only had two or three drinks.

"Eh, just wondering... Did you have any luck? With the keys and that?"

I pretend to misunderstand.

"The keys? What keys?"

"Aw, don't tell me you forgot. The keys for the flat."

I pretend I have just this moment understood.

"Oh, *those* keys. No, I wasn't able to get hold of Barry, sorry. I tried, but he's only around the town now and again."

He looks suitably unhappy.

"OK. So—no nookie the night, eh? Damn it, an' Ah'm as horny as hell."

He yawns, covering his mouth with his hand, and looks round. "Guess Ah'll just have tae settle for one off the wrist when Ah get home. Better than nothing, Ah suppose."

I reach into my pocket.

"No need, tonight."

I pull out a set of keys.

He grins, delighted. "What a little liar you are, you."

"No, not at all. These are not Barry's keys. They're just—keys."

In fact they are Shirley's. All the time I've known her, I never realised that she has a bed-sit in Wellington Street. I always assumed she lodged in the brothel.

"No, Audrey, I can't stay the night there," she told me. *"Once I finish my shift, I have tae leave. Rules of the house. But you're welcome tae borrow the place. I'll not be in till two or three. It's a big bed, make yourselves at home. I'll just jump in on the end, try not tae wake ye up."*

I explain this to Tommy.

"It's not ideal, but it's all I could come up with."

"No problem, it's fine, it's great."

He thinks for a moment, and frowns.

"Mind, though, Ah'm no' sleepin' in the middle."

"No, you're not, I am. Do you think I would let another woman near you? Oh, shit—another person, I mean."

Try as I may, to me Shirley is Shirley. It's just habit. But *he* seems happy.

He winks. "Aye, see, you're catching on. I'll make a man of you yet. Well—maybe no' *just* yet..."

This encounter is light-years away from our previous one. Tonight, the first time is urgent. The second infinitely more protracted. We are utterly comfortable with each other, and our interaction is unlike anything I have previously experienced. We enjoy each other physically and mentally. He is gentle and thoughtful.

And he is funny. We laugh as much as anything else. Shirley's bedsit is a dump, it's not even clean, but we couldn't care less. It is ours for an hour or two.

Because, I guess, we are alone, all his usual hang-ups seem to have disappeared.

It's nearly two o' clock. Sleeping time, and I want to spend the night next to him.

But as we share a final cigarette, I say, "You could go home now, Tommy, if you wanted to. So could I, if it comes to that. There's the late bus, George Square."

"But I don't want to," he says.

"Neither do I."

But when I realise he is warming up for an encore, I have to draw the line.

"No, no, stop it," I protest, like a silly teenager—and to be fair, that's exactly what I am. "I've got work in the morning."

And I have, Caldwell's calls.

A little rueful grimace. "OK, Ah'll stop, promise. Just a wee cuddle, eh?"

"Fine," I say. "But turn round. I'll cuddle you. I know what your cuddles can lead to."

"OK." He turns his back and I snuggle in.

Just before we drop off, he says, "And watch it, you—hands off the gorgeous bottom."

I am vaguely aware of Shirley falling into bed at some hour. Tommy is sound asleep, and—what a bonus—he doesn't snore.

But I don't sleep much after Shirley's return, because she *does*. And it's strange, sleeping between two people, I've never done it before. I am half-asleep, half-awake the whole night. In the morning, seven-thirty, we have to get up. I feel shattered, but spacey, and weirdly happy.

Tommy and I tiptoe around, getting dressed. Shirley is unconscious, snoring for the Guinness Book of Records. I have no idea what time she got in.

We whisper and giggle and yawn, like two naughty kids.

"Fancy a bit of breakfast?" Tommy says, as we emerge into the daylight.

It is deliciously cool this early, and I begin to feel better immediately. "You've got time, haven't you?"

I am suddenly starving. "Oh, yes, let's do that. I want bacon and eggs. And tea."

"OK, I know a wee caff that's open early. Only—it's a place I go into from work now and then, so—if you could just keep it toned down a wee bit..."

"Thomas!"

He holds his hands out. "OK, OK. Sorry, sorry. But..."

I yawn.

"I get it, stop worrying. Where is this place? I'll be embarrassingly masculine, I promise."

It's ten to nine. I will walk to work, it's only five minutes away. I wait at the stop with Tommy, for his bus to Maryhill. He doesn't work on Saturdays, lucky him.

He looks at me. "Thanks," he says.

"What for?"

"For a great night, what do you think what for, ya eedjit?"

"It's your pleasure," I say stupidly, and we're laughing again.

I see his bus turn the corner. He looks at his watch. "Next week? Same time, same place? OK?"

"Yes, next Friday."

His bus arrives, and he queues to get on.

"Oh, one thing..."

"Yes?" he says, over his shoulder.

"Next week, wear the jeans."

And I grab the gorgeous bottom and squeeze it.

He jumps on the platform and turns round.

"Count on it," he shouts, laughing, as the bus moves off.

He *is* wearing the jeans. And it's a huge improvement.

Tonight he seems totally comfortable when we meet, and is in full suggestive, jokey mood.

'*Maybe things are settling down,*' I think. '*Maybe he's getting used to it. Or resigned to it.*'

"So—did you get home all right, last week?" I ask him.

"Oh aye. Had a wee embarrassing moment though."

Oh, no. "Did somebody see us together?"

But he is smiling.

"No, no, nothing like that. But Ah was on the top deck of the bus, you see, needed a fag. And Ah started thinking."

"What about?"

"About what we did the night before. Picturing it, like. Big mistake, that. Between the bouncy bus and what was going on in ma head…

"Next thing Ah know, Ah've got this raging hard-on. Had tae put ma *Daily Record* over ma fly tae get down the stairs without embarrassment."

I've grown to enjoy it when he talks a little bit dirty. But I decide to play it cool this time.

"Oh, come on—as if anybody would have noticed that wee thing."

"What? Cheeky bastard!"

He puts his arm round my shoulder and squeezes me tight. He whispers in my ear, "Are you saying Ah'm not enough for you, then?"

His breath in my ear…

I want to turn my head and kiss him then and there, but daren't.

"More than enough, Thomas."

He mutters in mock despair. "Ah hope so. Ah think maybe you're wearing it out, Ah'm sure it's got a wee bit smaller."

I manage to keep a straight face. "God, let's hope not, I'll need tweezers."

He laughs long and hard and squeezes me again.

Well, I wanted a boyfriend, and I have one.

But I never expected this. This is not a game, a bit of fun. He's not a trophy to wave around, '*Look everybody—I've got a boyfriend!*'

No, this is serious.

How did I get so lucky?

It's Shirley's again this week. And certainly, it's fine for an hour or two. Then, damn, she gets home early, not long after twelve—'*Sorry, you two, but the brothel was empty, and Ah'm dead on ma feet, didnae sleep at aw last night.*'

Luckily we're respectable, and are lying in bed having a cigarette.

I am more grateful than I can say for Shirley's kindness in sheltering us. But when she throws herself into bed—*her* bed, I must remember—and starts snoring, I have to prepare myself for another sleepless session.

Tommy just shrugs. He seems to be able to sleep anywhere, him. I toss and turn all night, barely catching a wink. And I will have work the next day.

There has to be a better solution than this.

♦

We chat about it over breakfast, having left Shirley dead to the world. I'm having a bacon sandwich, though I have little appetite.

"We'll have to find something else. This is no good. I've not slept more than an hour or two, and I've got a day's work ahead of me."

I sip my tea. "Any ideas?"

He dips his toast in his runny fried egg.

"Well, any chance of thon Barry character being around? Maybe you could arrange something regular with him—like, maybe leaving the keys somewhere for you? Or even giving you a set? That would do it, wouldn't it? That wee flat was OK."

"Don't know. I've not seen him for a while. Nobody has, I've been asking around. He comes and goes, Barry."

"Oh, right."

I look over at him. "Like you the first time we got together—you came, then you went."

He nearly chokes on a chip. It makes me feel a little queasy, watching him. God, hope I'm *not* pregnant.

He munches away, still laughing. "How dae you know him anyway, that Barry? Ex-boyfriend?"

I reach over and wipe a spot of egg from his beard with a tissue. "No, nothing like that. I just know him from around."

I force myself to take a bite of my sandwich. Surprisingly, it's delicious; fatty bacon dripping with butter, or whatever it is.

"Oh, from around, eh?"

I sense that he has something on his mind.

He picks up another chip. I pinch one from his plate. I'm feeling better suddenly. Needed food, I suppose.

He looks down.

"But you must have had one or two boyfriends before you met me. Tell me about them, go on."

I look away.

"What's the matter? Are you shy?" He looks up again and laughs. "Don't be—Ah'll not be jealous or anything. Go on, tell me."

"Well…"

Why is he asking me this?

"Yes, I did, but not many, only one or two. There was a guy called Andy, for a while—he was weird and kind of sad. Then there was Bobby, a Canadian boy. He was in the pub the other week, that night you swept me off my feet. He was with his current affair, Vera—sorry, don't know her real name—*his* real name, I mean. She was sat next to you, remember?"

God this double-name thing is confusing!

"Bobby was nice, but a bit boring, it didn't last long. There was a guy called Tam McLain, but that was just twice—no, three times, and the last time it was as a favour to Angie—sorry, Gordon—really. Then there was…"

Oops. How do I explain The Three Stooges without sounding like a tart?

He is cutting into a sausage.

He looks up. "Then there was…?"

I want to be honest. "Well, there was a guy called George Cooper, but he was a bit of a mistake, he was married and I didn't know. And…"

If I rush maybe it won't sound so bad.

"…and his cousin Brian, and their friend Billy. That's it," I finish triumphantly, glad to have got it over with.

He looks up again. "Hold on, hold on. George and Brian and Billy? What, you had sex with all of them?"

My sandwich drips grease down my shirt. Why does he want to know all this ancient history? I'm getting a little bit pissed off. And that's because I would love to say that he was the only man I'd ever been with.

I take the bull by the horns. "Yes, all of them. But *separately*, not together."

He is laughing at me. "Oh, that makes it OK, then."

He takes a mouthful of sausage. "Boy, you're full of surprises, young George. You said one or two, but that makes six. Here I thought Ah was dating this innocent. Looks like Ah was wrong."

Now I'm getting almost angry with him. It's too early for all this. I scrub at my shirt, tired and fretful.

"What does all that matter anyway? It's past, done with. Why do you want to know?"

He pats my hand. "Hey, calm down, Ah'm not bothered. I don't care—as you say, it's past and done with. Ah'm not jealous, Ah'm not angry. Ah'm just curious. No, I'll tell you why I'm asking. How come, with this colourful past, you didn't ever—well, do it with any of them? You know—*that*, the business."

I am sick of this interrogation, and decide to be disgustingly blunt.

"Up the arse, you mean? Well, it just didn't happen."

"I see. So all this time you were saving yourself for me?"

He is laughing at me again. I could kill him sometimes. How is it only *he* can make me feel this stupid?

I know why. It's because I love him. Which is great, most of the time, but occasionally a bit trying.

"Saving myself? No, not at all. That's just the way it worked out. I wasn't saving anything for anybody. It was fate."

I look at him. "And you've got a chip in your beard, by the way."

"Oh—thanks."

He takes out his handkerchief. He is very particular about personal cleanliness.

I put down my sandwich. "Anyway, what about you? *Your* past? Go on—spill. How many affairs have *you* had?"

Suddenly I do actually want to know. And anyway it was him who started all this.

He looks serious. "Wis engaged tae a lassie for a while, years ago, Ah wis only eighteen, nineteen. But since then, none. Not one. Never."

"What?"

"Oh, I've shagged around as much as the next guy. Men, girls now and then, a bit of everything."

"Everything? Sheep and cattle?"

"Don't be daft. I'm trying tae be serious. It's important. No, I just mean… Sex, here and there, whenever the chance arose. This one and that one. But…"

He hesitates.

"No relationship. Not till now."

That's unexpected.

"Oh? This is a relationship, is it?"

He looks a bit hurt.

"Well—I don't really know. You tell me, you're the expert. I've never had one. Is it?"

I know he doesn't lie.

"Yes, I think it is," I say.

"Good," he smiles. "Ah was hoping it was."

I look at my watch. I always seem to be doing that when I'm with him, always cutting short, having to be somewhere else.

I've just got time for a cigarette. I pass him one, and try to answer his question seriously.

"Well, relationship, affair, whatever we're having, it's great, but it's going nowhere unless we can sort out this accommodation problem, find somewhere we can be together. Alone."

He does a solemn face. "Oh, aye, alone—so you can drain me yet again. Just after ma body, as usual."

I smile. But he's spot on. When we're together in private, I can't leave him alone. I find him eternally desirable, like an itch you can't scratch enough.

"Yes. Your body first. Followed by about twelve hours sleep."

He is quiet for a moment. He stares at me intently.

"OK. Ah'll sort it, leave it to me. You'll have both. My body, for as long as you want it, then sleep, ditto."

"Oh? How? Where?"

"I'll book us into a bed and breakfast somewhere. For tonight. Ah've been keeping a wee bit cash back from ma wages the last couple of weeks. Ah'll meet you from work and we'll have a bite to eat, then after… Whatever your heart desires."

"Really?"

He smiles. "Sure. But it'll just be a one-off, Ah'm afraid, Ah'm no' a millionaire."

He leans over the table, looks round, and takes my hand.

"Ah've been thinking about it for a while. OK with you?"

I touch the side of his face. Nobody is looking. "What do *you* think?"

"Ah think that's a *yes*."

Now it's his turn to look at his watch. "Here—you're going to be late for work, you. Better shift, come on."

We part on the corner of Sauchiehall Street.

'*Well,*' I think, as I walk into work. '*Imagine that!*'

I do feel a bit guilty about Tommy using up his wages when I've got a sizeable sum stashed away in my secret place.

But that money of mine is already earmarked for a very special purpose.

3. Teenager in Love

> One day I feel so happy
> Next day I feel so sad
> I guess I'll learn to take
> The good with the bad
> Each night I ask the stars up above
> Why must I be a teenager in love?
> **Dion and the Belmonts, 1959**

That first night we spend completely alone within four walls, in a bed and breakfast place near the Glasgow Art Gallery, is a turning point, and leads me to take a firm decision. This is how we should be together, he and I. Not now and then, not here and there, not once or twice a week, but all the time. I need to be with him permanently, to live with him, to be husband and wife, or husband and husband, whatever we are. And I can make that happen, I have the means.

But will he want it too?

I will leave home again without a qualm—my unfortunate parents are by now resigned to accepting that I am going to do pretty much what I want to do, that I am in fact a monster of self-interest where my own desires are concerned. They don't understand the irresistible forces that drive me to behave in this ungrateful and inconsiderate way, the overwhelming need I have to be my own person, to live by my own rules, to wring life by the neck in order to squeeze a bit of happiness out of it.

I doubt they ever will. I'm not sure I do myself.

But Tommy, as far as I can tell, is perfectly settled with his family. When he's not with me, he's either working or with them. Best of both worlds. Why would he want to give that up for me?

This is something I need to work on, or to work out.

It is wonderful, this one time, to finally have somewhere entirely to ourselves. He meets me from work as promised, and suggests fish and chips before we head off to the room he has booked for us.

"No," I say, "not fish and chips. Not tonight."

Despite my exhaustion from the previous night, those disturbed and sleepless hours at Shirley's place, I have had a profitable day.

"I've got a couple of quid, it was a birthday present, I'm treating you to an Italian."

"Oh? Make sure he's young and good-looking, then," he jokes.

We gorge on avocado with prawns (me) and minestrone soup (him), lasagne (me) and pizza (him), beer for him and wine for me. Real wine, no *Barchester Ruby* here in the *Rapallo*. *Chianti Classico*, an entire half-bottle, imagine, all mine. I discover that in fact I quite like the taste of wine, after all.

We arrive at the bed and breakfast around nine, are shown to our room, and fall into bed immediately. And after the familiar intimacies, slow and languorous, we sleep and sleep.

In the morning, we laugh together quietly at the miniature old lady who serves us our full Scottish breakfast. She must be seventy. Tiny, with strong glasses and a mane of obviously dyed bright red hair hanging to her waist behind. I wonder fleetingly if, in mediæval times, she might have been a king's mistress? Under the pension-book doddering she has a decidedly whorish look. But she is sweet and charming, and hopes we will visit again.

I think we might. This is the way our life should be, his and mine. This is the way I will *make* it be, whatever the cost.

We say goodbye at the bus station that was the scene of our romantic breakthrough. I have to get back to Rutherglen for my weekly devotions, playing the organ in Greenhill Church and trying not to nod off during the sermon.

September 1963.

Tommy is never completely relaxed when we are out together in one of the recognised pubs in the city. He puts up with it, for my sake. But he is not entirely comfortable in these surroundings.

Just opposite the *Strand* is a bar called *McColl's*, a small place, a bit of a dump, to be frank. Though it is not by any means a recognised gay haunt, it does now and then play host to the occasional queen or couple who fancy taking a breather in somewhere that is quieter than the *Strand* or *Guy's*. Tommy and I go in there from time to time, usually when the *Strand* is uncomfortably crowded, and the volume of noise and the excesses of rampant queenery are on the point of setting his teeth on edge.

McColl's Bar has one very regular *habitué*, a horrible old queen known as Patricia, or 'Pat', Medina. I have no idea what this character's real name is, no-one seems to know or care. But Patricia is universally loathed. And she returns that loathing with compound interest; indeed, she hates everyone. She took strong exception to me the first time I set foot in what she sees as her private territory, *McColl's*, abusing me as a 'queer', a 'poof,' and other such things loudly and repeatedly in front of the rest of the customers.

After Tommy had a quiet word, her abuse of me gave way to an apparent unawareness of my presence.

Physically unattractive, short and squat, hairless of head, probably fifty, possibly more, Patricia has nevertheless carved out a little niche for herself. Detested and despised as she is by the rest of the gay community, she is rarely seen in any of the regular watering places.

Instead, she sits in *McColl's*, a bloated, toad-like presence, nursing a pint all night, and keeping a sharp eye on the goings-on in the bar. Patricia has a very specific goal. She is looking for someone who is drunk, so drunk he can barely stand up, so drunk that he is only vaguely aware of what is going on around him.

Such sights are not at all rare in Glasgow. The phrase '*Sorry, pal, can't serve you any more, you've had enough*' is not in the lexicon of the average Glasgow barman. Unless the person in question is about to start a fight, or is vomiting or pissing on the floor, he can drink until he falls over. And if he can still hold onto a glass and pay for his pints, he can drink *after* he falls over.

When Patricia spots such a one, one who is on the verge of collapse, she moves in for the kill. She offers to buy the chosen one a drink, engages him in some kind of meaningless conversation, and waits, one eye on the clock, for closing time. Then she will offer to assist him to his bus or train.

More often than not, the befuddled one will decide he needs to relieve himself *en route*; and that is what Miss Medina has been waiting for. She will then conduct the unfortunate into some dark corner and as soon as he is unbuttoned and drained, she will sink to her knees and engulf him. Usually the victim is too far gone to resist; occasionally, I suppose, he may choose not to resist. More often, I suppose, he has little idea what is happening to him. If by any chance he should rally, object, and cut up rough, she will turn tail and flee—she is sober and he is drunk, after all. If he passes out completely, or pretends to, she is not put off. She continues to have her way, simply transforming sexual assault into a kind of necrophilia.

This is not just gossip. She boasts about these exploits to any of the very few people who actually speak to her or listen to her. Elaine is one such, and it was she who passed on the information to me.

The lovely and generally popular Miss Dorothy Provine is not, it must be said, universally adored. Certain of the older and less saleable queens dislike her. They begrudge her her youth and success, and they resent even more her popularity with others, the admiration her cabaret appearances elicit, and her acceptance of this homage as no more than her due.

Brenda Lee doesn't care much for Dorothy. Indeed, on one occasion, and in my presence, Brenda threw a pint of beer over her in the *Strand*. Unfortunately for Brenda, Dorothy moved out of the firing line at just the right moment, and the contents of the glass went over a certain Big Robert, who is a hulk, as well as a hunk. Robert was wearing his best suit—it was, after all, Saturday—and Brenda was thoroughly chastised for her temerity. She is no mean fighter herself, but Robert is twice her size and three times her weight. As a result of this, Brenda made the erroneous assumption that he was in some way Dorothy's protector, and avoided crossing swords with Miss Provine subsequently.

But if Brenda dislikes her, Patricia Medina detests Dorothy with an unreasonable and unreasoning ferocity.

In *Guy's* one night, she decides to lay into her. The insults fly forth, pretty much the same ones she had launched at me, but relentlessly, more highly coloured, and at top volume.

Dorothy is no slouch when it comes to a slanging match. But this unstoppable flow of filth and offensiveness is unanswerable. After contriving to ignore it for a few moments, she decides she will leave.

As she passes me on her way to the door, she mutters, "Mark my words, Audrey, that fat ugly cunt will *pay* for that."

It is only a day or two after this that I learn that the hideous 'Pat' Medina is dead.

Unregretted and unmourned, as far as I am aware.

"Aye," Elaine tells me, "went under a forty-two bus in Union Street."

"Oh?"

"Aye." She shrugs. "Did she fall? Or was she pushed?"

Given Patricia's unpopularity and her predatory sexual habits, the latter seems not impossible.

"Really? Oh, how sad," says Dorothy, with a little smile and a patent insincerity, when I pass on the news to her. "I always felt that there was probably a nice person under that vile exterior, didn't you? Shame so much potential should end up under a number forty-two."

Oddly, I hadn't actually mentioned the number of the bus.

Dorothy pauses, head on one side. "Still, Audrey, you reap what you sow, isn't that what they say?"

'*Oh? I wonder...*'

No, of course not...

"Thanks," I say to the attendant at the left-luggage office, Central Station, handing him the five shillings I owe. I take the small suitcase from him, and move away from the counter. I need to find a quiet spot.

The station buffet seems ideal. No-one I know ever goes in there, and at this time of day, ten in the morning, it is practically empty. I order a coffee, and seat myself at a table in the corner. I unsnap the catches of the case, raise the lid, and examine the contents.

One white shirt-waister dress, full-skirted, size fourteen; four frothy net underskirts; one bra, size thirty-six, complete with padding; panty-girdle, also white; stockings, beige, three pairs, with suspender belt; shoes, size eight, white, sling-backs with a low heel; assorted jewellery and make-up. All this bought months ago, thanks to my Caldwell's depredations, at a time when the prospect of another outing in drag was still an intriguing possibility. It is that no longer. I have very different things on my mind right now. I look at all this stuff, most of it still in its packaging, and wonder why I bothered.

I move the clothes towards the front of the case so I can reach the little closed pocket at the back. I unzip it, and take out the bulky envelope inside. Nearly four hundred pounds, all in pound notes. The fruits of crime, the wages of sin.

And more than six months of my Tommy's take-home pay.

He is unquestionably *my Tommy* now. I am head-over-heels, hopelessly, desperately in love for the very first time in my life. When I'm not with him, I'm thinking about him. Does he feel the same? The truth is, I don't really know. I think he does, but I don't know. He has never said to me '*I love you,*' although I have tried to encourage such a declaration. I have said it to *him* a couple of times, certainly, but so far never received the response I want.

Why is it important?

Because I am naïve and have been heavily influenced by the romantic literature I have read, the films, plays and television offerings that have shaped my expectations. If someone loves you, they're supposed to say so. He is older—eight years and four months older, to be precise, and much more down-to earth than I am. He was in the army, National Service, he's seen a bit of life, I suppose; and although this is his first relationship, if he's telling me the truth (and I have no real doubts that he is), his attitudes are tempered by an experience that I lack.

But in spite of his reluctance to express his feelings in words, I am sure, sure as I can be, that Tommy is just as besotted as I am. He must be. I feel his eyes on me all the time when we are together, even if we are on opposite sides of a room. He touches me discreetly whenever the chance arises, not sexually, not even romantically, he just seems to relish every opportunity for the least physical contact. And I am just the same with him, although, wary of his constant worries about his true nature being recognised outside our private sphere, I am more restrained than he is.

I have gradually come to really know him—and it is still early days, only a few weeks—and I realise how lucky I was to meet him. And how easily it might not have happened, how easily he might have slipped through my fingers.

'*Just tell me tae piss off,*' he had said that first night we met.

What if I had? It doesn't bear thinking about.

For, alongside the relentless, always satisfied but ever unsatisfiable physical attraction I feel for him, I have learnt that he is a truly good and decent man. He is kind, considerate, thoughtful and generous. And he is tough. Not in a bruiser-and-brawler way, that's not his style at all. But when I am with him, even in the roughest and most dangerous parts of Glasgow—and there are many such—I never have the least concern. I know he will look after me, come what may, that I will be safe with him.

And he is funny. Amusing, observant, and witty, often at my expense, and in a very *Glasgow* way, dry and ironic. I have come to accept his little joking remarks on my occasional vulgarities and my odd modesties, my naïve expectations, my youthful follies and my rare affectations. I no longer get angry with him when he picks on some trait or other of mine and makes me realise how ridiculous I sometimes am. I laugh along with him.

And, in any case, I am not exactly inexperienced in the art of the gentle put-down myself, and I give as good as I get.

Mid-September, during my lunch hour, I go looking for a place for us to live. The area round the west end of Sauchiehall Street, Charing Cross and St George's Road, teems with bedsits and flats to let. It is but five minutes from the town centre, and money is no object, I have plenty. But with unaccustomed common sense, I don't look for a flat at seven or eight pounds a week. Maybe that can come later, when I have convinced Tommy that our lives are destined to be lived together. I look for a bedsit, no more than two or three quid. The selection advertised in various shop windows is mind-boggling, so I simply pick one at random. And miraculously, for once, fall right on my feet.

Carnarvon Street is a street of tenement buildings, the mouths of closes lining either side, each leading to a series of flats, two on each floor. It is hardly a glamorous address, but both the street and the buildings are clean and well-maintained, and just opposite number thirty-nine, where I am heading, Baliol Lane runs down to join Woodlands Road and the University District. Fifty yards to the south, Carnarvon Street debouches into St George's Road, a busy main thoroughfare, and the route to the city. Caldwell's is easily reached in five minutes on foot. The Odeon Cinema, where Tommy works, no more than ten. Glasgow town centre is very small. This is looking good.

It becomes perfect when I discover that the landlord, a polite and respectable-looking middle-aged man, does not even live on the premises. He comes round once a week on Fridays to collect the rent. Other than that, the place will virtually belong to me and the other tenants. I will be able to live exactly as I want.

The flat is small, and only has two letting rooms, plus a shared bathroom and kitchen. I ask about the two lodgers who occupy the other bedsit—it might be tricky if I found myself sharing a house with a pair of elderly, nosy spinsters, or a brawling couple.

"Oh, they're students, the same as you. Mr Wright and Mr O'Brian. Nice lads, been here a year or more, never any trouble. Oh, the odd party now and then, but nothing to worry about. I'm sure they'll be happy to invite you along, if you fancy it."

This place just couldn't be better if I had ordered it from a catalogue. No landlord, own front door, young people, male, in the other room.

It's a small point, but just the fact that I can tell my family honestly that I am living with other students is a plus.

"I'll take it," I say. "It will suit me down to the ground. What's the rent?"

"It's two pounds a week, plus two pounds deposit. Hope that's not too much for you? I know you students don't have a lot of money. Spend most of it on drink and riotous living, I daresay."

He smiles, and for a moment I wonder if I can maybe knock him down a bit. Then I decide it's not worth the trouble, I can easily afford two pounds a week.

I hand him four pound notes, and he gives me a rent book. We shake hands, and he is gone. I stand in the hallway with my cases at my feet and the keys in my hand.

The keys to the kingdom.

The room itself is nothing special. But it is spotless, and obviously has recently been decorated. The furniture is cheap, modern and plywoody, but the recessed bed is large and clean, and there is plenty of storage space. A small dining table with two chairs sits by the window, an unattractive but comfortable sofa with two easy chairs is in front of the surprisingly modern gas fire, and there is a tall armoire and a spacious chest of drawers along the opposite wall.

I discover a spare set of bedding in the wardrobe. We tenants obviously attend to our own laundry, instead of having a changing day once a week, which suits me. The less interference I have, the less surveillance, the better. There is a launderette just a minute away in St George's Road, couldn't be more convenient. I drop my cases on the floor, to be tackled later.

I check out the rest of the flat. The kitchen looks as if it has never been used at all. There are dozens of eating places of all sorts within a few minutes' walk, and to me, as to most teenagers, cooking is an arcane science. *'Maybe I will learn to cook,'* I think. I am envisioning the occasional dinner party for the great and good of Glasgow society. As usual, my ambition knows no bounds.

The bathroom, however, is something else. It is grubby, a faint grey ring adorns the bath, the floor tiles are stained, while the condition of the toilet is better left to the imagination.

'What kind of animals am I sharing a house with?' I wonder.

I decide that this needs to be put right immediately—I can picture Tommy's face if he saw it—and hurry off to the shops to arm myself with the necessary equipment. If I have to do this every day, I will.

Less than an hour later, the bathroom is gleaming. The dirt was just on the surface, easily eradicated with a bottle of bleach and some scrubbing. It is just as I finish that I hear the front door open. I wonder if it is the landlord coming back, but when I step out into the hall, I see two young men, strangers, who must be my fellow tenants.

"Oh—are you the new lodger?" says the shorter of the two, before he turns to close and lock the door. He is small, fair and stocky, ordinary-looking, wearing a suit, and not more than eighteen or so, I would guess. He is balancing two boxes in his arms from which come a delicious aroma. My stomach growls embarrassingly.

The other is older, mid-twenties, tall and thin. Handsome, despite the beginnings of a receding hairline, he has an intellectual air, wears a long-sleeved jumper and jeans, and sports wire-framed glasses.

"Yes," I say. "I was just cleaning the bathroom, it was in a bit of a state. Hope you don't mind?"

The older one laughs.

"Mind? We're delighted, man, you deserve a prize. Colin was going to tackle it after that tart and her boyfriend moved out, but he's not had a minute, he works all hours."

Colin agrees. "Yes, sorry you had to take it on, I should have found time, but it's just a couple of days since Isabel and Martin left, and I've barely been here since."

The other takes over. "Aye, and we've hardly ever used the bathroom since they arrived here. Dirty cow, she was, that Isabel. Luckily we've got a wash-basin in our room, and if pushed, we have a piss in the back court, so for us the toilet has been strictly for emergency use only."

They survey my handiwork.

"Well, you've done a grand job... sorry, don't know your name?" Colin says.

"I'm George, George Logan," I say.

"Right," says the elder, "He's Colin O'Brian and I'm Geg Wright. Nice to meet a civilised person for a change, George."

He holds out his hand which I shake.

"Greg?" I say, thinking I have misheard.

"No, no, it's *Geg*, not *Greg*. Short for George, the same as you. Doesn't matter though, most people make that mistake, I answer to either."

The younger one is still gazing in admiration at the bathroom. The very first time, I think, that I have ever cleaned anything.

"What a difference—look at those taps, Geg—can't wait to have a bath. Oh, sorry, I should have said *hello* properly."

And he in turn shakes my hand.

"Would it be all right," he goes on, "if we take week about for the cleaning? I'll do next week, and after that you, and so on? That OK?"

It's fine with me, and I say so.

"Great," says Geg, "that'll work out well. Don't do cleaning, myself, sorry."

"What about the kitchen?" I say.

"Oh, we never really use the kitchen. Just wash up the odd glass or two, that's about it. Got a kettle in our room for tea and that. We usually eat out. But if you plan to cook, that's fine. Don't think the cooker's ever been turned on. I'll clean the kitchen as well as the bathroom when it's my turn, then you next time, like we said. OK?"

It seems we have a system arranged already. We are still standing in the hall.

"Gosh, where are my manners?" says the one called Geg. "Come into ours, man, and have a glass of wine before you get settled in. Do you like pizza? We've got plenty."

Their room is a bit bigger than mine, and has two beds. It overlooks the street, while mine looks out over the unprepossessing back court. It is, I notice, immaculately clean—the work of Colin, I guess, since Geg 'doesn't do cleaning'—but nevertheless every corner is occupied by tidily arranged stacks of books and records, posters, magazines, newspapers.

"Excuse the clutter," says Geg as he pours three glasses of wine. "I'm a bit of a collector, you see."

"A bit of a hoarder, you mean," puts in Colin with a smile, cutting up pizza and putting it on three plates.

Geg grins. "OK, OK, a bit of a hoarder, if you like."

He sits down and then immediately gets up again.

"Some music, maybe? What do you go for, George, what's your taste?"

"Oh, I don't mind, up to you, Geg."

He shuffles through a pile of LPs, selects one and puts it on the turntable of the surprisingly up to date and expensive—for a student—record player.

I am expecting something a bit esoteric—an album of modern jazz, maybe, which is my pet hate. Or perhaps the answer, my friend, will be *Blowin' in the wind*.

But no—the music is obviously classical, though I don't recognise it at all. I listen, and try to work out what it is. Turn of the century, got to be—the harmonies are heavily chromatic, and the orchestration translucent and brilliant. Late romantic, post-Wagnerian, I think. But it is melodious and—yes—sensuous in mood. But from where? Maybe French? Not German. Not English, either, nor Italian. Russian, perhaps? Early Stravinsky or late Rimsky-Korsakov?

"Know this?" says Geg, lounging back in his seat, looking smug. Colin hands out wine and pizza.

"Thanks," I say, as I take a plate and a glass from him. "No, I don't. But it's beautiful, whatever it is."

He smiles lazily. "Go on then—let's have your best guess."

I am realising that this one is a bit patronising and superior, though pleasant enough.

I take a bite of my pizza. "OK. Give me a minute."

I enjoy a challenge. I listen some more. It is very unusual music. The mood it conjures up is languorous and, yes, erotic.

"OK. It's early twentieth century, or very late nineteenth. *Fin de siècle*. It might be French, but no, it's not Debussy or Ravel, it's too—well—explicit."

I come to a decision.

"I guess Russian. Or maybe Polish—is it Szymanowski?"

He raises his eyebrows. "Wow, man, well done. No, it's not Szymanowski, but you're close, oh so close. Try again."

I have it now. Although I have never heard a note of this man's music, I know his reputation as the arch-exponent of perfumed musical decadence.

"Scriabin," I say decidedly.

He sits up in his chair and applauds.

"Yeah, spot on. Third symphony, second movement. Like it?"

The music rises to a brass-riven climax of bombastic frenzy, then subsides into a delicate murmuring of strings over which woodwind bird-calls flutter and trill.

I am entranced. "I love it—how come I never heard this before?"

"Hard to get hold of. This is an LP from Russia, picked it up in London."

Colin sits down and joins us.

"Well, you caught him out there, George. He tries that on everyone, and you're the first person to get it right. How come?"

I explain a little of my student background. They in turn tell me that Geg also attends Glasgow University, studying Philosophy and Art.

But Colin is not a student at all. He works in a hardware shop in Partick.

"Oh? I thought you were both students. That's what the landlord said."

Colin laughs as he sips his wine.

"Well, that's what he thinks, we don't tell him everything, you know." He smiles secretively. "You shouldn't either. I'm a student of life, George, that's about it."

Geg has lit some joss-sticks, and the slightly sickly perfume permeates the room. The music is once more in the throes of erotic frenzy, and Colin leans back in his chair.

"Oh, I love this part. It's music to make love to, don't you think?" he says to no-one in particular.

"Music to fuck to, you mean," scoffs Geg. "Why must you always be so *Woman's Own*, Col'? Say what you mean."

Once again I note the condescending and critical tone.

Colin doesn't reply, but the little smile never leaves his face.

This pair are puzzling. The Colin one is so wifely, so domesticated, ensuring Geg is comfortable and has all he wants, getting up to light his cigarette, taking it from him to put it out, forever moving things that have strayed out of place. I would have said they were undoubtedly a couple, were it not for the fact that the name of Geg's girl-friend, Valerie, is mentioned occasionally.

"She'll be here a bit later on, George, stay and meet her, she's a lovely girl," says Colin.

But I am tired, and have had enough for one evening of this slightly strange pair. I make my excuses, after thanking them for their hospitality, and I tell them it's time I headed off to my own room to unpack my cases and settle in.

"OK," says Geg, getting up. "It was great to meet you, man, I'm sure we're all going to get along really well."

He sees me to the door. "Drop in any time, any time at all."

I cross the hall to my room, close my door and lock it behind me. I could murder for a cup of tea, but there's no chance of that, I've not done any proper shopping as yet.

I don't bother unpacking, I'll do it in the morning. I just have a cigarette, fall into bed and sleep like the dead, my first night in my new home.

I have not given any hint of my move to Tommy up till now, I plan to surprise him. We meet up as usual, in *Guy's*, the following Friday evening. As we leave the bar, heading off for a coffee, he sighs.

"Don't suppose you managed to arrange anything for the night, did you?"

"No, sorry, Tommy, there's been nobody around to ask. I tried, but no luck, I'm afraid."

"Dammit. Don't suppose you could cope with Shirley's place again?"

He catches sight of my face.

"No, forget that, Ah'm just being selfish. Shame we're so poor, the two of us, eh? An' after last week an' all…"

He grins and I can tell something naughty is coming.

"Ah'll just have to settle for a bit of solitary later, Ah suppose. Hope Charlie's still out when Ah get home. He likely will be, the dirty wee bastard, always off on the pull at the weekend."

He sings between his teeth.

'Green door, one more night without sleeping...'

How weird to hear him sing my old anthem.

"How old is Charlie?" I ask, as we head down Hope Street. It has never occurred to me to wonder before.

"Nineteen, same age as you. An' about as daft. And we share a bedroom, the two of us, so privacy can be a bit of a problem now and then."

It's hard to imagine Tommy has a brother just my age.

We head for the *El Guero* and find a quiet table in a corner. The Friday night crowd are soon piling in, and as usual under these circumstances, I sense that he is not entirely at ease. Although he has become more relaxed in general with some of the people I know, he is still relentlessly on the alert for anyone or anything that might expose him to detection. It doesn't always make for a comfortable atmosphere.

Surprisingly, though, he has taken a liking to one or two of my friends; for the most part those who are not too obviously gay, those who can turn it on and turn it off. He has plenty of time for Elaine Stewart, for example, because she is witty and amusing, and because in appearance and behaviour she is so utterly ordinary. Of course, he's never had the pleasure of seeing her in her Thursday night *'Miss Stewart is pissed'* mode. That might change his ideas. He gets on well with her boyfriend, Little Joe, too. He and Tommy are alike, in a way, straight-appearing men in a queen's world, though Joe is devoid of Tommy's hang-ups.

A few others, he tolerates; Kay Kendall, Elaine's bosom friend, for one, who is from the same mould as Elaine herself. He likes Dorothy Provine, in spite of her outrageousness, because, once again, she has a vivid personality, and witty and amusing dialogue. He has time for Wilma Flintstone for much the same reason. Wilma is so outside the norm, both in appearance and behaviour, that she is almost a cartoon, like the character she is named for. If anyone he knows were to see him in her company, they would just put her behaviour down to some mental imbalance.

But Angie he has never warmed to, and never really will. His jaw tightens in that familiar way if she is anywhere in our vicinity.

I feel a little guilty about Angie. Our long closeness is gradually evaporating. Now and then, when Tommy is not around, we are able to resume our old camaraderie. But when he's there she tends to avoid me.

"You've changed, Audrey," she says. "And you used to be such a *fun* person."

I'm not sure I *have* changed, deep down. But I certainly moderate my outward behaviour when Tommy and I are together, for his sake. It's my fault she and I have lost something of our close friendship. But it's a hard world, and nothing puts it better than the old song:

'Lord help the mister
Who comes between me and my sister.
And Lord help the sister
Who comes between me and my man.'

As we sit and sip our coffee, Tommy gradually comes to look more and more gloomy. And I can guess why.

"This is crap," he says eventually.

"Yes, it's not very good coffee," I agree.

He smiles, for a wonder.

"Not the coffee, eedjit. The situation."

"Oh—yes, you're right."

He puts his hand over mine, after ensuring we are unobserved.

"Look," he says after a moment, turning back. "Ah don't like to ask, but—if we could find a quiet corner somewhere... "

He is looking down at the table, pink with embarrassment.

"Yes, I know. Relax, Thomas. OK." I stub out my cigarette. "I know somewhere. Up the road, Charing Cross way."

He grins, surprised, delighted.

"You do? Come on then, come on, what are we waiting for? Let's go. Ah'll see you to your bus after, make sure you're OK."

As we turn into the entryway of thirty-nine Carnarvon Street he is suddenly not sure.

"Maybe this is a mistake, George. Ah shouldn't have suggested it. This kind of back court stuff is not for us. Let's leave it. Ah'll sort something out for next week, Ah promise, OK?"

Now it's my turn to be eager.

"No, it's fine, come on, come on."

He can't resist. So, albeit a little reluctantly, he follows me into the close.

When I stop at the foot of the stairs, he hesitates and whispers, "Through the back, is it?"

"No, it's up there, first floor."

"Eh? Upstairs?"

"Yes, trust me."

"OK, OK, this is your show."

We reach my front door and I take out my key.

He takes a step back. "What the hell?..."

I open the door, have to virtually propel him through it, and close and lock it.

We tiptoe down the hall. There isn't a sound to be heard from my neighbours.

"Whose place is this?" he asks, too loud, looking around.

"Ssh. Never mind that, just keep quiet."

I unlock my room door and open it.

"Come on in, then."

He walks in, and I see him look suspiciously round the cosy room. I have left the gas fire on low, as the September nights are getting chilly now. Only a small lamp is alight, on the chest of drawers beside the bed. On the dining table candles wait. Also on there is a bottle of wine— *Chianti Classico*—and on the window sill are some bottles of beer. The table is set for two.

I have anticipated the look of total bewilderment on his face. I close the door behind us, lock it, and lean against it.

"So—what do you think? Will this do?"

He turns to face me.

"But—whose place is this? Who lives here?"

I take a step or two towards him.

"We do. Us. You and me."

I explain that I've left home. I keep it brief, just the outline, no details. No mention of my bank raids on Caldwell's, though he must be wondering how I can afford this. He will have to know that story eventually, but not right now.

"So," I conclude, "we have no problem about where to go. This is where we spend our private time."

I indicate the table. "Let's eat. Have a beer, they should be cold. Have you tried Chinese before?"

I have recently discovered the joys of the take-away and the magic of a low oven.

He looks around again. At first he doesn't know what to say. Then after he's taken it all in, he puts his arms round me.

"Wow."

"Wow? Is that it?"

He chuckles and looks into my eyes. "You're a wonderful woman,

Audrey."

I can't help laughing. "Hey, stop taking the piss, Thomas."

"I'm dead serious. You're a wonder. How did Ah come to get this lucky?"

Now where have I heard that before?

And how could I have forgotten to buy a corkscrew?

Our routine is quickly established. Friday night, Saturday night, he is there, always. We now have a warm and private place to be together. We go out for a drink now and then. We eat together, sometimes out, sometimes in. Sometimes he pays, sometimes I do. Once in a while I phone him at work and we have lunch, if I feel I just have to see him. But that's it. There is never any question, any discussion about taking things further. No, if he's not with me, he is at work or at home. Or maybe at a T.A. meeting, or the famous sports club.

I come to realise that this is a job only half-done. OK, we now have all the privacy we need when we are together. But in a way I have made it easier for him to retain his separate life. Maybe if I had been less anxious to push things forward, if I had allowed him to languish unsatisfied more often, and made it more difficult for intimate moments to take place, eventually he would have been the one to make a move to improve our situation. But then again, maybe he would just have got tired of the frustration and moved on. It's a puzzle, and I am at my wits' ends to solve it.

Things at Caldwell's have taken an unexpected turn. I arrive one Saturday morning in September to discover the place in chaos. Iris, the boss, has been replaced overnight, without any warning. The new person in charge is a Mrs Olszyinski, a Polish lady, pleasant on the surface, but a far cry from the primped and painted, fun-loving and easily manipulated Iris. Mrs Olszyinski is affable enough, but her little close-set eyes are shrewd, and she is utterly rigorous where things like time-keeping and order books are concerned. It is a whole new regime, and I am not too impressed with it.

Rosemary explains to me that Iris didn't just leave; she was sacked.

"Problems with the accounts, George, apparently. Police called in and everything. I don't know all the details, but it seems they think Iris was on the fiddle. I can't believe it myself—I've known her for years."

'Oh dear,' I think. *'Poor Iris. I hope my merry high-jinks with the cash register had nothing to do with this.'*

Rosemary and I have become friendly, and even go out socially once in a while. She has met Tommy, we've had a pizza together once or twice, the three of us along with her boyfriend, Graham, and, although personal details are never discussed, I know that they understand our situation, and do not disapprove. Tommy likes her a lot, gets on well with Graham, and enjoys our occasional get-togethers. The presence of a woman makes him much less self-conscious.

She goes on.

"Mary upstairs in the office says there's more than two thousand unaccounted for, mistakes in the books, unpaid accounts, National Insurance not kept track of properly. Stock missing, orders charged for but never filled, or filled and never charged for... Imagine, Iris... No wonder she could afford all those holidays abroad."

Oh good, I'm relieved. More than two thousand? So nothing to do with me, then. Well, maybe one or two of the orders.

"And," she murmurs, "this new woman bears watching. She's as sharp as a knife, misses nothing, so look out. We're all going to have to be careful in the future."

I wonder briefly if my friend is trying to tell me something. Does she have some idea of what I have been up to? Is she perhaps up to something herself? Have I been working with a gang of ruthless embezzlers, thinking all the while I was the only one?

At any rate, *Audrey's Disco* is closed down permanently, never to re-open. And my raids on the tills are reduced to a minimum, although I find myself unable to abandon this source of income entirely. Just a couple of quid now and then.

October 1963.

One Friday evening Tommy turns up with his guitar case under his arm. I already know he plays a bit, but he has never really talked about it much.

We go out for a drink or two, and come back around ten. After we have a bite to eat, I pick up the case.

"Go on then," I say. "Give us a sample. Play something for me."

He looks down. "No, no, George, you don't want tae hear me picking away."

I call his bluff. "Well, if you'd no intention of playing the thing, what did you bring it with you for?"

He grins sheepishly. "OK, it's a fair cop, Ah suppose. Ah *did* think you might enjoy a wee bit of Country instead of all that opera stuff you usually listen to. Just now and then."

He unpacks his guitar, which I can see has been lovingly looked after, and tunes up.

And he sings. Inevitably, it's *'If you loved me half as much as I love you.'*

Our song, I suppose.

And I am astonished at how good he is. Why has he never shown me before? His voice, when he's unaccompanied, maybe in the street or in our room, is ordinary, if pleasant. But it is totally transformed when he plays his guitar. It is a lovely voice, light, but mellow and tuneful, and he gives the words meaning and truth.

And he sings in a pure, natural Scots accent, no fake American twang. His guitar playing, if not virtuosic, is the ideal accompaniment. He strums gently, his eyes closed, and when he finishes, I have a lump in my throat, he interprets the sad and simple lyrics of the song so well.

"Tommy," I say, as he finishes. "Why did you never tell me you could sing like that? It was just—well—perfect."

He is immediately embarrassed.

"Och away, it's nothing. But I enjoy it, that's what counts."

"No, really, listen, I'm telling you… I wasn't expecting it."

"Well, I'm glad you liked it."

After a moment, with a little smile, he adds, "That's our song, after all."

Oh? This sounds hopeful. *'Yes, go on,'* I think.

But he doesn't. Instead he starts strumming again. *'Oh jealous heart, oh jealous heart, stop beating…'*

For a moment I would quite like to beat *him*. Then that's forgotten, and I am caught up again in the sincerity and charm of his singing.

And I am not alone. A little later, as he finishes *'Hey, good-lookin', what ya got cookin'?'*, we hear a smattering of applause from the hallway. And when I open the door, there are Colin and Geg, along with a girl whom I guess must be Valerie, the girl-friend. She is plain, as tall as me and as thin, with spectacles and lank, long brown hair. She looks like a school teacher. Later I will discover that's what she is.

"Hello there, you two, sorry to interrupt, but we couldn't help stopping to listen," says Geg. "Hope you don't mind."

He looks at Tommy. "Man, that was brilliant, just the best. Love a bit of Country and Western. Hank Williams song, yes? Great, man, great."

Colin chips in. "Want to come over to us for a glass of wine or two? You're very welcome, we'd enjoy the company."

I look at Tommy. "Want to?"

He shrugs. "Sure. Why not?"

I stand up. "Thanks, that's nice of you."

"Great," says Geg. "And bring the guitar, please."

Tommy keeps us entertained for more than two hours. He seems to know dozens of songs off by heart, many in the suicide style, but a few more upbeat numbers. I can tell by the way he sings them, though, that broken-hearted misery is his preference.

'Oh, look around you
Look down the bar from you
The lonely faces that you see
Are you sure that this is where you want to be?'

"He your boyfriend?" whispers Colin in my ear at one point, as he is serving drinks.

"Yes, he is," I reply proudly.

"Good for you. He's nice," he says as he moves off to top up Geg's glass.

I end up chatting to the girl-friend, Valerie, for most of the night. Although she is very plain in appearance, I discover that she is not only intelligent, well-read and well-educated, but she has a shy charm that is immensely appealing. Her accent marks her as coming from a similar background to my own, and she explains that, like me, she tends to keep her family in the dark about her private life.

"Oh, they don't approve of Geg," she says at one point, looking over at him, "not at all. They think he's a layabout, that I'm wasting my time with him. They want to see me with a chartered accountant, or someone with *'a good job and prospects'*."

She laughs, and I realise that when she is animated, her features become almost pretty. "No chance of that, though…"

'Gosh,' I think. *'We're not that different, her and I.'*

I wish I could figure out this strange threesome. Despite her presence, Colin continues to play the wife assiduously, and Valerie seems to have no problem with that. I must ask Tommy later what he thinks.

A fair bit of wine is drunk, and it is nearly one in the morning when we finally leave. As we say goodnight, Geg claps Tommy on the shoulder.

"That was great, man, you're a natural, a real star. Drop in any time."

There is no question Tommy is pleased and happy. As for me, I am just about bursting with pride.

♦

Remains the question of university and my education. Well, in September I had enrolled for my classes, English II and Logic. I had decided to choose the latter over Moral Philosophy, as I am pretty certain that I'm more logical than moral. And classes and lectures? No, I haven't attended even one, and we are now four weeks into the term. Compared with what is going on in the rest of my life, study doesn't seem very important.

I have been sacked from Caldwell's!

Well, not actually sacked, made redundant, officially. But that's only because nothing can be proved. Anyway, it comes to the same thing.

Rosemary tips me the word one lunchtime, so I am prepared.

"They've got people in this afternoon, George, watching us, checking up on us," she whispers. "Watch your step. Mary upstairs warned me."

She heads off to serve a customer. I head off to the toilet.

Once there, I remove three pound notes from my sock, this morning's takings, and burn them to cinders with my cigarette lighter.

I am in a mild panic.

'Maybe they've been marked in some way, maybe the serial numbers have been noted down.'

The ashes I flush down the toilet, and then return to my duties.

I feel an enormous sense of relief after getting rid of the evidence. And now that I have been warned there is an investigation in progress, it is so obvious it's funny. I register an occasional customer spending ages browsing in the racks, then heading to the counter as soon as I, and only I, am unengaged.

OK, obviously it's me they're watching. There are at least two of them. I serve both scrupulously, give them their receipts and their exact change. I am sunny and charming, helpful and polite. I call them *Sir* and *Madam*, although Sir looks like a bit of a Madam to my experienced eye.

But it is clear to me that they know my game, and know that I am onto theirs.

Luckily, there is absolutely no way these thefts can be traced to me—I have been careful never to pass any of my ill-gotten gains through a bank account, I have dealt solely in cash, and that is well hidden away where no-one will find it. It's no longer in the left-luggage office—though my suitcase of clothes still rests there, and indeed may well continue to rest there into the distant future. I have found the perfect cache for my cash.

No-one ever looks inside an organ pipe.

In addition, because sales rung up on the tills do not require a staff number to be keyed in, even questionable amounts (and I have avoided those for the most part) cannot be brought home to any specific individual. And the shop is so busy no-one can remember what they sold yesterday, let alone a week or a month ago. There is no paper trail to follow. So unless I were to be actually caught in the act, I am safe. And that is not going to happen now.

But I have to accept that the game is finally up. When Mrs Olszyinski tells me she wants to see me in her office after closing, I know what's coming.

She starts off amiably enough. "So sorry, George, to be the bearer of bad news, but I'm afraid we're going to have to let you go. The shop is cutting back on staff, and –"

"Let *me* go? Oh, I understand there are problems, Mrs Olszyinski, what with all the business with Iris, the frauds and the fiddling we've all heard about, the police being called in—so, yes, I appreciate the situation. But surely it should be 'last in, first out'? Isn't that the way it usually works? And I've been here longer than anyone except Rosemary. So—why me?"

We both know exactly what is going on, and what has been going on, but neither of us is going to say what we are thinking.

Mrs O. looks a little nonplussed by my proactive attitude. So she decides to up the stakes.

"Yes, I understand. But it's not that simple, George. It seems from what we can gather that the former manageress was not the only person involved. The police are still investigating –"

"I devoutly hope, Mrs Olszyinski, that you're not suggesting that *I* may have been concerned in these matters? That you are getting rid of me because you suspect me of dishonesty? If that were the case, I would feel compelled to seek redress."

'*Go on,*' I think, '*accuse me to my face. See where that gets you.*'

Her expression moves from puzzled to flustered.

"No, no, no-one is suggesting that, George," she says. "But with all that has been going on –"

"I'm glad to hear it. I have worked in Caldwell's for nearly three years. I have given all my energy and devotion to this place and I never expected to be treated with such a lack of regard."

I wonder if a tear or two might be too much? I've always understood that the Polish are a susceptible and emotional people. I briefly consider using the *'But weren't you received here graciously when you had to leave your ghetto and your war-torn homeland? Didn't we Scottish people invite you to our country, provide for you, welcome you?'* routine.

But I decide that there is such a thing as over-egging the pudding.

I can tell that she is both confused and annoyed by my effrontery, but is not sure how to respond. The little close-set eyes crease into an unconvincing fake smile.

"Yes, of course, George, and your work here has always been appreciated, I know." She gives a little pretend sigh. "I'm truly sorry, but I'm afraid that's just the way things have to be."

I wait a moment. Then make a phony display of reluctantly accepting the situation. "Very well, Mrs Olszyinski, I accept your apology, inadequate though it is."

I have already prepared my final piece of brazenness.

"Naturally, I shall expect a reference, and a glowing one. I trust that will be forthcoming?"

She stares at me with mingled dislike, frustration and bafflement, eyebrows arched, challenging me. But she is backing a loser. Audrey is lurking behind my eyes, and Audrey is a bold bitch who fears no-one, and who is never going to lose a staring contest.

Eventually she drops her gaze. "Yes, very well, I will see to that. I can hardly do more."

"On the contrary, Mrs Olszyinski, you can hardly do *less*. I shall expect to receive it in the post within the next few days, along with the overtime and holiday pay that is due to me."

She says nothing, and I turn to go. Just before I sweep out, I turn back.

"And good luck with your new job, Mrs O., however short it's duration may prove. I suspect you're going to need it."

Damn, damn, damn! Despite my bravado, this is going to cause me problems. Although I still have most of my (or rather Caldwell's) money left, my weekly earnings have dropped at a stroke from about twenty pounds to five. All I will have is my student grant, and the measly one pound I earn on Sundays. And even the grant I am not really entitled to, since I have completely given up attending lectures.

What to do?

If Tommy would only fall into line with my plans for our future, we could manage well together. I would find a job, and his is reasonably well paid. But so far he has shown no signs of a desperate inclination for us to share a hearth on a permanent basis.

I will be working on that.
But in the meantime, I am going to need a new source of income.

4. A House is Not a Home

> A room is still a room
> Even when there's nothing there but gloom
> But a room is not a house
> And a house is not a home
> *Dionne Warwick, 1964*

Suddenly everyone I know wants to visit my *Little Grey Home In The West*. In the West End, that is. Not at weekends, when callers are definitely discouraged—Friday and Saturday Tommy is in residence, and Sunday I spend in Rutherglen, visiting the family and performing my religious duties. But during the week there is nearly always someone there with me. Because most of my friends live in the suburbs with their families, it suits them to have somewhere comfortable to pass an hour or two, away from the draughts of the Central Station, somewhere where they can be warm when the pubs are shut, where they will be offered a cup of tea and maybe something stronger.

My room at thirty-nine Carnarvon Street becomes a kind of drop-in centre.

It is only my close friends who are encouraged to call. Angie knocks now and then, I welcome Wilma and Connie from time to time, and Shirley makes the odd appearance between shifts at the brothel. But Elaine is my most regular visitor, usually with Little Joe, and often with her friend Kay Kendall.

Kay is about Elaine's age, and the same shape, short and stocky. She has a thick mop of wavy blond-brown hair, a large mole on the side of her face, described by her as a beauty spot, and a noticeable lack of teeth in the upper jaw. In personality she is outwardly agreeable and pleasant, but inwardly calculating and self-interested.

Her domestic situation is a singular one.

Kay's 'husband', Johnny, forty-something, is a married man with two sons. He, his wife and children, and his lover, Miss Kendall, reside together in a two-room apartment, in an unusual 'design for living'. According to Kay, the wife has no idea of the true situation, and thinks of her, Kay, as 'the lodger'.

I am dubious. It may not be the only family setup where the wife sleeps with the children in one room, and the husband with the male lodger in the other, but it can't be a common arrangement.

Kay has a fixation about *tootsie trade*—that abhorred entanglement where a queen, nominally the passive partner, may occasionally take the active rôle in a relationship. This, as I have mentioned, is not all that uncommon, although rarely admitted to—my own brief encounter with Juliet Prowse remains my one personal experience of it, and there I have no complaints at all. But Kay is obsessed, condemning out of hand those who dare to transgress what she sees as The Great Universal Law. It sometimes occurs to me to wonder if the lady, perhaps, doth protest too much.

Naturally my relationship with Tommy meets with her full approval in this regard. I could scarcely be more fey, and Tommy could hardly be more masculine, so in the Gospel According To Saint Kay, we are the perfect orthodox, God-fearing couple. If she's in her cups and in our company, she rather likes to sing:

'Audrey and Tommy were lovers,
He wanted to give her everything.
Flowers, presents,
And most of all a wedding ring.'

Yes, if only.

With these fixed ideas, Kay would be horrified to know that I would not be entirely averse to my nocturnal activities with my beloved taking a rather more flexible turn now and then.

One Monday evening, late October, Elaine, Little Joe and myself are sitting in my room, having a beer or two and chatting idly. I won't be seeing Tommy again till Friday, so we are just passing the time, but Elaine has been keeping a revelation back.

"Well, Miss Hepburn, have I got some news for you. Have a look at this."

She passes me a creased and tattered newspaper, folded open to an inside page. I take it and look at it carefully, but can see nothing of particular interest. The Glasgow Corporation is apparently considering pulling down the little that remains of the old Gorbals, despite vociferous protests, but that is nothing new. Forty-two year old Mrs Frances Macintosh has produced quadruplets in the Royal Infirmary. So what? That's not a birth, it's a litter.

I look up, puzzled.

"Bottom of the page, right hand side, Audrey..."

I look down again. And see the paragraph she is referring to.

Beehive Wilma Turns Out To Be William, I read. It is a report of court proceedings.

A police witness relates how a very tall and striking young lady sporting a beehive hairstyle, heavy makeup, slacks, a sweater and kitten heels was stopped by the officers of the law in Argyle Street just as she was about to enter Lewis's department store.

'*The defendant came swivelling towards me,*' avers the unfortunately named PC Piggot. '*I asked for her particulars, and demanded to know what her purpose was. The defendant said his name was Wilma and that he resided at Lancefield Street in Anderston. He claimed he was on his way to use the ladies' facilities in Lewis's, as he had very tight knickers on. And I quote—"and they've worked their way right up the crack of my arse." Sorry, that's the defendant's arse, your honour, not...*'

I can picture the laughter in the court, and this nervous young constable. The newspaper replaces the offending word with asterisks, but the point is clear.

The article goes on.

'*Anyway, sir, when I conducted him to the police station in Cowcaddens, the defendant admitted his real name was William Mitchell and that he—once again, I quote, your honour—"was much more comfortable in female attire and didn't see what business it was of mine or anybody else's." The defendant then made a suggestive gesture to me, followed by a proposition. He was subsequently charged according to the indictment, after the usual caution.*'

Sentence—six weeks imprisonment, for conduct liable to lead to a breach of the Public Order Act.

"Not *our* Wilma, surely?" I ask, folding the newspaper and looking up.

Elaine scoffs. "Oh no, Audrey, it'll be some other Wilma."

She tuts. "For God's sake, Miss Hepburn, how many William Mitchells do you know who live in Anderston and call themselves Wilma?"

She's right, of course.

'*Poor Wilma,*' I think. '*Still—six weeks? She'll do that standing on her head, she's a tough character. Probably have a whale of a time in there, in one fashion or another.*'

"Anyway," continues Elaine, "that paper's more than two weeks old, so she'll be back with us in no time. It was Connie that passed it on to me, she's planning a welcome home party when Miss Flintstone gets out, and we're all invited, it seems."

Just at that moment, there is a ring at the doorbell.

"Wonder who that is?" I say, looking up, not really very interested.

I'm not expecting anyone. I imagine it will be someone looking for my neighbours across the hall—they have a lot of rather strange visitors; but then so do I. So I make no move to answer the door.

"Oh, that might be Kay, Audrey," says Elaine. "Saw her earlier. Said she was having a drink with some friends in town, but might drop round here later. If ye don't want her here—Ah know you're not that keen on Kay—just don't answer the door. We can always say we went out if she asks."

I get up, yawning. "Oh, I don't mind, just as long as she doesn't stay too late, I could do with an early night. Hope she's brought a contribution, if it *is* her."

I open the front door, and it is indeed Kay. But she is not alone. Standing behind her is a statuesque blond girl, and, of all the unlikely things—a black man.

"Oh," I say, rather inadequately. "Hi, Kay... Er—come in."

She is apologetic. "Audrey, sorry, but dae ye mind if ma friends come in for a wee while?"

She smiles winningly, showing the gaps in her teeth. "We've brought a couple of bottles."

I take a look at this diverse company. "No, that's fine, come in, come in, it's a cold night and you're letting all the heat out."

They do so, and I close the door behind them. The two newcomers crowd into the hallway, not sure in which direction to head.

I size them up.

"Are you going to introduce me to your friends then, Kay?"

"Oh, sorry, hen. This is Elsie—she's a hoor, just up from London, and this here is her pimp, Ernie."

'*Well, tell it like it is, Kay,*' I think.

I shake hands with the new arrivals. Elsie is big and buxom, attractive in a slightly overblown way, mid-twenties, earth-mother type. Ernie is a good looking man of perhaps thirty, tall and broad-shouldered.

I can't take my eyes off him, and try not to stare too obviously. I have never seen a black man in close-up before. Well, only Harry Belafonte in *Carmen Jones* and *Island in the Sun*. And Harry was only slightly black.

Kay leads the way to my door, we enter, and introductions are made. Not that Elaine needs one.

"Elsie! Well, there's a surprise," she says, standing up to embrace the lady. "Last time I saw you was in Piccadilly Circus, getting arrested. You, that is, not me. Anyway, welcome tae Audrey's Palace of Fun. When did you get back to Glasgow?"

"Just the day, Michael, goat the train fae Euston this morning, had enough of London for a wee while. And they'd had enough of me."

"Getting a bit too hot for you two doon there, was it? Aye—Ah can imagine. Same here."

Elsie settles herself into the most comfortable chair, kicks off her shoes, and nods towards her friend.

"You remember Ernie, don't you?"

"Oh aye, of course Ah do." Elaine shakes hands with the dark gentleman.

"I prefer *Ernest*, personally," the latter puts in. "*Ernie* is rather common."

He laughs. "Makes me sound like a barrow-boy, don't you think?"

I don't know what to think.

"But to his close friends he's Dirty Mary," say Elsie with a chuckle.

"Dirty Mary?" I say.

"Oh aye. Remember that night, Michael?"

"How could I forget?" says Elaine with a snigger.

"Yes indeed, Mary is fine too, or even Dirty Mary, if you prefer," Ernie goes on, and laughs again, with a lot of teeth. He has a distinctly public school English accent. Angie would be highly impressed.

I decide not to enquire further. "OK. Well, whatever your name is, sit down, please."

He does so, and Elaine goes on to introduce them to Joe, who in his usual self-effacing manner is very quiet.

"And this is ma man, Little Joe."

Her face crinkles in a smile. "And before you ask, no. He's little by name but not by nature."

Joe turns pink, but says *hello* politely. The wine and beer are broached, and we all settle down for a merry evening.

It turns out that Elaine knows Elsie and Ernie from her most recent visit to London, where they shared lodgings. These three reminisce happily, while I chat away to Joe, making sure he is not left out of the conversation. Shame Tommy's not here, the two of them could talk about man-things. Kay is in charge of the drinks and ensures no-one's glass is empty.

It must be about ten o' clock, and Elaine is telling a rather *risqué* story from her distant past.

"Aye, it was a few years ago now, Miss Kendall and me had been tae this party over in Paisley Road—it was before you and Johnny were together, Kay, Ah think? And at the end of the evening there was just me and Kay and this one glamorous guy left. The three of us and the hostess, Diane Varsi, her an' her man, Ray.

"Anyway, Diane says it's OK if we stay over, an' she and her husband show us intae the spare room, me and Kay and this other fella. So the three of us piles into this big bed, me an' Kay on the outside an' the guy—nobody seemed tae know his name—in the middle. Well, it's about half an hour later, and by this time the guy is snoring his head off. Ah'm still awake, and…"

She hesitates. "How can Ah put this tastefully?"

She pauses again. "Oh, go on Kay, *you* tell it, Ah'm too embarrassed."

Kay takes up the story.

"Och Elaine, for Christ's sake… aye, well, the fella is snorin' away like Elaine said, and Ah think, '*Why waste an opportunity like this? Elaine will be asleep by now.*' So Ah lifts the covers and creeps down the bed, thinkin' Ah'll gie a wee blow-job tae this fella. Well, Ah gets down there, groin level, an' Ah'm just about tae apply lips, when Ah looks up and what dae Ah see lookin' across at me fae the other side o' this guy's cock? The face of Miss Stewart, wi' the same idea in her heid."

Everyone rocks with laughter.

"Aye," says Elaine, when she's recovered her composure. "We called it The Powder Puff Derby."

As the laughter subsides, I say, "So who won? Who came first?"

"Oh, *he* did, the fella," says Elaine. "Remember, Audrey, the customer *always* comes first."

Hysteria arises anew.

This is turning out to be a fun evening.

When we've all calmed down, Ernest digs around in his pocket and pulls out a twist of brown paper.

"Anybody fancy a tablet or two?"

I'm not sure if I have heard him correctly, but Little Joe's hand is already out.

Ernest unwraps the little package and produces a pile of small blue pills. And I understand.

I have heard of *purple hearts* or *pep pills*. But I have never had the occasion to indulge, myself.

But I am in the minority, it seems. The only other person in the company who has never had them before is Kay. The others take a pill with their drinks. She looks at me.

"What dae ye think, Miss Hepburn? Should we give it a go?"

I hum and haw. "Well—I'm not sure…"

"Aw, come on, Audrey, what's the matter with you?" chaffs Elaine, swallowing hers. "Harmless, they are, just now and again, a bit of a laugh. Come on; as Angie says, you used to be such a *fun* person."

I allow myself to be persuaded, and both Kay and I have just one tablet each.

By midnight we have all had another pill or two, and I have realised that these people, these dear friends of mine, this specific little group, are actually the most wonderful people in the world. They are charming, interesting, witty, and I love them all. Even Kay, who has never been one of my favourites.

As she and I sit on the sofa, heads together, discussing the finer points of current ladies' fashions—a subject about which neither of us knows anything at all—I decide that I have misjudged Kay, and that she and I are actually bosom buddies. Her eyes are sticking out of her head like a pair of bloodshot marbles, she is grinding her few teeth non-stop, and as I look round the rest of the group, I realise that she is far from the only one in that condition.

The room is blue with cigarette smoke. Little Joe is more animated than I have ever seen him before, and tears of laughter are coursing down his cheeks at some bawdy remark Elsie has just made. Elaine sits back in her chair, looking at Ernie and Elsie, singing and chuckling to herself—'*Ooh, Ernest, I'm so crazy for you*'. She has a happy, dazed-looking smile on her face.

Only Ernest himself seems relatively normal. Until he suddenly lets rip with a resounding fart, and says solemnly, "Damn, Elsie, I knew I shouldn't have had that black pudding—sorry, folks."

It is his utter seriousness and the impeccably correct accent in which he delivers the remark that has us all suddenly laughing like hyenas.

"But Ernest," I say, coughing and spluttering, but unable to resist the opening, "I thought it was Elsie there who was on a diet of black pudding?"

Little Joe nearly falls off his chair in convulsions of mirth, I have to slap Kay hard on the back to stop her choking, and Ernest himself roars with laughter.

Elaine suddenly comes out of her reverie. "Aye, ye see, Audrey, that's it, exactly. It's the importance of being Ernest…"

And this, it seems, is the funniest thing anyone has heard yet.

The next morning I feel beyond dreadful. A dazzling low autumn sun beams through the thin curtains. The inside of my mouth is sore where I have been chewing it. My head pounds, and my stomach feels rather as if it would like to get away from me.

I turn over in bed and open one eye. Next to me on the pillow is another bloodshot eye staring into mine. It takes me a minute to realise that it belongs to Little Joe.

'*Oh my God,*' I think, '*surely I didn't... surely we didn't...*'

Elaine comes through the door, singing.

'*Oh, what a beautiful morning, oh, what a beautiful day...*'

She is fully dressed and is carrying three mugs of tea. She seems as bright as a button, totally unaffected. But Joe looks about as bad as I feel.

Elaine puts the mugs down on the bedside table and seats herself on the edge of the bed.

"Morning, Miss Hepburn, sleep well?"

"I don't know," I mumble fuzzily. I look round. "Er—why is Joe in bed with me?"

"Don't you remember?" She sips her tea. "You said Joe and me could stay over, after Kay and the others left. It was late, and you said it was fine... I hope that was OK?"

I yawn and stretch.

"Yes, of course, Elaine, it's no problem, you're welcome. Er—but where did *you* sleep?"

"In the bed with you two, where else?" She smiles. "Ah put Joe in the middle, I know you like to wake up in the morning feeling a new man."

'*Oh no,*' I think. '*I hope I didn't... I hope we didn't...*'

I decide a direct approach is best.

I turn to Joe. "Well, I just hope you weren't tempted to interfere with my person in the night, you."

He mutters something incomprehensible.

Elaine laughs, and puts her mug down. "No chance of that, Audrey, they pills have a very bad effect on the sex drive. Joe there couldn't have raised a smile for you even if he'd wanted to."

The man in question suddenly comes to life, and sits up.

"Aye," he says with a cheeky grin, "but that was then and this is now. Normal service has been resumed."

And to prove his point he whips back the bed clothes. "Yes, Houston, we have lift-off."

I see he isn't exaggerating.

"Go on, Audrey, spoil yourself," he laughs, making a grab in my direction.

"Oh, Joe, *stop*," I groan, burying my head in the bedclothes, half in agony and half in embarrassment, as I have just realised that both of us are stark naked.

"Ah need a piss."

Joe bounds out of bed and heads for the bathroom.

I shake my head, looking after him. Joe, like Tommy, is completely unselfconscious.

I reach for a cigarette.

"He's great, your Joe. You picked the right one there, Elaine," I say, lighting up.

"Aye, Ah know. But no more than you, Audrey. Tommy's one of the best."

"Yes, he is," I agree.

We are quiet for a few moments, contemplating how lucky both of us have been in love's lottery.

I pick up one of the mugs of tea and slurp it down. It is scalding hot and burns my tongue, but I don't care, it's delicious.

After a moment I put it down again. I can't stop yawning.

"Oh Elaine," I say, "I feel awful. Queasy stomach, and as for my head…"

"Aye," she says equably, "Ah must say, ye look terrible."

"Oh, thanks very much!" I grouch.

Joe returns from the bathroom, whistling, and is just about to leap back into the bed.

"No, no," I say, pushing him off. "Not back into bed, Joe. Put some clothes on, please. Your irresistible masculine nakedness is distressing me."

Elaine agrees. "Aye, come on Joe, get dressed and drink your tea. We've things to do, signing-on day the day, and Miss Hepburn here has to prepare herself for her new career."

I put my tea down. "Eh? What are you talking about?"

Elaine looks at me, eyebrows raised. Little Joe starts climbing into his clothes.

"Dae ye no' remember the conversation you and Elsie had last night, late on?"

I ponder. And gradually it comes back.

♦

"It's no easy, Audrey, ye understand. Ernie an' me are stayin' at a friend's place, and it's miles out of the toon. So Ah have tae take ma customers up a close, or into a car park, or something."

Elsie puffs on her cigarette. I've no idea at all what time it is. I just know that this Elsie is a warm and wonderful person. Joe and Elaine are curled up on the sofa. Ernie and Kay are dancing to the drinking song from *La Traviata*. They're doing a kind of quick waltz, and doing it rather competently, all things considered.

"Ah need tae find a wee flat in the toon," Elsie goes on. "Somewhere like this wid be perfect. But that's difficult. There's not many places wi' nae landlord on the premises. If ye hear of anything, be sure tae let me know."

I say I will.

She nods reflectively. "Ye see, out in the open Ah cannae ask mair than a couple of quid, but with a place tae take the punters, Ah can get a fiver a time. Makes aw the difference."

A daring idea is forming in my mind.

Elaine raises her eyebrows. "Oh, ye remember now, do you?"

Joe trips on the hem of his jeans, sprawls full length on the floor and bangs his head on the new coffee table, my latest purchase. I hope he hasn't damaged my veneer.

Elaine looks round unsympathetically.

"Get up Joe, ya clown. Audrey doesn't have a licence for acrobatics."

She turns back to me. "Elsie's goin' tae be usin' your place here for her punters. Just during the week, you were most insistent about that."

Yes, so I was.

We agree that she can borrow my keys Monday to Thursday, seven till eleven, and I will arrange to be out. At first she suggests the arrangement should be one pound per client, but I object. Despite the over-indulgence, and my deep affection for this wonderful person, my hard-headed side kicks in.

"No, Elsie," I say. "You give me three pounds a night, flat rate."

After all, how am I going to know how many clients she has had? Her system is open to abuse. And I am quite familiar with how easily systems can be abused.

Eventually Elsie agrees that that seems fair.

I have some conditions.

"And make sure you keep the place tidy, OK? Be as discreet as you can coming and going, no fights or arguments, and *no* johnnies in the fireplace or down the toilet. Put them in a bag or something. And take them away with you when you go off-shift."

"OK, it's a deal."

Then she looks at me quizzically. "If Ah didnae know better, Audrey, Ah'd think you'd done this before."

After Elaine and Joe leave, I ponder the situation. I'm not sure my arrangement with Elsie was one of my better ideas. But—and it's a big but—it does mean that my income will return close to its previous comfortable level, and I can always find something to do to fill in the hours when Elsie is on-duty. If nothing else, there are about twenty cinemas in Central Glasgow. I just hope there are no problems with the police or anything. After all, I suppose that, technically, I will be living off her immoral earnings.

I am beginning to feel slightly better, though my head is still throbbing, and my stomach churns. I think about the previous evening, the booze, the pills, the laughs. Yes, it was fun, no question. But this fragile, sick feeling is a high price to pay. The pills are to blame more than anything, I feel sure.

'*So,*' I think, '*maybe just once in a while, eh?*'

Elsie starts work at my place a day or two later.

'*Should I sort of—well—supervise?*' I wonder.

'*No,*' I think, '*I will just leave her to it initially and see how things work out.*'

She calls round to pick up the keys around seven o' clock, bringing Elaine with her. I suggest to Elaine that she and I perhaps might go to the pictures for a few hours—she is a huge cinema fan, I know. And it will help pass the time. I'm going to have a lot of time to pass, one way and another.

"Oh yes, good idea," she says. "As long as you can pay for me. Ah'm skint. Don't get ma money till tomorrow."

"No problem. Anything you fancy seeing?" I ask her as we head down towards the town centre. "I've no idea what's on—should have got a paper, I suppose."

"Well—there's always *Cleopatra*," says Elaine.

"No, seen it, it's crap."

I try to think what else I have seen advertised recently.

"What about *The Haunting*? I enjoy a good horror movie."

Elaine shudders. "No, never, Audrey. Claire Bloom's in it. Can't watch anything with Claire Bloom. I can't stand her."

"Oh? Always thought she was a good actress, myself."

"She is, she is," says Elaine as we cross Sauchiehall Street towards the La Scala. "But she's a cow."

"Oh? You've met her then?"

"Aye, if you can call it that. She was doing personal appearances on tour with the film of *Look Back in Anger*, a few years ago—don't suppose they could talk Richard Burton intae it. Anyway, I went round to get her autograph afterwards. There was about a dozen of us waiting, and she just swept right past. '*No autographs, no time, far too busy*', she says. Snooty bitch."

We have reached the La Scala, one of Glasgow's largest cinemas. It's showing something called *Charade*. With Cary Grant and Audrey Hepburn.

"Well, there you are, Audrey—that settles it," says Elaine. "We'll go and watch you in your latest vehicle. You've not seen it yet, have you?"

"No," I say, a little reluctantly. "Not sure I fancy it really."

The truth is that, much as I admire my namesake, I can never understand why she always seems to be cast with old codgers like Humphrey Bogart, William Holden, Gregory Peck, Fred Astaire. Maybe she likes older men. But I don't.

I had been delighted to see her appear with the young and handsome George Peppard in *Breakfast at Tiffany's* a while back, thinking that perhaps it marked a change of direction. But no; it seems that now she is back among the coffin dodgers.

"Any other ideas, Elaine?"

She thinks for a minute. "Well—I *do* have a suggestion. But not sure you'll go for it."

"Go on."

"Well, the Cosmo is showing *They Flew Alone*. Old black and white movie with Anna Neagle, nineteen forty-two, the life story of Amy Johnson. It's not great, but it's a bit of a special occasion."

Elaine's voice is full of a mounting enthusiasm.

"Anna Neagle herself is making a personal appearance, there's a sort of question and answer thing afterwards."

The Cosmo in Rose Street, later The Glasgow Film Theatre, is the nearest thing we have to an art cinema. It specialises in European films, obscure American offerings, and re-runs of old British movies deemed to have some artistic or historical value. Elaine catches my expression, which despite my best intentions, must be registering 'less than enthralled'.

"Och, forget I mentioned it, Audrey. Ah know it's no' your cup of tea. Maybe there's a Bette Davis on somewhere."

"No, it's fine, Elaine, really, I don't mind. If you want to go, that's what we'll do. The Cosmo? Just round the corner, isn't it?"

In fact it turns out to be an agreeable enough evening. The film, relating the life story of Amy Johnson, the renowned British flying ace, is distinctly average, but Anna Neagle, CBE, is full of charm. And after she has finished her question and answer session with the audience, Elaine is enthralled to find that the First Lady of British Film is quite happy to sign an autograph or two and have five minutes private chat with us.

We are Michael and George for the occasion. Miss Neagle is smart in a tailored suit rather like a uniform, and Elaine asks her about the decoration in the form of a pair of wings attached to her lapel.

"Ah, yes, that," says the great lady, looking down at it. "One of my proudest moments, that, Michael. This was presented to me by the Royal Canadian Air Force, in recognition of my contribution to the war effort with this very film. In the States it was retitled *Wings and the Woman*. I've no idea why, sometimes I think the Americans change titles just for the fun of it."

Elaine continues to admire the delicate ornament, praising both it and its owner extravagantly. I think that possibly she is hoping there is a faint chance that Anna will offer it to her. But no, she doesn't.

November 1963.

It's time, I realise, that I brought Tommy up to date on things. I seize the moment the following Friday when we are out having a drink or two in *Guy's*. I know that if I want to keep him, I should always be as honest with him as he is with me.

Honest? Well… Honesty tempered with kindness, and seasoned with just a hint of self-interest, that's the ticket.

"I won't be going back to Caldwell's," I say baldly, as we sit down. "I've left."

Which is the truth and nothing but the truth, if not quite the whole truth.

He looks up with a knowing little smile. "Oh—got the sack at last, did you?"

What?

"Well, no," I prevaricate. "I was made redundant, actually. Found surplus to requirements. They're cutting back. They explained that they couldn't afford to keep me on there."

"And that would be because of your thieving, I suppose? No,"—he raises a hand to stifle my protest—"don't make excuses. I'm not daft. Do you think I couldn't work out that you were getting money from somewhere? How could you afford your place for a start if you weren't? And I heard you'd left, Rosemary told me, ran into her the other day. A couple of weeks ago this happened, isn't that right? Of course, she thought I would know about it already."

"Oh." I look away.

I'm not quite sure how to continue.

After a moment, I say, "I suppose you're angry with me? For not mentioning it before, I mean?"

"No—not angry. Maybe a bit disappointed."

He shrugs.

"But it's your business, not mine. And I knew you'd get round to it. But you could just have told me the truth straight off."

Yes, and I should have. I am at a bit of a loss as to how to proceed.

"And what about the actual—well, thieving, as you rather unkindly describe it. What do you make of that?"

The bar is quiet, no more than half-a-dozen customers.

I wheedle. "Do you think I'm a bad person?"

I put my arm through his, squeeze it, and look up at him in a manner I imagine is irresistibly appealing.

He laughs, and shakes his head from side to side.

"No, no, George, it's no use, don't try your tricks on me, all that butter-wouldn't-melt stuff. Ah know you too well."

He disengages my hand from his arm, and turns to face me.

"Look—Ah don't disapprove, you're an adult, yer hardly the first tae help yourself, and you won't be the last. But I'd rather you didn't lie to me."

After a moment, I say, "I did it for us, you know."

"Oh? Is that right?"

"Yes."

"You're such a liar. I bet you've been doing it for years, long before you met me. Come on, admit it."

So I decide to have done with excuses, and simply tell him the whole story. *Audrey's Disco*, the lot. I explain that, although my taking ways began a long time ago, if it wasn't for them, we would still be hunting around every night for a place to be together.

"We'd probably still be spending our Fridays at Shirley's place."

I put on a bright smile.

"So, it's a good thing, really. And I've still got quite a bit left. But sorry. I should have told you all this long ago. Sorry."

"No, not at all. You don't have to tell me anything. But if you suddenly feel an urge to confess something, just make it the truth."

"Yes, I will in future, I promise. Sorry."

He smiles.

"And stop saying *sorry*, you're starting to sound like me."

He takes my hand and squeezes it gently. I'm pleased to see he seems to have regained his sense of humour to some extent. I stand up and head off towards the bar to get us another drink.

While I'm waiting to be served, I think about what he's been saying.

After I come back and sit down, he says, "So—anything else I should know about?"

While I am ahead, I explain my new arrangement with Elsie the tart. Better, I think, to get everything out in one go.

He is a little dubious.

"So—who is this Elsie? I mean, can you trust her?"

"Oh, I think so, yes. She's a nice girl."

His expression becomes serious again. "I'm not sure, George, it all sounds a bit iffy to me. And what about the other two, the ones across the hall—what is it, Geg and Colin? They're bound to notice something, no?"

I hasten to reassure him. "Oh, I've explained all about it to them—I thought it was best that they knew, with the comings and goings and that. And they're quite happy about the arrangement. Geg even said he might ask Elsie to introduce his girl-friend Valerie to the business as well. I think they could do with the extra cash."

He guffaws. "Valerie? That tall skinny thing? Ah can't really see her as the temptress of Blythswood Square. Thought she was a school-teacher or something?"

"She is, but…"

"An' as for all this *girl-friend* business—Ah thought thon pair of guys was a couple of poofs."

He grins. "You know, like you and me?"

"Yes—so did I at first. But—well, I'm not sure exactly what is going on there. They're definitely a bit on the strange side, all three of them."

The bell sounds for last orders.

"Yeah. I don't really like the Geg fella much. The other one's OK, nice enough, but Geg… Somethin' no' right there, Ah can feel it."

It's the first I've heard of it.

"Well, they like you—Geg thinks you're Hank Williams reincarnated."

"Aye, maybe so, just the same…"

Something occurs to him, and he changes the subject.

"Oh—did I ever tell you the name of Hank's wife? Sang wi' him a bit sometimes?"

"No, I don't think you did. What was it?"

He smiles as he stands up. "She was called Miss Audrey."

"No! You're kidding me!"

"Naw, it's right enough. Maybe we should try a wee duet or two, eh?"

I would never dare, he is too good as a solo. Anyway, I can't really sing.

"OK," says Tommy, stretching. "One more drink, and then it's off tae bed for us. Right?"

Naturally that's fine with me.

Before making for the bar, he turns back to me.

"Just be a wee bit careful, George, wi' all that bunch of weirdoes. Don't get too involved. Especially in the week, when Ah'm no' around tae keep an eye on you. Ah can't be there all the time."

He heads off to get our drinks.

'*Yes,*' I think. '*But you* could *be there all the time. So why aren't you?*'

All unexpectedly, Angie turns up on my doorstep one Monday afternoon in early November. It's been a couple of weeks since I last saw her. She is dressed up to the nines, smart and stylish, which is more than I am. Indeed, domestic independence has led me to neglect my appearance to some extent, and some days I am positively slovenly. Not at weekends when Tommy is due, then I am looking my best. But at other times I have definitely let myself go a bit.

Angie on the other hand is elegance personified. She is wearing a cream, round-collared shirt—'*a Doctor Kildare shirt they call it, but it's more correctly a mandarin collar*'—a lamb's wool sweater in dark grey, and smart matching trousers with patch pockets. A beautiful coat in beige wool is slung across her shoulders. She looks quite the fashion plate.

She surveys the room. "I suppose you're still with that Tommy?"

"Yes, I am."

"Hm—I don't care for him, sorry."

She makes herself at home in my most comfortable chair.

"And I know he doesn't like me very much."

"No, he doesn't. But that's because he doesn't really know you."

"Yes, I suppose you're right."

"Oh, it is. If he did, he would hate you."

She assumes I am joking.

"Oh, Audrey, don't be so *uncamp*."

I comment on her appearance, and her outfit.

"Oh—like it? Thanks. This way of wearing a coat over the shoulders is all the rage in London these days. Capewise, I call it. Rather chic, no?"

She stands up, does a catwalk twirl, and the coat lands on the floor.

"Very," I say, clearing up some papers and magazines. "So how do you suddenly know what's all the rage in London? Been swotting up in *Vogue*?"

She smiles a little condescendingly as she bends down to pick up her coat. "No, not at all, Audrey. As a matter of fact, I've just got back from London. Had ten days there. I had that money I'd saved up to go to Canada with The Bastard, so thought I might as well have a bit of fun."

Angie in London?

"Wow, London, Ange. Sit down. Tell me all. Cup of tea?"

"Oh, OK. Thanks." She sits down again. "Unless you've got anything stronger?"

I find her a beer, which she necks straight from the bottle, rather spoiling her sophisticated image in the process.

I make myself a cup of tea and join her.

"So—where did you stay in London, Angie? Hotel? Hostel? I suppose it was expensive?"

She leans back in her chair, legs crossed, after taking a giant swig.

"No, no, surprisingly reasonable, actually. A nice little establishment in Victoria. Lots of single girls like me."

"The YWCA?"

She scoffs. "Don't be ridiculous, Audrey, as if... No, a private hotel."

She takes a deep breath. "And guess what? I found the man I've been looking for all my life."

"Really, Ange?"

She nods. "Yes."

Nods again. "Jesus."

I have a fleeting vision of Angie in a novice's habit, prostrate before the altar, the Bride of Christ.

But I get it suddenly. "Ah, you mean—"

She carries on without letting me finish. "Or rather, *Hay-soos*, to give it its correct pronunciation. Spanish, you know."

"Yes, I know," I confine myself to saying.

She clasps her hands together soulfully. "He was *fabulous*, Audrey. Tall, dark, really good-looking. A little greasy, or perhaps swarthy is more the word, a wee touch spotty here and there. But oh, wild, dangerous, bit of a *bandido*…"

She continues to coo in reminiscence for a few more moments, then hesitates.

"And—pardon my frankness, but—a whopping great popsy, if you follow me."

I follow her perfectly. I just don't want to follow her any further down that particular road. But I am pleased to conclude from what she says that *Angie the Conflicted Virgin* has finally discovered *The Joy of Sex*.

I am about to congratulate her, but she has more to tell.

"And—you'll never guess—he taught me Spanish. Oh just a few words, but the real *español*, you know. The language of love, the language of—well, the guy who wrote *Don Quixote*, him."

She pronounces it carefully, correctly, *Don Kee-ho-tey*.

"Miguel Cervantes," I help her out.

"Yes, that's the one. The language of Che Guevara…"

"And General Franco…"

"Eva Perón…"

"And Fidel Castro…"

"Vera Cruz…"

"And—ah—no, Angie—Vera Cruz is a place in Mexico," I point out. She raises her eyebrows. "Really? No, Spanish film star, surely?"

Before I can correct her, she takes another swig of her beer and carries on.

"The language of hundreds of people at any rate."

"Millions."

She swallows and gazes off into space.

"It was a fabulous week. Shame you've never been there Audrey. Life in Glasgow is *sew* provincial, it's time you broadened your horizons."

I decide to let the implied criticism go. It sounds as if she had a wonderful time. And I am happy for her, she deserves a bit of luck after the Al Fraser fiasco.

"OK, Ange," I say. "Give us a bit of the *español*, go on."

She blushes. "Oh, as I said, it's just a few words."

She clears her throat. "*Olà, Audrey, qué hora ès? Hello Audrey, what's the time?*"

"Ten past one," I say.

"*Muchas gracias*! Of course everybody knows that one. Then there's *La cucaracha*—that's a song."

"The cockroach?"

She smiles. "Yes—he used to call me that; *mi cucaracha* he would say. Affectionately, of course."

Once again the bottle is raised to the lips.

"*Buenas dias, Audrey, cômo estás? Buenas noches, Audrey.*"

She is silent for a moment. "Oh—and *tu culo*, and *mi carajo*. He used to say these phrases a lot."

I am sipping my tea, and have to turn my laugh into a cough.

"Oh? So what do they mean, Ange?"

She is vague. "Oh—hello, goodbye, something like that. They're sort of slangy, not the kind of Spanish you'd learn in school."

"No, definitely not in the school curriculum," I say when I have recovered my composure. "Angie, *tu culo* means *your arse* and *mi carajo* means *my cock*."

She is once more in the process of imbibing, and nearly drops the bottle.

"No! Really? Are you certain?"

"I'm quite sure. I can say these words in pretty much any European language."

She looks thoughtful. She ponders for a moment, then her brow clears. "Oh—so *that's* what he was after."

I have to revise my earlier idea as to the state of my friend's maidenhood.

Suddenly she is worried. "Oh dear, Audrey—and I said these words to *loads* of people. At the airport, getting into a taxi, in a restaurant. Just dropped them into the conversation" She giggles. "Just hope none of them understood Spanish."

"Let's hope not."

I am curious. "So—what happened to him, this fascinating *Hay-soos*? How come you didn't pack him in a suitcase and bring him back with you?"

She is suddenly serious.

"Oh, Audrey, that was terrible, the whole thing ended badly, I'm afraid. You see, I didn't know, but it turned out *Hay-soos* was an illegal immigrant and a drug dealer. He was arrested, and I suppose they'll send him back to Madrid or Barcelona."

'*Yes, or Bogotá or Buenos Aires, more likely,*' I think.

"And, worse than that—I was with him when the police picked him up, I wasn't carrying my passport, and they assumed I was like him. Imagine it—they thought I was an alien!"

At this, I simply can't control myself. Angie starring in *It Came From Outer Space*.

"Oh, stop *lar-fing*, Audrey, it wasn't funny at the time."

But she too is trying to control her giggles.

"It's because my diction is so clear. I don't really sound Scottish, I realise that. And they didn't believe I was."

I calm down. "So what did you do? Give them a chorus of *The Bonny Banks Of Loch Lomond*?"

"No," she says, quite seriously. "I recited a bit of *Tam O'Shanter* for them, we learned it at school. I put the accent on really strong, and they finally let me go."

She clears her throat.

> '*When chapmen billies leave the street,*
> *And drouthy neibors, neibors meet,*
> *As market days are wearing late,*
> *An' folk begin to tak the gate*'

I laugh. "Angie, you're incorrigible."

"Yes I am, I know. So you shouldn't encourage me."

This line is so good, I applaud. It's quite like old times.

One night I am lying in bed, alone. It is midweek. I have spent a couple of hours with my neighbours, just chatting and listening to music. There was no sign of Valerie, the girl-friend, who, they told me, has so far resisted strenuously Geg's attempts to persuade her to join my friend Elsie on the mean streets.

"But don't worry, she'll cave in given time, she always does," said Geg, in his usual unanswerable and self-confident manner.

I am just on the point of drifting off, my mind blank, when gradually I become aware of a rhythmic noise. A noise I am not unfamiliar with; a noise that no doubt issues from my own quarters regularly. It is the sound of sexual congress.

As I listen more carefully, sitting up in bed, I hear other things, sighs and grunts, that confirm my suspicions.

"Well," I think, lying down again and smiling to myself. "So those two *are* at it, just as Tommy thought. Wait till I tell him."

And in two minutes I am asleep.

I bump into Colin the next day on my way to the kitchen, and invite him in for a cup of tea. I am determined to solve this mystery. But I don't want to embarrass him. I like Colin—much more than I like the slightly intimidating and superior Geg—and wonder how to broach the subject in a manner that won't offend him.

I make him a mug of tea and offer him a cigarette.

"So, Col," I say, "how are you?"

"Oh, I'm fine, George, a wee bit tired today, but nothing a day off work won't fix."

He yawns.

This is an opening but a rather oblique one. I try a more direct route.

"Colin," I say, "you know how Tommy and I are—well—together, if you know what I mean?"

He smiles. "It's pretty obvious. And anyway, you told me. Together a long time? You two, I mean?"

"No, not very long—three months now."

"Good." He sips his tea. "Hope it works out for you, I really do. He's a great guy. You're dead lucky."

"Yes, I know."

I pause.

"Only—I was wondering… Please don't think I'm just being nosy, but—are you and Geg in a similar—well—situation? Together, I mean?"

He looks down, as if embarrassed.

"Yes. Well—sort of. I thought you would guess. But don't tell Geg that you know, he would go mental, he hates anybody knowing."

Aha!

"No, I won't say anything, of course not. But… 'Sort of'? How do you mean, 'sort of'?"

He eventually explains that he met Geg at Art School when he, Colin, was sixteen, and they almost immediately became a couple.

I still don't understand.

"But where does Valerie fit into this? He calls her his girl-friend, I've heard him, many times. And she's around a lot. So—what's going on there?"

He lights his cigarette. "Well—it's like this. Geg likes women as well as men. Oh, not as much, but once in a while."

I wonder why Geg, who is not at all unattractive, would, if he wanted a woman, settle for the sweet but plain and unprepossessing Valerie. I put this to Colin.

"Yes, I know what you mean. But, you see, Val's family is well-off, and she's got a good job. And Geg needs money, all the time."

I laugh. "Don't we all, Colin?"

But he is very serious. "No, not like that. He needs lots of money. For his habit."

"What habit?"

"His drug habit—he's an addict, Geg, has been since before I met him."

I am still confused.

"But surely—a few pills now and then, maybe a joint or two…"

Colin smiles, but his eyes are full of sadness.

"We're not talking about pills or puff here, George. I wish we were. No—Geg shoots up. Heroin."

"Heroin?"

I am horrified. I know nothing about heroin at all, except that it is reputed to be a killer. And *shooting up*, I know, means injecting.

I raise a hand to my mouth in shock. "No, Colin, surely not? Heroin?"

He sighs. "Aye—that, and anything else he knows won't kill him straight off."

He goes on to explain that Valerie supplies the money to Geg for his needs, in return for the dubious honour of being his girl-friend.

I have to know more.

"But when we say *girl-friend*, do they…?"

He laughs, but his expression is bitter. "Oh, once in a very odd while he throws her a fuck. Maybe four times a year."

His voice sounds choked. He clears his throat. I can see the tears in his eyes.

"Or tries to. The big joke of the whole thing is that he's so wrecked most of the time, he can't get it up from one month's end to the next. So neither of us is getting much in that department."

Suddenly, horrifyingly, embarrassingly, he starts to cry. I get up, sit down on the edge of his chair, and put my arms round him.

Eventually he calms down enough to speak.

"It's shit, eh?" he whispers, wiping his eyes. "Shit, the whole thing."

"But why do you put up with it? Why does she?"

He smiles through his tears.

He sniffs "We love him, both of us, God knows why."

We are silent for a moment or two.

Then he says quietly, "You're lucky. You've got someone who loves you, that's obvious. But Geg loves no-one but himself, and never will."

He gets up.

"I'd better be going, sorry. Just in case he needs anything. He doesn't look after himself properly, somebody's got to do it."

Just before he opens the door, he says, "Please—promise me you'll never say anything to Geg. Or to anyone else."

I am just about to speak when he says, "Oh—you can tell Tommy."

He gives a watery smile. "And that's as it should be, it's not good to have secrets from each other if you're together. And that's one thing I *can* say. Geg has no secrets from me. I know him inside out. Right down to his rotten core."

And he is gone.

I can't get our conversation out of my head. The tragedy of it, the utter waste. And Colin is a kind, loving and sweet-natured person. Valerie is an interesting, intelligent woman with a mind of her own. Why do they throw themselves and their youth away on someone who, at bottom, cares for nothing but his own needs?

I wonder if maybe Geg will die soon? I know heroin addicts don't tend to be long-lived on the whole. Maybe he will take an unintentional overdose. That would be a happy release for two people. Or for three.

I tell Tommy the whole sad story when the weekend rolls round.

"Aye," he says. "Ah thought there was something weird about that setup. Now I understand. Have you noticed how the Geg one always wears long sleeves? That'll be tae cover up the track marks. The needle marks in his arm."

And he's right, when I think about it. I've never seen Geg's arms. It makes sense.

We are in bed, just chatting and catching up.

After a while he says, with a shake of his head, "Ah'm no' sure it's a great idea, you living here. Not with that goin' on across the hall. Not when I'm not here."

He lights up a cigarette.

"Maybe you should look around for somewhere else—what do you think? I'd be happier, certainly."

'*Well, you know the answer,*' I think. '*Either move in with me, or let's find another place, together.*'

But I don't say that. Instead I say, "Oh, but I like it here. It's convenient for everything—and no landlord. Which means Elsie can operate as she likes, and that pays the bills."

The Elsie arrangement has worked out, on the whole. There is an odd night when she doesn't show up; sometimes she's on the go till twelve; one slow night she only gives me two pounds, though she makes up for it the next. But by and large, we manage to function pretty well. She has had a chat with Valerie across the way, and explained to her that, in her own words, *'There's nothing to it.'* Where that will go, who knows?

"Yes, you're right, I suppose," yawns Tommy. "Anyway, maybe you should just cut down on the amount of time you spend with them. I don't like to think of you spending your evenings in a drug den."

"OK," I say, "I see that. I'll have to stay friendly, at least on the surface. But I won't hang around with them, if that's what you mean."

"Yeah, that's right. Anyway, you've got plenty of other friends to knock about with. Go out with them instead. Elaine and Joe. Dorothy Provine. Wilma or Shirley. Even Angie."

He smiles.

I say nothing.

"Lights out, OK?"

I remember what Colin said. *'You've got someone who loves you, that's obvious.'*

"Tommy," I say nervously, after a moment. "Do you love me?"

He looks puzzled. "What?"

Then he adds after a second, with a laugh, "Well—I fuck you, don't I?"

I simply can't believe he said that. I sit up in the bed.

"What? That's horrible! Is that all this is to you? Sex?"

He is immediately contrite.

"No, no, sorry, that was nasty. All I meant was, well, actions speak louder than words, something like that."

I don't think he knows *what* he means.

I have calmed down a little.

"OK. But why can't I have the actions *and* the words?"

He doesn't say anything for nearly a minute. Neither do I.

He puts out the light. Another minute passes. We are far apart, not touching as we usually are. It's a small room, but it's a big bed.

I still say nothing. He turns to me and tries to pull me towards him.

"You see, Ah worry…"

I don't respond.

"…maybe you'll get bored with me, find someone else."

I smile in the dark. He loves me, I know it.

"I'd never do that. I love you."
"Good. Then if you do, get over here and prove it."

Later, I say to him, "Colin says you love me. He says it's obvious."
We are sharing a final cigarette.
"Oh, Colin says that, does he? Oh aye, an' he's the great expert, Ah suppose? Isn't he the one that's living wi' a hopeless drug addict? Who uses him when it suits him, and shags a lassie when he needs some money?"

That is unanswerable.

"Anyway," he concludes, turning over, "these heavy conversations wear me out. Time we got some sleep, you and me. As for the rest of them, fuck 'em all."

5. Jail-house Rock

> Number forty-seven said to number three
> 'You're the cutest jailbird I ever did see
> I sure would be delighted with your company,
> So come and do the jailhouse rock with me'.
> *Elvis Presley, 1958*

November 1963.
Wilma is out of prison. It's Sandra Dee who passes on the news to me.

So who is Sandra Dee? Well, in the wider world she is the pretty *ingénue* heartthrob, the wet dream of many a teenage boy, the youthful star of *Gidget*, and the wife of pop singer Bobby Darin.

But in the Glasgow microcosm, 'Sandra Dee' is a small individual, real name Don, who looks no more than fifteen. He claims seventeen, and mentions a previous career as a jockey, which is unlikely, given his age. But not completely impossible, as he is not more than five feet four or five in height. He wears horn-rimmed glasses, and bears an uncanny resemblance to a fair-haired version of Freddie of *Freddie and the Dreamers*.

Sandra seems to have taken a notion to me, and is in the habit of calling round to my place in the morning from time to time. In spite of the name and the diminutive height, the blond curls and the youthful mannerisms, there is something disconcertingly masculine about 'Sandra Dee'. I am pretty certain that in a year or two 'she' will metamorphose into a 'he'.

This impression is borne out when she rings my bell one day while I am still in bed.

After a quick '*Good morning, Audrey*', she starts undressing. I climb back into bed, still half-asleep. Sandra is carrying a sports bag, and I assume that she is going for a change of clothes. I turn away to give her some privacy. But the next thing I know she has jumped in beside me, stark naked, and is immediately ready for, and expecting, some action. She fastens her mouth limpet-like to the back of my neck, and pushes into me, her intention unmistakable.

"Hey, what are you doing, Sandra? Get off me! Stop that, I'm a married woman, remember?"

Undeterred, she is biting the back of my neck hard.

"Ow! Stop it, Sandra, that hurts!"

I finally manage to dislodge her, turn, and smartly push her out of the bed onto the floor, which is not exactly difficult, she is small and light. She lands on her back with a thud.

I am more than a little ruffled and embarrassed by this unsought intrusion.

"I don't know what you're thinking of, trying that on with me," I yelp, pulling the shattered remnants of my dignity together. "I may be many things, but I'm not a *lesbian*. Come on, you're a *woman*, Sandra."

"Eh? No, I'm not a woman. I'm a man."

Sandra is completely unembarrassed by the rebuff. Her tumescence gradually subsiding, she picks herself up from the floor.

"Well, I'm a bit of a woman when I feel like it, but when I don't, I'm a bit of a man. What's wrong with that, anyway?"

And the answer is '*nothing at all.*' Face facts, we're all men when it comes down to it, and who am I to tell anyone how they should behave?

But quite apart from the unexpectedness of the attempt, and despite my occasional heretical thoughts re the gorgeous bottom of my beloved, I am still living under The Immutable Rule. In my head I can hear the voice of Kay Kendall: "*Tootsie trade! Audrey, really, shame on you!*"

And anyway, were I to contemplate travelling across that invisible line, little Sandra Dee isn't a destination I would consider.

"Well, you can forget it, Sandra. Quite apart from anything else, you know perfectly well that I already have a boyfriend, and I'm not interested in anyone else. Least of all you."

I pull the bed clothes up to my chin. "Now put your clothes on, please, and turn your back, I need to get dressed. And keep your hands to yourself."

She does as I ask.

"Sorry, Audrey, I just couldn't help myself."

She pulls on her jeans—no underwear, I note, the slut.

"I wasn't thinking. And you're right, he's lovely, your Tommy." She draws a comb through her hair. "I wouldn't mind throwing him a length myself."

"*Sandra*! Now look here, you, I'm warning you, one more word out of place, one more move, and you're no longer welcome here. Is that clear?"

She is dressed by this time.

"OK, Audrey, OK. Sorry."

She looks over her shoulder and winks. "But you don't know what you're missing."

"*Turn round*, Sandra—I'm not dressed yet!"

Sandra is philosophical. She sits herself down on a chair and starts filing her nails.

"Really, you're very old-fashioned, Audrey. Things are changing, nowadays you can be whatever you want, whenever you want."

Me? Old-fashioned?

She goes on, "As for me, I do as I like, butch, bitch, whichever—I even chase after a woman now and then."

This revelation really *does* surprise me. But Audrey has an answer for everything.

"Sandra dear, you chasing a woman would be like a dog chasing a car. If you caught one, you wouldn't know what to do with it!"

This does finally shut her up. But her remarks give me some food for thought.

Though Sandra, judging from her accent, is obviously from a middle-class background, she constantly endeavours to ape the mannerisms of the in-crowd, the heavy drinking, the endless smoking and the occasional rough language. Not a million miles from myself, if truth be told.

The very next day she turns up again, eight in the morning, when I am once more still abed.

'I must try to break her of this early morning habit', I think.

She has obviously realised that making moves on me is going to get her nowhere, so she restrains herself and heads toward the dining table.

"Oh?" she says, looking down. "A bit of a night last night, was it?"

"Not really," I yawn.

Half a dozen beer glasses, one half-full, the rest empty. It was hardly a party, just one or two drinks with my neighbours.

"I'll just help myself, you don't mind, do you?"

She picks up the half-full glass.

I sit up in bed, my hand out. "No, Sandra, wait…"

But it is too late. She has downed the lot.

Oh dear.

"Ewww…" She shudders. "Tastes like piss."

"Yes…"

Unfortunately, when Geg has had a few, he sometimes can't be bothered trying to make it to the toilet. A disgusting habit. Colin hates it too. He usually deals with the fall-out, but last night he must have forgotten.

Sandra seems unfazed. "Oh well—a first time for everything, I suppose."

I pull the bed-clothes up to my chin

"Just don't ask me whose it was," I mutter. "You wouldn't like it."

She heads over towards the bed, where I am now sparking up the first of the day.

She is looking annoyingly smug.

"Take a look at this, Audrey."

I am anticipating another assault, or at the least an indecent exposure, but instead she dives her hand into her pocket and pulls out a small roll of notes, pounds and fivers. She throws them up into the air, and they flutter down onto the bed. There must be a hundred quid there.

I watch Sandra with some curiosity. Geg's voidings must contain a fair proportion of illegal and intoxicating substances. But thus far she seems to be showing no effects.

"Had a punter last night and dipped him for the lot," she says, obviously highly pleased with herself. "Come on Audrey, rise and shine, get dressed, we're going shopping."

Sandra treats me to an entire new wardrobe. Tight ice-blue jeans, two pairs, sweaters, shirts, trousers and a smart winter coat. The trouble is she buys exactly the same things for herself, same colours, same styles, just smaller sizes. We're going to end up looking like the Bobbsey Twins. Apart from the difference in height, which must be a good seven inches.

And nothing beats a good seven inches.

It's when we're having lunch in the *Rapallo* later—no expense spared, four courses, wine, the lot, thank-you Sandra—that she mentions Wilma.

"Oh yes, out of prison, Wilma," she says round her *tiramisú*. "Saw her and Connie last night in the station. Said she had a great time in there, the toast of Barlinnie she was, according to her."

I smile. "Yes, I thought Wilma would make an impression."

"Well she did, it seems. Big celebration party at their place in a couple of weeks, a Saturday, I forget which one. Connie'll tell you. I'm invited, naturally, Connie's put me in charge of the music. In fact the whole town is going to be there. You as well, I hope?"

I'm not too sure. Tommy is not really a fan of big parties, especially when all the campest in the land are going to be flaunting there, and weekends are our private time. I'll mention it to him and see what he says. If he doesn't fancy it, we won't go. But it would be a shame to miss it.

"We'll see, Sandra."

This next bit is difficult. I do a bad thing, a shameful thing.

First the excuses.

One: Tommy and I have been together about three months. It's three months, rather, since we met, maybe a little more. I love him, there is no question of that, none at all. I have done my best to make things work for us. I have left home, I have found a place for us to be together; I make sure everything is comfortable; that he wants for nothing, that he has food, drink, and as much sex as he is able to handle.

So why the hell doesn't he tell me he loves me? Does he? Or is this just an ultra-convenient interlude for him? Why doesn't he seem to have any interest in taking our relationship to the next level? Why doesn't he suggest we live together?

But he hasn't. And I can't understand why.

Two: I am bored. Oh, not always, and not for very long at a stretch. But though I have company most of the day—one or other of my friends is usually around—the nights are difficult, except at weekends, when he is there.

I suppose I am more lonely than bored. The idea that I might alleviate my boredom and loneliness by showing my face at the classes that I am supposed to be attending never occurs to me. That's how far gone I am.

Three: I am young and impatient.

No, scrub that last, that's not really any kind of valid excuse. And if it is, it is one I have well worn out already.

Really, there is no excuse at all.

It is Little Joe who introduces us. In the *El Guero*. He and Elaine are sitting with someone I don't recognise when I arrive. I wave over to them, collect my coffee, and head across to their table.

"Miss Hepburn, actress, sit down, sit down," says Elaine. "Joe here was just telling us a funny story, he's just out of the jail."

I am puzzled. I look at Little Joe.

"Well, it seems—"

"Hang on a minute, Elaine. What do you mean, just out of jail? What happened?"

Little Joe guffaws. "No, no' *me*, Audrey. She means Joe, *this* Joe. Yes, another Joe, that's right."

"Oh aye, sorry Audrey, two Joes here the day. Joe, this is our very good friend, Audrey," says Elaine. "Audrey, meet Joe. Ah suppose we'll have tae call him Joe Two, or something."

I take him in. Maybe twenty-four, twenty-five, this Joe is tall, dark and handsome.

No, he is more than just handsome. He is so handsome that it is practically indecent. He has Hollywood looks, regular even features and a warm smile. On top of that he has broad shoulders and a trim but muscular physique.

He is one of the best-looking men I have ever laid eyes on.

He looks at me enquiringly, almost challengingly. I can feel myself turning red, I have no idea why.

This Joe is every queen's fantasy; every woman's, too. I bet even straight men go weak at the knees when he looks at them as he is looking at me. He is so beautiful that he shouldn't be allowed to walk round the streets without a health warning on his forehead.

To hide my embarrassment and my confusion, I go for the humorous.

"Well," I say, "we've already got Little Joe. You must be Big Joe."

He smiles lazily.

"Well, if ye ever want tae find oot, just tip me the wink, Ah'll be happy tae satisfy yer curiosity."

Elaine laughs. "Och, you've nae chance there, Joe, Audrey here's a happily married woman, is that no' right Audrey?"

"Yes, of course," I say with a smile.

But Big Joe knows better.

He and I spend the next two days in bed together. With breaks for corned beef sandwiches, cigarettes and cups of tea.

I hear Elsie battering at the door Wednesday night, ready to start her shift, but I don't answer it. Let her assume I'm away, or dead, or something.

Big Joe is a beautiful animal, he is charming, enthusiastic, and utterly and completely frank.

"This is great, but that's as far as it goes. Ah don't hang around the town. Ah'm married, two kids, live down in Dumbarton, so we'll probably never see each other again. But if we do, this never happened, OK? You've got a boy-friend, anyway, is that no' right?"

"Yes," I say, not used to being on the receiving end of instruction, and quite enjoying the novelty.

He smiles. "So we'll not get in each other's way then, will we? Now, if that's OK wi' you, let's have some fun."

That's OK with me.

No more than twenty seconds after Big Joe leaves forever on the Friday morning, Wilma is knocking at my door, accompanied by Elaine.

"Well," she says, looking over her shoulder, "thon wis a sight for sore eyes. Gorgeous guy, just passed him on the stairs."

"Oh yes," I say hurriedly, adding the first thing that comes into my head. "It was the gas man. For the meter."

Shit, shit, shit! Why did I not just say, *'Oh yes?'* Or nothing at all.

"The gas man? Well," says Wilma in a Mae West drawl, as she comes in, "he can come an' check ma consumption any time he wants."

"Oh? The gas man, Miss Hepburn?" Elaine mutters, eyebrows raised, as she follows Wilma. "Well, Ah hope ye got yer rebate."

"Oh, he just popped in for a cup of tea, Big Joe," I whisper to her, flustered.

"Yes, of course he did," she replies. "Popped in on Wednesday for a cup of tea. Then popped out on Friday lookin' completely shagged out and disguised as a gas man. Some people, eh?"

I give her a warning look. Luckily, I know Elaine will never give me away. That's the kind of friend she is.

"Get the kettle on, hen," says Wilma as she and Elaine enter my room. "Ah've a right drouth on me."

She is dressed normally, or as near to normal as I have ever seen her. Which makes the new-born breasts look rather incongruous. Yes, they are definitely in evidence under her sweater. Small and pointy, but unmistakably there.

She looks surprisingly well. I comment approvingly on her restrained attire.

"Oh aye, Audrey, got tae keep a low profile these days—every polis in Glasgow knows ma face an' ma figure efter ma escapades."

She chuckles. "Ma figure especially, wi' ma new assets. Like them?"

She primps and poses in front of my mirror.

It's true that Wilma does have a good shape. Despite her height and muscularity, she has a trim waist and slim hips. Indeed, she would make a fine figure of a man, were she not Wilma, and did she not have a noticeable bosom.

She and Elaine settle themselves down and request refreshment. I hasten to oblige.

I get up and put a record on the player. It's the Caravelles singing *'You don't have to be a baby to cry.'* On my way back to my chair, I contrive to tuck a hand-towel that will definitely need washing out of sight under a cushion.

I serve tea, and as we sip our drinks, I ask Wilma how she is, and how she got on during her incarceration in notorious Barlinnie prison.

She smiles. "Oh well, it's the jail, Audrey, when all's said and done. It's what ye make of it. Ah just thought of it as a wee change."

She leans back in her chair. "But Ah wis fine, in there, really. Ah wis known fae the wan end of the place tae the other, as ye can imagine. Aye, they aw knew me, Big Wilma, so they did.

"An' Ah had a *load* of guys after me. It wis ma personality that did it. Well, that an' the tits, if Ah'm honest. Ah satisfied as many as I could in the wee while Ah wis there, but there was plenty of others left wi' their tongues hanging out. Ah made the most of it, Ah'm tellin' you."

She makes four weeks in Barlinnie sound like four weeks in paradise.

"Tell Audrey the story, Wilma, the one you told me, aboot the black man," says Elaine.

"Oh, aye—well, there wis this one fella, big black guy he wis, as big as me if no' bigger. He wis mad for me. But Ah didnae fancy him, somethin' about him made me uneasy. He wis in for manslaughter."

"God!—manslaughter? I don't blame you, Wilma."

"No, no, it wisnae that that pit me off, come on, we all make mistakes. But ye know whit he says tae me when he's chattin' me up? He says, '*Are you a white wog, Wilma?*' Now whit did he mean by that, dae ye think? A white wog? Me?"

One look at Wilma's crinkly hair, where the orangey-blond is growing out to reveal the dark original, and I have the answer to her question.

But Elaine and I look at one another in pretend bafflement. As one, we say, "No idea, Wilma."

"Naw, me neither. Anyway, he didnae have his way wi' me, no' after that."

"And go on, tell Audrey about the photo, Wilma, she'll be interested," says Elaine, who seems to be acting as prompter to Wilma's reminiscences.

"Oh aye, thanks, Elaine, Ah near forgot. Audrey—did ye know that yer a pin-up in Barlinnie?"

"A what?"

"A pin-up. Aye, bet ye never knew that. But Ah'm tellin' ye. Yer there on the wall in all yer glory for the perverts tae wank over."

She laughs as she lights up a cigarette. "Naw, just kiddin'. It's a nice picture, ye look good."

What on earth is she talking about?

"Sorry, Wilma, what do you mean—a pin-up?"

"Yer photey, ya daft hoor. It's pinned up in a fella's cell. He showed me it. You an' the fella thegither, in the photey. He says tae me, '*That's ma girl-friend, Audrey.*' Nice wee guy. Brian something."

Oh.

"Och aye—ye remember Brian, Audrey? Worked on the dodgems, you had a wee thing with him," puts in Elaine helpfully.

I fake nonchalance. "Yes, I remember."

Brian. The photos we had taken together, ages ago. I haven't given a thought to him or them in months, indeed I have forgotten all about our fling.

Wilma is still chattering on.

"So Ah telt him Ah knew ye well, a good friend of mine, Ah said. Told him ye were still around the toon, said I wid mention it tae ye, that Ah'd seen him an' that."

It is suddenly silent in the room, and Wilma looks round.

"Oh, the record's finished, Audrey, put on something else."

"OK," I say, not really listening.

I pick the first thing that comes to hand. It's Patti LaBelle and the BlueBelles. *I Sold my Heart to the Junkman*, an old favourite of mine.

My mind races. Brian, imagine that. Still in prison. How long is it now? Nearly nine months.

My God, how bad can I get? Not only have I just committed repeated and enthusiastic adultery and jeopardised the present—it now looks as if my past is coming back to haunt me as well.

Elaine joins in with the record.

"*I sold my hole to the gas man*," she warbles. "*And I'll never fall in love again.*"

I shoot her another warning look.

"Any more tea in that pot? Elaine, top me up, there's a guid lassie," says Wilma.

She returns to her theme. "Aye—he's getting out in a couple of weeks, he said, this guy. '*Ah cannae wait. First thing Ah'll dae when Ah'm oot is look up Audrey*,' he says tae me."

"Look Audrey *up*, Wilma, I hope he said," says Elaine fastidiously, pouring more tea.

"Aye it wis wan or the other," says Wilma, unconcerned. "That'll be nice for you, Audrey, won't it?"

Elaine adds milk to Wilma's tea.

"No' too much milk, Elaine, Ah like ma tea like Ah like ma men—hot and strong."

"But not black," mutters Elaine to herself.

Wilma's exaggerating, surely?

"That was ages ago, Wilma, me and Brian. And it was just a couple of nights, nothing serious. And I'm with Tommy now, anyway. Brian—I'd pretty much forgotten all about him."

"Thanks, Elaine," says Wilma. "Nice tea, that, Typhoo, is it? The tea in the jail wis shite."

She takes a sip and resumes. "Well, he's no' forgotten aboot you, Audrey, that's for sure."

She leans back in her chair and is suddenly philosophical.

"Aye, it's like that in the jail—ye get an idea in yer head, an' it's all ye can think aboot, getting' oot and getting' back tae the way things wis before."

I don't like the sound of that. I don't want things the way they were before. I can tell from her expression that Elaine understands what I am saying, and the reasons for my concern.

"Well, how about you, Audrey, eh?" she says quietly. "Men coming out of your ears. Tommy. Jailbirds. Gas men."

Luckily Wilma's prison diary turns a sudden page and she's off on another topic.

"Anyway, Ah met this other guy in there too, great dancer, professional, he wis in for public indecency, he taught me a load of new steps. Huv ye got yon record, *The Turkey Trot,* Little Eva, Audrey? Pit it on, Ah'll show ye."

"No, sorry," I say. "Got *The Locomotion*, though."

I can't concentrate, my mind is too full of the news I have just heard.

"Naw, no' *The Locomotion*, Ah'm sick of that. Got anythin' else?"

I'm not paying attention. I put on something called *Piltdown Rides Again.* I am so distracted, it could as easily have been Beethoven's Fifth.

"Aye, that'll dae," says Wilma, standing up.

"I like the other side better. *Bubbles In The Tar,* it's called," says Elaine, my concerns forgotten, as she moves the coffee table to one side and joins Wilma on the floor. "Ah often think Ah could dae a good striptease to that one."

The two of them dance together. I notice that Wilma's new acquisitions wobble a bit as she shimmies.

'Brian,' I think. '*Oh dear, this could cause some problems.*'

But maybe not. Once he gets out, he'll forget all about it, surely? I hope so, anyway. And he's a nice guy. He'll understand the situation.

I've absolutely no desire to see him again. He's the past. Tommy is the present, and that's a boat I don't want rocked.

Though I may just have rocked it myself to the point of 'man overboard.'

Tommy rolls up that evening, as is usual on a Friday. And I am racked with guilt. What was I thinking of? How did I let myself be seduced so readily?

And that in itself is an inventive fabrication. I was not seduced at all. OK, the guy made the first move. But I was only too ready to go along with it. If I love Tommy…?

I feel horrible, dishonest and deceitful. I long to tell him on the one hand, to try to explain and ask him to forgive me. And am terrified to do so, on the other, in case I end up throwing away the only relationship that has ever meant anything at all to me. How could I have been so utterly stupid?

The weekend passes without incident. If Tommy notices anything different in my behaviour—and he should, how can he not, I wonder?—I see no sign of it. Is he maybe a little quieter than usual? No, that's just my guilty imagination.

I hate myself. Oh, I can excuse everything, naturally.

'Well, if he would just bite the bullet, finally tell me he loves me, move in with me, that wouldn't have happened.'

So it's his fault, not mine, I convince myself.

I wonder how he can be unaware, how he can fail to sense it. I feel dirty, disgusting and altogether unworthy. I know this will have to come out eventually, he deserves my total honesty. But expert in self-justification that I am, I manage somehow to get away with, *'Not now. Later, maybe.'*

Elsie and Geg between them have finally managed to persuade Valerie, school mistress and part-time girl-friend, to grace the commercial alleyways of Glasgow with her presence.

Valerie's surname is Fletcher, and I have an irresistible image of one of her pupils presenting an apple to the teacher.

"*There you are, Miss Fletcher, this is for you. By the way, didn't my Daddy shag you up a close last Tuesday, miss?*"

Intellectual, quiet and rather shy, she certainly seems an unlikely whore.

"Well, she wears glasses, Audrey, and they're strong, Ah'm tellin' ye," Elsie says. "Nothing wrong wi' that, it's no' her fault. But Ah said she should take them off when she's workin'. No' a big call for specs in this business, unless it's for some perv wantin' to be caned or something. And that's a bit specialised, ye don't get a lot of requests for that sort of thing up The Drag."

'The Drag' is the slang name for St Vincent Street, which is, along with Blythswood Square, the centre of the red light business in our fair city.

"So she took them off, an' Ah did a nice wee make-up on her, she looked no' too bad, considering. She's got nice eyes, it's just a shame she cannae see a lot out of them."

We are having this conversation in my room. It's about eight o' clock, and Elsie has called to pick up the keys and start work. I have apologised, and explained to her that I was called away the previous Wednesday and Thursday, and was unable to let her know. She is philosophical.

"Nae problem, Audrey. Next time, jist stick a note on the door if yer away, it'll save me hangin' around. But it's OK for the night?"

"Oh yes, it's fine, Elsie, hope you have a good session."

I have arranged to meet Connie and Alec in the *Strand* later. We'll have a few drinks, Connie wants to discuss her plans for Wilma's coming-out party, which has been announced for this Saturday, the twenty-third.

"OK," I go on, "tell me more. About Valerie's debut."

"Oh aye... Well, Ah found her something half decent tae wear. Trouble is, she's goat nae shape tae speak of—nae tits, nothin'. Ah mean, wi' thon long hair hangin' roon her face she looks the same fae baith sides. Ye cannae tell the back fae the front."

"Maybe if she put her glasses back on that might supply a clue," I laugh.

Elsie smiles. "Anyway, Ah takes her oot early evening for her first time, it's easier around seven or eight, the punters are no' sae drunk. An' Ah say Ah'll stay with her for a wee while, an' handle the negotiations till she gets the hang of it. But then one of ma regulars turns up, so Ah have tae leave her on her own.

"Ah'm nae mair than half an hour, but when Ah get back, she's vanished. Ah'm thinkin' maybe she's goat cauld feet. But Ah ask around the other lassies jist tae be sure, and that Big Marion wan tells me Valerie's gone. Her eyesight must be even worse than Ah thought, because Marion says she went up tae a polis and asked him if he wanted business. A policeman in uniform, can ye believe it?"

My mouth drops open.

"Imagine it—five minutes oan the street, an' she's lifted, right off. Ah didnae know whit tae dae. '*Whit are the boys goin' tae say tae me?*' Ah'm thinkin'. Ah wis supposed to be responsible for her."

"Oh my God, Elsie, that's terrible," I say, genuinely shocked. I have come to like Valerie. "But it wasn't your fault. It was a mad idea, Geg should be shot, making her do it. I just hope she's OK."

Elsie raises her eyebrows.

"Ye hope she's OK? Oh, don't you worry, she's fine, Val, yiv no' heard the rest of it, wait, it gets better. Aboot twenty minutes later, she wanders round the corner, aw smiles. '*Yes, it was fine, Elspeth, I think I'm getting the hang of it. I got four pounds from that soldier, and he wants to see me again next week.*' An' she smiles like the cat that goat the cream. '*And you know what, Elspeth?*' she says. '*I rather enjoyed it.*'"

Her imitation of Valerie's educated accent is flawless, and has me convulsed.

"So Ah have tae sae somethin' tae her. Ah mean, a polis... So Ah says, '*A soldier? What about his helmet, Val? Did ye no' notice his helmet?*' But she's no' paying attention tae me. Her eyes are everywhere, lookin' for another punter. '*What was that, Elspeth?*' she asks me, without turning round. '*The helmet!*' Ah say. '*Oh yes,*' she comes back. '*A lovely bell-end he had, right enough.*'"

I am almost crying with laughter. "No, Elsie, stop, you're making that up!"

"No, no, it's as true as God, honest. Then Ah'm just tellin' her how relieved Ah am that she's OK, and next thing, while ma attention's distracted, she's goat her heid in the windae of a car, an' she's off again. Ah bet she made more than me yesterday, and on her first day, too."

She smiles philosophically. "An' good luck tae her."

She roots around in her handbag for a cigarette. "Men, eh? Never can tell what they'll go for."

Later that evening, Connie explains her plans for the party.

"Shirley's goin' tae help me oot, Audrey. Is that no' right, Shirley?"

"Aye, mistress of ceremonies, me, Audrey," says Shirley as she settles herself on her bar stool. "Now—I was goin' tae ask your opinion—whit dae ye think? Whit aboot a cake? It wid be great if we could get a cake—any ideas?"

She is suddenly struck by a thought. "Could you maybe bake one?"

My cooking has definitely improved now I have my own kitchen. Indeed, I am getting quite a reputation among the undiscriminating. But the truth is that I can only manage a few basic things, some more successfully than others. Tommy is the regular guinea pig in these culinary adventures, he's not a fussy eater. A cake, however, is well beyond my skills.

"Why don't you think about buying one, Shirley? Just a wee one, maybe a few candles? Wouldn't cost much, and it's the thought, isn't it? What do you think, Connie?"

Connie draws in a breath. "Cannae afford tae buy one, the whole thing is goin' tae cost a bit as it is. Naw, Ah'll hiv a word wi' ma maw. She's an expert wi' cakes, won competitions an' aw that. Jist like a professional. She's a master bater."

"Jesus, Connie!" says Shirley.

I have to turn away and stuff my knuckles in my mouth.

Connie, all unaware, leans past me and raises her voice.

"And Ah'll be wantin' some cash off *you*, so Ah will."

This last is addressed to Alec, who is not taking part in this conversation and has turned his back to us. Women's stuff, beneath his dignity to join in.

"Eh? Whit's that, Jim?" He turns round.

"Ah said, Ah'll be lookin' for a few bob off of you for Wilma's party. Cannae pay fer it aw masel'. A fiver, that's what it's gonnae cost ye."

The plump face creases into a frown. He shrugs and spreads his hands in the familiar manner he obviously thinks is irresistible.

"Aw c'mon, Jim, Ah'm skint, so Ah am. Ah can let ye have a quid, two quid maybe, but nae mair."

He raises an eyebrow.

"Don't know whit aw the fuss is aboot anyway? Wilma wis only inside for a couple o' weeks. Nae need for a big do—just wan or two pals and a few bottles, that wid dae it."

Shirley interrupts. "No, Alec, no, that *widnae* dae it. Connie wants tae treat Wilma tae a special evening. She's been a good friend tae Connie, lettin' her share the flat, pittin' the rent book in her name, an' aw that."

Alec shrugs and turns his back again.

"Will ye excuse me a minute, girls?" Shirley says, moving away, "Powder room. Back in a tick."

I am a bit puzzled, wondering why Wilma would put her flat in someone else's name. I ask Connie.

"Don't really know. It wis her idea, Audrey. She's got some notion in her heid, she's no' sayin' too much. Anyway, she jist said it wid help me oot, gie me a bit of security. Nice of her."

Alec has overheard. He sniffs. "Probably worried aboot gettin' lifted again and disnae want yiz tae lose the flat," he says over his shoulder.

Connie nods. "Aye, maybe. She did say she might no' always be around, might have tae disappear. Ah think masel' it's somethin' tae dae with this apparition thing she's keen on."

"Oh yes." I can't resist. "You mean the sex-chair?"

"Eh? A sex-*change*, Audrey, no' a sex-*chair*! Anyway, maybe it's that, maybe it's no'. Whitever it is, she's keepin' it tae hersel'. But it wis a kind thought. So this party's just a wee thank-you."

She gives a little flirtatious smile in Alec's direction.

"An' you should be thankin' Wilma too."

He turns round to face us. "Oh?—and how's that?"

"It wis doon tae Wilma that you an' me ended up thegither. She telt me how tae capture yer heart. Her an' Audrey here, baith o' them."

"Is that right?" He looks at me in mock disgust. "So—it's you that's responsible for for this torture, is it? Thanks a bunch!"

Alec turns away again. But I don't miss the happy little grin on his face.

Connie waxes girlish as Shirley re-joins us.

"Och, he disnae mean that, Audrey, not a bit of it. He cannae resist ma charms, an' well he knows it."

"Yes, Connie, he's a lucky man, Alec," I say. "Don't you agree, Shirley?"

Shirley shrugs, glancing at Alec.

"Alec? Lucky? Oh aye—he's lucky awright, nae question. Lucky Big Olivia's no' had him kneecapped."

She goes on before Connie can protest.

"No, Connie, Ah'm awfy sorry, but Ah don't agree wi' the way he just dumped Olivia for you the way he did." She drains her glass. "Ah just hope the bastard disnae end up treatin' you the same way, eh?"

She smiles. "Still, none of my business, is it?"

She looks at her watch and gets down from her bar-stool. "Anyway, Ah have tae shift, Ah'm on duty in ten minutes."

She turns to Connie. "So—that's all agreed, Connie? Keep in touch and let me know numbers an' that. You try an' sort the cake thing oot wi' yer maw. Ye know where tae find me."

"Aye, OK Shirley, thanks."

"Bye, Shirley," I say.

"Be seeing you, Miss Eaton," says Alec.

And Shirley heads off into the night.

Connie is suddenly quiet.

I am curious. "Look—I don't want to raise an unwelcome topic, but I've been wondering—what *about* Olivia? What's her take on this, you and Alec being together?"

Connie shudders. "Ah've nae idea. She's gone quiet. We've no' seen her for ages, neither of us."

She raises her voice, and it takes on a querulous edge.

"Unless that bastard there has been sneakin' off tae see her oan the sly. Ah widnae pit it past him, mind."

She pushes Alec's shoulder none too gently. "Here, you, dae ye hear me?"

He turns round again.

"Ah said, Ah hope you've no' been creepin' round Big Olivia's place while ma back's turned. Eh?"

"Naw, naw, Jim, no' seen Olivia in months, ye know that."

His cunning little eyes crinkle.

"Mind, Ah could always take a trip over there if ye like, an' get some money off her fer this party o' yours. A quick shag, maybe ten quid, that should do it, back within an hour or two. Whit dae ye say?"

Connie is not impressed.

"A quick shag? Well, if ye dae, Alec, make the most of it. It'll be the last shag ye ever enjoy. An' Ah'll attend tae that personally."

Alec backs off, grinning a little nervously.

"Och, Ah wis kiddin', ye know that, surely? C'mon, if Olivia wis tae set eyes on me she'd go mad. She'd probably batter me."

He laughs gleefully, dismissively, at the improbability of this.

Connie is not amused.

"Aye—an' after that, *Ah'd* batter ye. So you be careful, Alec."

He shrugs, disarmingly.

"Aw c'mon, Jim, take a joke, fer fuck's sake. You know you're the only one for me these days."

"Hm. Ah hope so."

Connie seems finally to accept his explanation.

Just at that moment, someone taps me on the shoulder, and I turn round.

"Jesus, Audrey, at last."

My mouth drops open. Jesus, indeed. It's Brian.

If I had seen him in the street I doubt I would have recognised him. Gone is the Brylcreemed quiff, his hair is short and neat. A prison haircut, I suppose. And he's bigger than he was when I last saw him. Not taller. Wider. He has filled out. The tee-shirt he is wearing—and it is November, it is cold outside—shows off muscles I don't remember. His appearance is completely different from that of the boy I knew. So different that I have some difficulty in believing it is actually the same person.

How did he change so much in a matter of months? It looks as if he has been doing the Charles Atlas course for about three years.

He smiles at me. The smile and the mouth at least are familiar.

"Great tae see you, Ah've missed ye." His voice drops. "Did you miss me?"

No, I haven't missed him at all. Well, not after the first couple of weeks.

I smile in what I hope is an enthusiastic manner. "Well—yes, of course I did. But—you just vanished, what was I supposed to think?"

He frowns. "But Billy told ye where Ah was, didn't he? Aye, he did. He wrote tae me. Said he'd seen you, said he'd told you that Ah wis in the jail."

I am flustered, and not sure how to respond.

"Well, yes, that's right…"

I am floundering.

"He said you were goin' tae write. How come ye never wrote tae me?"

He sounds angry.

"Well…"

I really don't know what to say to him. I realise that not only has he altered physically, his personality seems to have undergone some profound change. Where is the sweet-natured, shy young man I remember?

I rack my brains for a way round this.

The other two, Connie and Alec, have been following our conversation with some interest.

"Look, Brian," I say, "let's find a seat, we need to talk in private."

"Aye, Ah think we do."

As we head away from the bar I cogitate furiously. How do I deal with this? How do I calm him down? I am going to have to do that. Underneath his words I am aware of a low-level, simmering anger.

We sit down together at a table.

"OK," he says. "You were going to tell me how come you never wrote."

I take a deep breath. Time for honesty, it's the only solution.

"I decided not to."

He is about to speak.

"No, wait. I thought of it, I did. I asked Bill how to go about it, and he told me what to do."

Once again he tries to interrupt, but I don't let him. If I just keep talking, try to explain everything to him, maybe I can defuse this situation.

"But then everything went wrong. Personal problems, family problems…"

I run out of steam at this point.

He is silent for a moment or two.

Then he says, quietly, "Ah spent nine months in the nick. Ah thought about you a lot of the time. Ah wondered if ye'd wait, hoped ye would. Ah wondered why ye didnae write. Ah wis goin' mad, in there, sometimes."

"I'm sorry."

I wait a beat. "But– it was only a couple of days. You and me, I mean."

"Four days it was."

"OK, four days. It's not much."

He looks down. I can barely hear him.

"It was tae me."

Our conversation falters. I try to change the subject now that things seem to have calmed down.

"What happened to George, George Cooper, I mean?"

He looks up. "Oh, he's still in the nick, Big George. Two years, he got."

Suddenly the anger I thought I had quelled rises again. His tone is vicious.

"Anyway, fuck George, who cares about him?"

"He's your cousin, and I just wondered…"

He is quiet for a moment. He is struggling with that hair-trigger temper.

"Yeah, sorry, it's OK, Ah don't want tae lose ma rag wi' you. Ah shouldn't."

After an awkward silence, he seems to come to a decision. His expression brightens and he takes my hand.

"Anyway—forget aboot aw that. It's over and done with. Friends?"

Thank the Lord. The situation seems to have settled down, and he appears to have accepted the inevitable.

"Yes, of course." I try to keep the mood light. "Would you like a drink, Brian?"

"Yeah, why not? I'll have a pint of heavy, thanks. Then we can get off, you and me. Ah hear yiv a nice wee place up the Cross? Time tae pick up where we left off, eh?"

I sit down again.

"Oh?" he looks at me. "Thought ye were getting' me a drink? Is something wrong?"

I grit my teeth.

"Yes, there is something wrong."

My tone remains even and smooth.

"Look—I enjoyed our time together, it was fun. I really liked you, we liked each other, right? We had some good times."

I turn away slightly. "But that was ages ago, and things have changed. I've met somebody else. We're together. We have been for a while. You and me—that's over and done with."

I am ready for anything—anger, tears, violence, recriminations, blame. Whatever comes, I will have to deal with it. What I am not expecting is the blank look in his eyes.

He nods slowly.

"Ah see, that's how it is," he says, getting up. "Well—I wish you luck, you and whoever he is. Hope you treat him better than you treated me. See you around."

"Goodbye, Brian," I say.

And he turns to leave. Relief surges through me.

But suddenly he swings back and leans over the table towards me. I look at his face, and see the blazing anger is back.

"Yer a cunt, you. You just use people. Ye have enough of Big George, so then it's ma turn. Oh, and don't think Ah don't know Billy was in your bed a couple of days after Ah got lifted."

I am about to protest. But he doesn't let me speak.

"Oh aye, he told me aw aboot it, so don't you bother lyin'."

Kiss and tell. And I thought we girls were gossips.

His head comes down lower. I back off from his glare. His voice is low, his tone bitter.

"Yer just a slag, you, that's all. Ah hope this new fella of yours finds that out. And he will, soon enough, when ye chuck him away like ye chucked me away. So fuck you, Audrey, yer no' worth ma trouble."

Now there are tears in his eyes.

He takes a kick at the table where we were sitting, turns and disappears.

After a moment, Connie and Alec wander over.

"Are ye all right, Audrey?" asks Connie.

Am I?

"Yes, I'm OK."

"So who wis that?" says Alec.

Who indeed?

I look towards the door.

"Just somebody I used to know."

"Glamorous guy," says Connie.

"Shut it, you," says Alec.

For the next few days I ask myself, *'Did I do something wrong?'* If I did, I don't understand how, or what it was. We spent a few pleasant nights together. It was maybe the beginning of something. But there was no commitment, there were no promises. We liked each other, we enjoyed each other's company, each other's body, end of story. Then he disappeared.

There remains the possibility that, if he hadn't got himself into trouble, things might in time have got more serious between us, but it didn't last long enough for that. And I am as sure as I can be that, at the time, it meant no more to him than it did to me. It was an agreeable interlude, nothing else.

I try to puzzle it out. I *did* miss Brian at first, I remember. But other things soon took over and pushed him out of my mind.

But it may have been different for him. During the months he spent behind bars, perhaps he built it up in his head to be more than it was. Maybe he had nothing else to think about. Maybe it made his sentence more bearable to have something to cling onto, something to look forward to. And maybe it came to assume an importance that it didn't deserve. This is about the only theory I can come up with that explains the facts.

I go over all this Brian business with Tommy when the weekend rolls round. He is sympathetic and understanding. The other matter, the guilty secret, has ceased to trouble me quite as much. As my unsavoury adventure recedes into the past, I manage to convince myself on one level that it wasn't important, not really. It's something I will deal with when I have to. If I have to.

But I'm feeling a bit down, even a bit guilty, about Brian, though I would be hard pressed to explain exactly why. Tommy knows about him, he knows it was only a brief fling, long ago.

"So—this guy was in prison for what, nine months?"

"Yes, about that. But it was only four days we were together. Four days."

He smiles dismissively. "Aye. Well, sounds like he's just been brooding on his own too long, an' built it up into something it wasn't."

"Maybe. But I still feel bad about it, and I don't really know why. I feel sorry for him."

"Well, don't, you shouldn't. You wait, in a wee while he'll have got over it. He'll meet somebody else, and you'll be history. Stop worrying."

I brighten up a bit at this.

"Yes, I suppose you're right." I laugh. "Yes, you are. He'll have no trouble. Every queen in Glasgow will be throwing herself at his feet."

Tommy raises his eyebrows. "Oh—that good-looking, is he?"

"Well, yes, you could say that." I rib him gently, with a smile. "You don't think I would be with some ugly bastard, do you?"

Now it's his turn to tease me. "Oh? Better looking than me, then?"

I look at him critically.

"Hm—well—yes, maybe," I say, not really meaning it, but knowing it will get a reaction.

The truth is that neither of them is wildly handsome, not at all. Brian is big and muscular—well, he is now—but facially, he's fairly ordinary. And Tommy? Well, he's Tommy. To me, he's just about perfect in every way, although I doubt anyone else would share my opinion. He's attractive-looking, but quite average, in reality. It's who he is that does the trick.

But neither of them is in the Big Joe league, looks-wise.

"Oh—Ah see. And is he bigger than me? His build, Ah mean, just in case yer thinking Ah meant something else."

"Bigger than you? Well, no offense, Tommy, but he makes you look like Mighty Mouse."

"Aw, thanks, ya cheeky swine," he laughs. "Just you remember—the bigger they come…"

He is suddenly serious. "Don't you worry, like Ah said, he'll have forgot all about it in a few days. An' if he hasn't, if he gives ye any problems, Ah'll be here tae sort it out."

'*Yes,*' I think. '*You'll be here today. You'll be here tomorrow. But what about when you're not here?*'

But I say nothing. I have learned that he doesn't respond to pressure, he digs his heels in. Just like me.

"Anyway," he goes on, "how come yiv settled for me, and no' this Greek god?"

Well, maybe a tiny bit of pressure.

"That's easy," I say. "I love you. I don't love him. Simple as that."

He is, naturally, embarrassed. He looks away and clears his throat before he says, "Aw, right, Ah see. That's nice."

That's nice. And that is all I am going to get, it seems. So I change the subject.

"Oh—I forgot to mention—there's a party tomorrow at Wilma's place.

It's her coming-out party."

I look at him in what I hope is an appealing manner.

"Don't suppose you want to go? I know it's not really your cup of tea. But it might be fun."

He considers it.

"A party, eh? Well—Ah suppose it wouldn't do any harm. Might cheer you up a bit. An' Ah like Wilma."

He comes to a decision. "OK, let's go, if you fancy it."

I am astonished; so surprised that I feel it's the least I can do to mention a caveat or two.

"Angie will be there. And probably half the screaming queens in Glasgow. Are you sure you can deal with it?"

He smiles. "Well, they'll all be droolin' over me, of course. But if you can handle that, Ah think *I* can."

He takes a cigarette from his pack, passes me one, and abruptly changes the subject.

"Oh, by the way—did you hear about Kennedy? Shot this afternoon, he was, he's dead."

"Kennedy?"

"John F, the president. In his car, in a parade or something. Dallas, Texas. Heard about it at work. Terrible, eh?"

They say everyone remembers where they were when they heard that President Kennedy had been assassinated.

'That's sad,' I think. Five minutes later I have forgotten all about it.

I don't care very much. Events that happen in the big world outside are pretty much irrelevant to me, unless they are likely to affect me personally.

For others, however, important matters are afoot.

6. Standing on the Corner

> Standing on the corner,
> Watching all the girls go by.
> Standing on the corner,
> Giving all the girls the eye.
> The Four Lads, 1957.

Friday November 22nd, 1963.
9 pm.

Central Station. At the bottom of the Union Street stairs, the wee man who sells newspapers calls out his '*Late Fine-awl! Kennedy assassinated!*' for possibly the hundredth time this evening.

Maggie Wilde, trench-coated, stands by the weighing machine. Bored and broke, out of fags and out of patience, she is considering heading for home, when she becomes aware of a commotion down by the Gordon Street entrance. A small figure in a shiny blue coat, carrot-top and a drinker's complexion, is screeching abuse at no-one in particular and everyone in general.

Maggie recognises Brenda Lee, otherwise Kenneth Shelton, the Townhead Terror, and quickly moves off to avoid recognition. Brenda is a nightmare when she's drunk, and the last thing Maggie wants is to be screamed up this early in the evening. So she sways off with the exaggerated hip swing that has provoked Elaine Stewart to say, '*Every time Ah see Miss Wilde mincing across the station, it reminds me… Ah must get that grandfather clock fixed*'.

Maggie positions herself further up the concourse by the platform entrance, as inconspicuous as it is possible to be in a coat that white.

But she needn't have worried, Glasgow's finest are already on the case. The two officers head towards Brenda to attempt to reason with her. Maybe they are new to the Central Station beat, or maybe they just haven't come across Brenda in the past. If they had, they would know that reason is unknown to her, and that her speciality is police assault.

No sooner have they got within reach than she rises on her toes—Brenda is about five foot seven—and lands one on the younger of the two—a good solid punch that nearly knocks him off his feet. The pair are so taken aback that for a moment they don't know how to react.

Maggie watches from a distance, riveted.

Brenda's head goes down, and she charges the second officer, knocking the wind out of him when her head connects with his not inconsiderable belly. He crumples with an '*oof*'. But his colleague has recovered and, sizing up the situation, has by now got a death grip on the collar of Brenda's raincoat. He hoists her about a foot into the air, her legs windmilling. Not a wise move, as officer two has just struggled to his feet, and the added altitude allows Brenda to connect her size five brogue with his chin and down he goes for a second time.

By this time a bit of a crowd has gathered. With a '*Gawn, son, gie'm it!*' and a '*Nut the bastard!*' they encourage Brenda's efforts. There's nothing a Friday night Glasgow audience likes more than a good rammy, especially if the polis are getting the worst of it.

Eventually the still struggling Brenda is subdued (*'The prisoner was restrained'*), and the victors somehow manage to contain her between them, one still holding the collar and the other those lethal feet. She is carefully carted off, and the crowd, booing and disappointed, parts to allow her escort to conduct her towards the rear of the station.

No doubt Brenda will pay the price a little later in the peace and quiet of the Railway Police's cosy offices (*'The prisoner's injuries were sustained while he was resisting arrest'*), and, sometime after that—this is far from Brenda's first offence—she will enjoy a short stay in Barlinnie, the Bar-L, Glasgow's notorious prison.

Maggie has thrilled to the drama—what a story to pass on. Unfortunately there is no-one around to share it with at the moment. Never mind, the pubs will be out soon, the station will be rammed, and she is sure to find an audience. She heads back towards her former spot now that the coast is clear. And is annoyed to see that her vantage point has been pre-empted. Some idiot is in her place.

'*Fuckin' drunks!*' she mutters.

It's a young man she had noticed earlier slouched in the far corner by the Travel Office. Nevertheless, she is not to be ousted so easily. She is, after all, a major Glasgow star.

She takes her place next to him. Not that close at first, you can't be too careful. He squints at her.

"Huv ye goat a light, pal?" he asks, as he places a soggy dog end in his mouth.

Maggie looks at him. He could do with a shave, but he's clean-looking, young and solidly-built. And very drunk.

Maybe too drunk to know exactly what he's doing? Or, supposing he does, too drunk to care?

"Aye, sure," says she, mind racing, eyes darting to check if anyone she knows is around.

She passes him her matches.

He lights the stub with some difficulty and drags on it.

"Did ye hear some bastard shot Kennedy?" he slurs.

He suddenly has Maggie's full attention.

"What? Jackie Kennedy? Shot? Oh no, that's terrible!"

He spits out some shreds of tobacco and laughs.

"No, no' Jackie, ya eedjit. Her man, him, the president. Of America."

Maggie is reassured.

"Oh, that's OK then, ye had me worried for a minute. Ah've always loved Jackie Kennedy," she says, her eyes once more scanning the station.

He shakes his head, and looks away. A moment passes.

"Are ye waitin' on somebody?" Maggie asks, just to make conversation.

He stuffs his hands in his pockets and rocks forward on his feet, still puffing on his dog-end.

"Naw, naw, no' me, pal," he says round it. "Just been drownin' ma sorrows, that's all. But Ah've run oot o' the readies."

"Drownin' yer sorrows, eh?" Maggie says, assuming a sympathetic tone. "That's a shame, son. Whit sorrows is that?"

She couldn't care less what his sorrows are—it's his body she's interested in, not his life story. But she knows it always helps to display at least a token show of concern.

His eyes fill with self-pitying tears. He takes one hand from his pocket, and the half-smoked cigarette from his mouth.

He looks down at his feet. "It's ma girl-friend. She's chucked me."

Maggie screws her eyes up in a half-hearted attempt to achieve a concerned expression.

"Aw no, that's a shame. A nice lookin' boy like you, too? She must be mad, yer girl-friend."

He wipes his eyes, and smiles at her. "It's nice of ye tae say so…"

'*He's not as drunk as I thought he was at first,*' she realises.

"…but she's met somebody else, so she has."

He puffs on his cigarette morosely once more.

"Well, more fool her, if ye ask me. Och, yil soon find another one."

"Naw, naw." He won't be side-tracked. "Ah don't want another one. Ah'll get her back, so Ah will."

He looks around. "Ye know, it was here Ah first met her."

His eyes once more fill with beery tears. "Last year it was, right here, in the Central Station."

Maggie couldn't care less when or where he met his girl-friend. What were they doing anyway? Train-spotting? Maybe she should move on, try her luck somewhere else.

All the same, she'll give it a few more minutes.

"So—where have you been drinking the night?" she says brightly. A safe topic surely?

He drops his cigarette and grinds it out with his foot. "Och, all over, here and there. Finished up in the *Strand*, just up the road. Ah ran oot o' money."

Maggie knows the *Strand*, of course. But ever cautious, she says nothing.

He suddenly seems to brighten up. "Here—ye'd no' happen tae huv a wee drink on ye, wid ye?"

He grins ingratiatingly.

This is just the opening Maggie has been waiting for.

"Well—aye, maybe. Ma place is just up the road a wee bit."

It's not really her place—the ancient and decrepit Queen Mother allows Maggie the use of a room in her large house in Renfrew Street, in return for which Maggie is supposed to do 'cleaning' once or twice a week. Maggie's standards are not remarkable. Fortunately for her, neither is the Queen Mother's eyesight. They rub along in a sort of armed truce; each needs the other, but would never admit it.

"An' Ah've goat a drink in, if ye fancy it." Maggie smiles winningly.

And she has, she was saving it for later. It's only half a dozen cans, but no matter.

"Aw, smashin' pal, that'd be great. It wid cheer me up, that wid."

Maggie takes another look. Well—it's nearly a quarter past nine, and there's nothing else doing tonight. She makes her mind up.

"Right ye ur—let's go. It's no' far."

"Aw, great."

He looks up at her. "An'—yil no' mind me sayin', Ah hope—yiv goat lovely eyes, so ye huv."

Maggie does indeed have lovely eyes, they're her best feature, dark and lustrous.

"Aw—thanks, son," she says, flashing them alluringly. "Yiv no' got a spare fag, hiv ye?"

He digs in his pocket and passes her a crumpled cigarette.

"Aw, thanks."

And off they go, weaving a little from the combination of his unsteadiness and her idiosyncratic gait.

Just by the narrow Hope Street exit, she blanks Pat Calhoun and Susan Strasberg, who are coming into the station.

"Evening, Miss Wilde," Susan says, as she passes Maggie and her conquest.

Maggie is deaf and blind.

"Whit's the matter wi' her?" Susan wonders, looking back after her.

"Ignorant cunt," says Pat. "Fuck 'er."

He's not in a very happy mood.

Maggie leads her new beau out of the station. She feels a little bit guilty for having ignored Pat and Susan—she knows them well. But she just couldn't be bothered explaining what she was up to—anyway, it's none of their business—and she didn't want to risk her new friend being distracted and finding other company more to his taste. No, she's captured him for now, no point in hanging around.

"Where did ye say yer place wis?" he asks.

"Oh, it's no' far, son, Renfrew Street, five minutes, ten at the most—we'll be there in no time."

And they turn right into Hope Street.

9.15 pm

Pat and Susan make their way across the station, heading towards the recognised gathering point, top of the stairs that lead to the toilets.

"Funny that, Pat," says Susan, looking back again. "Maggie usually stops just tae see if she can bum a fag—it's no' like her."

"She's clicked, end of story."

Pat has other matters on his mind.

"Shit, Ah need tae find some young thing fer The Priest the night; and typical, there's naebody around."

"Should huv asked Miss Wilde when ye had the chance," says Susan. "She's nothin' special, Maggie, but he's no' fussy, The Priest."

"Naw, naw, like Ah said, she's goat somethin' on wi' that fella she wis wi'. Ah'll huv tae find someone else."

He hesitates and looks at his companion speculatively. "Unless..."

"Eh? Me?" Susan shakes her head. "Naw, naw, Pat, ye can forget that. Ye cannae expect yer *wife* tae go wi' yon auld bastard."

Pat raises his eyebrows. "Oh? Ur ye no' forgettin' something, Peter? That's how Ah met ye; fixed ye up wi' The Priest aboot two year ago. Whit were ye, seventeen? Ye were no' sae fussy then, anythin' for a couple o' bob, right wee slag ye were."

Susan is unmoved.

"Aye, maybe so—but things huv changed. Ah'm a married woman now. Ah'm surprised yiv goat the nerve tae ask me."

Pat tries to coax, assuming a wheedling tone.

"Aw, Peter, come oan, whit is it, ten minutes? Ye don't huv tae dae much, ten minutes and it's two or three pounds in yer pocket, no' tae mention a couple o' quid fer ma commission. C'mon, gie it a go. Please?"

Susan is adamant.

"No. No way. Look—we'll hang around here a wee while, somebody's bound tae turn up. Maybe Sandra Dee or Big Audrey, maybe Judy Garland."

Pat scoffs. "Wee Sandra, aye. Audrey, no, she's off the market, remember? Married woman these days. But Judy? She's aboot the last one Ah'd pit oan tae The Priest. Ye know whit Judy's like. All wee woman, sweet as pie on the outside, but five minutes alone wi' him and she'd have her cock up his holy arsehole afore he got his cassock off. And trust me, that's no' whit ma man's lookin' for."

Susan nods.

"Aye, ye're right aboot Judy—Ah wisnae thinkin'."

She hesitates.

She sighs.

"OK, Pat. Gie it another ten minutes, an' if naebody else shows up, Ah'll think aboot it. We could certainly dae wi' the cash—Wilma's big party the morra."

"Aye—an' the two of us skint."

He looks around and sighs. "No' a soul aboot. Where are they all?"

Susan takes out a cigarette and lights it.

"Probably at hame, watchin' the news tae see whit's goin' oan wi' yon President Kennedy business."

"Aye. The President of America shot. Big deal. Whit's that goat tae dae wi' us?"

He takes Susan's cigarette from her mouth and puffs on it.

He scans the station once more. "End o' the day, who gies a fuck?"

Maggie links her arm through that of her new friend. He's a little bit rocky, but she has decided that he must know the score, know what she is after, and will be happy to provide it.

On their progress up Hope Street, they eventually reach the doorway of the *Strand*.

He stops for a moment.

"Here, yiv no' a couple o' bob for another wee pint, have ye? This is the place Ah wis drinkin' earlier. Nice wee bar. Ah wis hopin' ma girlfriend might be in there, but there wis nae sign of her. Maybe she's in there now? Whit dae ye say? Goat a quid?"

Maggie is not about to be baulked. And anyway, the notion's ridiculous, what would anyone's girl-friend be doing drinking in the *Strand*?

"Naw, naw, son, Ah'm as skint as you."

She is indeed, and even if she weren't, the last thing she wants is for her pick-up to hook up with anyone else at all.

"C'mon, like Ah said, Ah've a bevy at the hoose, got a few records, we'll have a great wee time, jist the two of us. C'mon, it's no' far now."

He gives in.

"OK, pal, OK, lead the way. Lead on, Macduff!" He glances at her and laughs. "Is that whit ye said yer name wis?"

Just as they are about to set off again, a small figure making it's way carefully down the road, eyes fixed on the ground, draws level and narrowly avoids crashing into them.

"Aw, sorry aboot that, pal—Ah should be lookin' where Ah'm goin'."

He raises his head.

"Aw, it's you, Maggie. Sorry, Irving—didnae see ye there. How's it gawn? No' seen any sign of Michael, hiv ye?"

Maggie responds rather unwillingly. "No, Joe, sorry, Ah've no' seen her at all. Him at all."

The newcomer looks despondent. "Damn, Ah need tae find her."

He turns to Maggie's companion. "So who's this, then? Gawn tae introduce me?"

Pat and Susan stand together, top of the toilet stairs, peering here and there, searching, searching, when a familiar figure trots up from Union Street and sees them.

"Awright, you two?"

"Oh, here's Elaine," says Susan, turning round. "Yes, fine, hen, how's yersel'?"

Elaine shudders slightly. "Well, Ah'm better than I was last night—had a bit too much tae drink. Thursday, ma pay day, you know how Miss Stewart is when she's had a few."

"Aye, Ah do," laughs Susan. "Only too well."

Elaine settles herself next to Susan and Pat. The latter is looking off into the distance, still desperately hoping to find a warm body for his patron.

"One thing, at least I didn't get lifted last night," continues Elaine. "But Ah had a big row wi' Joe, no idea what about, God knows where he's disappeared to. He didn't show up at *The Pop*, Ah hope he's OK.

Yiv no' seen him, Ah suppose?"

"Naw, no' seen him at aw, but mind, we've only jist got here. Saw Maggie Wilde on our way in, though, she's picked up a fella by the looks of it. Completely blanked us, the ignorant cow."

"Miss Wilde wi' a fella? Well, ye cannae blame her, she disnae get many offers."

Susan is suddenly struck by an idea. She turns away and whispers to Pat.

"Here, Pat, whit aboot..."

She indicates Elaine, who is busy surveying the station. "Elaine could dae wi' the cash."

Pat looks unbelieving.

"Whit?" he scoffs. "Ur ye mental, Peter? Miss Stewart? OK, The Priest's no' that fussy, but there's limits. They huv tae be young, at least, and preferably no' stinkin' o' booze."

Elaine has heard this. "I am *not* stinking of booze, Patrick Calhoun, how dare you."

And indeed she isn't, and never is, despite her liking for it.

"Just you watch what you're saying, you. Remember, I know a thing or two about you that I could repeat. Like who you used to be before you were Pat Calhoun. Ring a wee bell, Margaret? Eh?"

Pat is suddenly desperately keen to shut her up.

"Aw, c'mon, that wis ages ago, leave it, Elaine, Ah'm sorry, OK?"

"Oh?" says Susan, suddenly interested. "Whit dae ye mean, Elaine?"

Elaine grins smugly.

"Oh, nothing, Susan, nothing important. But if this one gives ye any trouble in the future, jist you come to me and I'll tell you one or two wee facts that'll turn his gas doon tae a peep."

"Leave it, never mind aw that," says Pat, anxious to change the subject. "Whit am Ah goin' tae dae aboot The Priest? Ah've tae meet him at a quarter tae ten in the *El Guero*, an' Ah cannae seem tae lay ma hauns oan anybody. Any ideas Elaine?"

He continues to look round the station attentively.

"No, no' me," says Elaine with a shrug. "Anyway, Ah'm more interested in finding my husband than in helping you out with your grubby commercial arrangements."

Conversation falters for a moment.

Then, in the distance, Susan sees a small figure appear from the Gordon Street side of the station. Shoulders hunched, head down, hands deep in pockets, he stumbles along as if lost, heading in no particular direction.

"Here, is that no'…?"

"What?" Elaine follows the direction of her pointing finger. "Aye, that's him all right, silly wee bugger."

She cups her hands to her mouth. "Joe! Joe! Over here!".

He looks up, spots her, and his face breaks into a silly grin. He increases his pace, narrowly avoiding falling over, and Elaine heads towards him and supports him by the arm.

"Where the hell have you been? Ah've been worried sick," she clucks in a motherly tone as she leads him back towards the other two.

She takes a closer look at him. "And—Joe, you're *drunk*. How on earth did ye manage that?"

Little Joe grins sheepishly.

"Aw, Ah met an auld mate fae the nick earlier, spent the evening on a wee pub crawl, ye know how it is… Oh, an' sorry aboot last night, byraway, Michael, the row an' that, Ah don't know whit got intae me."

Elaine is too relieved to be angry. "Och, it disnae matter, just as long as you're alright. It was probably ma fault anyway, ye know whit Ah'm like when Ah've had a few. Where did you end up, anyway?"

"Ah bumped intae Big Audrey, she pit me up fer the night. Gi'ed me a right ear-bashin' an' all, for fallin' oot wi' you."

"Oh?" Elaine raises her eyebrows. She and Miss Hepburn are close, and Audrey has a steady boyfriend. But the truth is she's a bit of a slut.

'*She jumped on that Big Joe quick enough. Maybe she's been waiting to add my Joe to her list of conquests,*' thinks Elaine.

"Ah hope…"

But Joe forestalls her. "An' afore ye ask, Ah spent the night on the settee, just in case yer wonderin'."

While this happy reunion is taking place, Susan once more whispers in Pat's ear. "Whit aboot him? Wid he no' dae?"

Pat looks Joe over.

"Well—if it wisnae fer that daft wee moustache… Whit is he? Twenty-two, twenty- three? Ah suppose he could pass for eighteen, nineteen. Ah wonder…"

But Elaine has overheard.

"No, no, forget it, Pat. If you think you're enrolling my man in your charm school, you can think again. Is that not right, Joe?"

Joe looks up. "Whit's that then?"

Pat explains eagerly. "It's a punter, Joe, easy work, ten minutes—maybe ye could nip downstairs and huv a quick shave? It's a couple o' quid in yer haun'. Just strip off for this auld guy, that's it, ye don't have tae touch him, he disnae touch you or anything. It's ten minutes, nae mair, dead easy."

"Oh—well, maybe…"

But Elaine is adamant. "Under no circumstances, Patrick, will I let that happen. 'No' is the answer. *No, no, a thousand times no, I'd rather die than say yes!*"

She leans towards Pat and whispers quietly, "Got that, Miss Lockwood? Eh?"

Pat gives Elaine a look half-murderous, half-beseeching. But he hasn't quite given up—he has seen the avaricious gleam in Joe's eyes.

"Two quid, Joe, maybe even three, if he likes you…"

Elaine fixes her husband with the pop-eyed, intimidating glare that has quelled the aspirations of many a Bette Davis co-star.

Joe gets the message. "Aw, sorry, Pat. If the little woman here says 'no', Ah'm sorry, it's 'no'."

Elaine nods, satisfied. "Aye, quite right."

A thought strikes her.

"Here, Margaret—why don't ye give The Priest the benefit of yer own body for a change. That wid be a rare treat fer him, dae ye no' think?"

Susan joins in, laughing. "Right enough—why did I no' think of that, Elaine? Might really get the auld fella goin', whit dae ye say, Pat?"

"Aye," says Joe, "an' he might appreciate the change—bet he's no' had a wee baldy guy before!"

These three are in stitches at their own wit. But the follically challenged Pat is not amused.

"Aw, fuck it, fuck him, an' fuck you lot an' aw'," he says, turning away in disgust.

9.30 pm
Conversation has flagged.

Then, "Oh, look," says Susan, turning towards the Union Street entrance. "It's Jackie Kennedy—whit the fuck has she come as?"

A tall, slim young man clad entirely in black has reached the top of the stairs. Black jacket, black trousers, black shoes, black shirt. And impenetrable dark glasses, even though it's November and late in the evening.

"Well, come on, Susan, think about it," says Elaine, raising her eyebrows. "What did you expect? Her man wis shot the day, she's in mourning."

Comprehension dawns.

"Oh, Ah see," says Susan. She pauses. "Well, in ma opinion, there's such a thing as takin' yersel' too seriously."

Grumpy Pat is equally unimpressed.

"Aye, an' she looks a right fuckin' eedjit in they glasses. It's a fine line between Jackie Kennedy and Roy Orbison."

The new arrival has reached the group.

"Good evening, Miss Kennedy," says Susan politely.

"It's *Mrs* Kennedy, if you don't mind," sniffs the lady addressed.

"Actually, it's the Widow Kennedy now, to be accurate," says Elaine, ever the stickler.

Suddenly Jackie yanks a lace-edged handkerchief from her pocket and bursts into a flood of tears; simulated or real, it's hard to tell. She carefully pokes the corner of the handkerchief under the rim of the glasses, wipes delicately, then withdraws it.

Whether or not it has dried her tears, it certainly bears faint traces of mascara. *ScandalEyes*, by Rimmel, a new line.

"So sorry to hear the news, dear, it must have been a terrible shock," says Elaine, playing along.

The newcomer sobs. "Oh Elaine, it wis, it wis. He was the best of husbands, ma man wis, the best. Ah just don't know how Ah'm goin' tae cope."

And once again the sobs break out and the handkerchief is manipulated deftly.

"Aw, fer fuck's sake…" says Susan, turning away.

"Och, have a heart, Susan, can ye know see the lassie's upset?" says sympathetic Little Joe, putting a comforting arm round the widow's shoulder.

"Piece of fuckin' nonsense, if ye ask me," says Susan dismissively.

Pat says nothing, but he has a speculative look in his eye. The Widow Kennedy is no more than eighteen, and, under the all-concealing glasses, youthful and fresh.

But he looks away and awaits his moment, feigning disinterest.

"There, there, hen," says Joe, "Dry yer tears. Ye have tae be brave, so ye do."

"Aye," says Elaine, "remember, Jackie, the eyes of the world are on you. You have to carry on. The children need you."

Jackie looks momentarily confused.

"Whit children's that?"

Recollection kicks in.

"Oh aye, oor weans. It's the stress, Ah forgot aw aboot them fer a minute. Caroline, and whitsisname. Poor faitherless kiddies."

"Yiz are aw mental," decides Susan, shaking her head and lighting up a fag.

Meanwhile Pat has moved away slightly.

"Anyway, don't you worry, Jackie, you'll soon meet somebody else, a nice-lookin' lassie like you," says Joe encouragingly, giving the shoulder a squeeze.

But this is the wrong thing to say, it seems. The tears break out afresh, and the handkerchief is busy again.

"Naw, naw, never…"

Elaine gives Joe a look.

"Jackie, hen, huv ye goat a wee minute?" Pat calls over.

Jackie looks up. "Whit is it, Pat, can ye no' see Ah'm in bits here?"

He beckons. "Just a wee thought, hen, might cheer ye up. Over here a sec."

"Whit dae ye want?" Jackie says as she moves to join Pat.

He rises on tiptoe, and she bends down to allow him to whisper in her ear.

Susan smirks.

After a few seconds, Jackie shrieks in horror, "Patrick Calhoun, how can ye suggest such a thing? Tae me, a widow of only a few hours?"

And she hurries back to re-join Susan and the others.

"Dae ye know whit that bastard wants? Sorry Susan, Ah know he's yer man an' aw that, but Ah mean tae say, there's a limit. Dae ye know whit he wants me to dae?"

"Oh aye, Ah think we've a fair idea," says Elaine.

Jackie nods. "Aye, tae go wi' a punter—yon auld priest, fer a couple o' quid. Can ye imagine? Me? A president's widow?"

There is total silence for a moment or two.

"Ah mean, two quid? Bastard."

She looks round the group, awaiting a reaction.

After a brief pause, Elaine says, "Would ye dae it for ten quid, Jackie?"

Jackie's turns to her. She frowns, momentarily confused. Eventually, her expression clears.

"Oh aye, well, ten quid, Elaine, that's a different matter, isn't it? But two quid? Whit kinda woman dis he think Ah am?"

Elaine smiles. "Well, Ah think we've established whit kind of woman ye are, Jackie. Now we're just haggling over the price, is that no' right?"

This logic is unassailable. Jackie frowns again, but says nothing

Eventually, Little Joe speaks. "Well, Jackie, OK, it's only two quid, but cash is cash, when all's said and done."

"Aye," says Susan, now deciding to join in the game. "Think of the kids. New shoes maybe? Their education, college, aw that. A widow's pension disnae stretch very far."

"And remember, you're a star," says Elaine, encouragingly. "The show must go on."

Pat has re-joined the group, and delivers the *coup de grace*.

"It's what John would have wanted, Jackie," he whispers.

Jackie sniffs. "Dae ye really think so, Pat?"

"Oh aye," says Pat, turning away, sensing victory. "Nae question."

"Paint a smile on those trembling lips, actress. Life is for the living. Show the world you're maybe down, but you're not out," says Elaine.

Jackie rallies, takes a deep breath and squares her discretely padded shoulders.

"Aye, yiz are right."

She turns to Pat.

"Two quid, ye said? OK. Lead me tae ma fate, Pat. Ah'm ready tae face the press."

Pat takes her arm. "Nae bother at aw, hen, jist you follow me."

And together they head for the station exit.

"Ah'll be back in half an hour, Peter, OK?" Pat calls over his shoulder as they reach the top of the Union Street stairs.

"Silly cunt, that one," says Susan with a shake of her head, looking after them. "Still, at least Pat an' me'll have a bit o' money fer this party the morra. You goin', Elaine?"

"Oh aye, me an' Joe will be there, nae danger. The whole of Glasgow will be there by the sound of it."

After a moment or two, Elaine returns to an earlier topic.

"You were sayin' ye saw Miss Wilde leavin' here wi' a fella earlier on, is that right, Susan?"

"Oh aye, headin' intae Hope Street they were. No' a bad-looking wee guy, either. Mind, he looked paralytic tae me."

"Oh, that wouldn't surprise me. Maggie looks much better through the bottom of a bottle."

Little Joe offers a contribution.

"Aye, Ah saw them an' aw, staggerin' up Hope Street thegither. It looked as if she wis practically huvin' tae haud him up. She tried tae blank me at first, but Ah had a wee word wi' her. She wis tellin' me Brenda Lee goat lifted in the station a while ago, for fighting. Again."

"That Brenda," tuts Elaine. "She's daft as a brush. Gets a drink in her then makes an arse of herself and ends up getting' lifted."

"Aye," sniggers Susan. "Who does that remind ye of?"

"And that's quite enough from you, Miss Strasberg," comes back Elaine with a smile.

She turns to Joe again. "So tell me about this fella she wis with. Miss Wilde, Ah mean. Not a regular? A New Face? Young? Old?"

Joe wrinkles his brow and doesn't answer straight away.

"C'mon Joe, c'mon, I need information."

Joe ponders. "Well, she didnae introduce him or nothin'. But he wis young, nineteen, maybe, twenty? Nice-lookin' boy. Don't know who he wis, but Ah know Ah've seen him before somewhere. Maybe in the nick? No' sure."

9.45 pm

He seems to have sobered up a bit. But he stumbles, and Maggie has to help him negotiate the crossing at the Sauchiehall Street lights.

"Aw, thanks," he says, "Ah near went over there. Sorry aboot that, Ah've had a few."

"Nae problem," says Maggie, looking left, then right.

"Whit's yer name, byraway?" he slurs.

Now… Is she Maggie tonight? Or is she Irving?

She decides to risk it. Despite the fact that she knows he has been drinking in the *Strand*, Glasgow's premiere gay hang-out, she's not entirely certain what kind of reaction she will get.

But, come on, he's pretty far gone, and she is sure she can out-smart him if he cuts up rough. Cards on the table, then.

"Ah'm Maggie. They call me Maggie Wilde," she simpers.

He seems completely unfazed. He nods.

"OK—hello Maggie. Ma name's Brian, awright?"

7. It's My Party

> It's my party and I'll cry if I want to
> Cry if I want to, cry if I want to
> You would cry too,
> If it happened to you.
> *Lesley Gore, 1963*

Saturday 23rd November 1963.

By the time Tommy and I arrive at the party, about nine o' clock, there is already quite a crowd there. Angie has come with us.

"Oh, I hate turning up solo at a party, Audrey, it's *sew* undignified. Do say I can come with you two."

"Yes, of course you can," I say. And turning to Tommy, I add quietly, "And not a word, you, OK?"

He shrugs and grins. "No, no, that's fine. We wouldn't want poor Gordon to have to arrive stag."

She looks at him, dubious, scenting an insult but not quite able to pin it down.

For a wonder, these two actually seem to be getting along a little better. Tommy naturally insists on addressing Angie as *Gordon*. After ignoring him for a time, and then trying a vain attempt or two to correct him, she eventually decides she will respond to it as if it were her name. Which it is.

She reacts in kind by calling him *Thomas*, when she remembers.

"He's not *that* bad, actually, your Thomas," she confides quietly at one point. "I'm beginning to warm to him. A bit common, unfortunately, but lucky for you to meet someone who's not too fussy."

"Up your *culo*, Angie," I say.

Among the guests already present are Elaine, with Little Joe and Kay Kendall. Shirley, in charge of the evening, is rushing around serving drinks, assisted rather reluctantly by Alec, while Wilma, the guest of honour, is ensconced in the most comfortable armchair.

She is in full female attire. But not her usual slacks and sweater get-up. No, Wilma is wearing a dress; and the pale blue crêpe is protesting ominously at the seams. The front of her hair is so back-combed it resembles a cliff-face. It's lacquered into a solid mass, and she has a matching blue bow just over each ear. She wears low-heeled pumps—I imagine her feet must be about a size ten—and carries a dainty handbag. She is fully made-up, false eyelashes, the lot. All slightly undermined by just a hint of blue shadow round the jawline. She looks like a transvestite bricklayer. A bricklayer with a noticeable cleavage.

We take our bottles into the kitchen where the lady from downstairs, Betty something, is in the kitchen with Connie, cutting up sandwiches. It is the strictly observed rule in Glasgow party society that the host provides the location, and possibly—though not necessarily—some kind of food, while the guests are responsible for the liquid refreshment. I have contributed a bottle of gin, Tommy a case of beer, while Angie has brought two bottles of wine, *Lanliq*, Glasgow's premier vinous tipple. She'll be drinking that all alone, I have no doubt, unless everything else runs out first. Not that she will mind in the least. Angie is an enthusiast of the grape, however abused it may have been on its way to the bottle, and she's not fussy about vintage.

Sandra Dee and Kay Starr are chatting over by the sideboard. I wonder briefly if the vivacious but unpredictable and shameless Miss Dee is considering making a pass at the ever lugubrious Miss Starr. If so, it might penetrate the latter's habitual gloom, not to mention more tangible parts.

Sandra is in charge of the musical side of the evening, and has to rush to the record-player every couple of minutes to select a new hit.

Ava Gardner and Lana Turner are seated with Dorothy Provine round the dining table, which has been pushed against a wall to allow space for—well—dancing, I suppose. Their friend Vicky Lester is sobbing quietly in a corner, no-one knows why, or cares much.

I take a look round the flat. There's quite a difference since my last visit. Not only is the place tidy, but somehow storage space has been found for all Wilma's clutter. There is not a sign of disorder, and I can see that the flat is actually a rather cosy one, now it's been straightened up.

'*This would suit me and Tommy down to the ground*,' I think. But not here in Anderston, this particular area, with its proximity to the docks, is on the rough side, and anyway, I prefer the town centre.

When Shirley brings another drink over, I ask her, "Did you have any luck with the cake, Shirley?"

"Oh aye Audrey, it wis nae problem. Connie's maw made one, lovely it looks. Big enough for everyone to have a slice, fresh cream, icing, candles, the lot. Connie's that proud, you'd think it was *her* that made it. We just had a wee bit difficulty keepin' her mother from comin' tae the party. But Connie told her she widnae really fit in, it wis a class reunion."

In a sense it is exactly that, considering the very different backgrounds represented in the guest list.

"So—where is it?—the cake, I mean." I continue.

She lowers her voice. "Ssh—it's hidden away, in the hall cupboard, Wilma disnae know anything about it, we're saving it as a surprise. Yil see it later on, Ah'll just wait for the right moment an' get Connie tae bring it oot."

And she dashes off to open the door to some new arrivals.

We head over to greet the guest of honour, and Wilma welcomes us cordially.

"Audrey, good tae see ye. An' your husband too—glad you two could make it. Have ye got a drink? Oh, and Miss Dickinson. Well, Hollywood must be empty the night."

"And the jails too," sniffs Angie, looking round the assembled company.

"You'll feel right at home then, Angie, won't you?" Wilma smiles.

She turns to me. "Find a chair, Audrey, before the place gets too crowded."

There is a comfortable-looking armchair over near the fireplace, and I head in that direction, Angie trailing behind. But Tommy pushes past both of us, gets there before me, and sits himself down with a satisfied sigh.

"Oh—thanks," I say, surprised. "I had my eye on that seat."

"It's no problem," he says with a grin. "Here—sit on ma knee."

"Who? Me? Or Angie?"

"Oh, Ah'm not bothered—as long as I have a lovely lady on top of me, Ah don't really care who it is. Up for it, Gordon?"

"Really, Thomas, how *dare* you suggest such a thing! The very idea!"

Angie turns to me, breathing heavily.

"Audrey—please, control your husband, will you?"

"Yes, sorry Ange. Thomas, behave yourself."

And I sit down on his knee.

Angie, pink with embarrassment, has moved off to talk to the pretty but borderline-disturbed Vicky Lester, who has finally stopped crying, and is looking ravishing this evening in a pale grey pearlised plastic coat, and a pair of very smart and fashionable spectacles. The latter must be a recent acquisition, I've never seen Vicky in glasses before.

I put an arm round Tommy's neck. '*This is nice,*' I think.

"You OK there? Comfy?" he says, looking up.

I snuggle. "I'm fine, never better."

By ten-thirty the place is heaving. I see Vera-Ellen with her boyfriend Bobby Savage, the one that used to be mine. The pubs have turned out, and there must be forty or fifty people crowded into this tiny flat. Little Judy Garland arrives with her shadow, Bridie Gallacher, and they settle down to have a chat with Kay Kendall. All the chairs are taken, some people sit on the floor, a few stand around, others crowd the tiny kitchen. The drink, of which there appears to be no shortage, flows like water. Every new arrival clutches at least one bottle, which is then passed to Connie, who is in charge of refreshments.

And Wilma is not the only one to essay a little fancy dress this evening. Julie London and Shirley Temple, in their matching blonde wigs and mauve cocktail dresses, look like a couple of the Beverley Sisters. Dame Margot Fonteyn has come as Dame Margot Fonteyn, in, perhaps, *The Firebird*. At least, I assume that's who she is meant to be. No, she is not actually featuring a *tutu*, but she looks breath-taking, beautifully made up, her enormous green eyes outlined in kohl. And she has done something remarkable with what I eventually come to realise are a couple of nylon hairpieces and a jewelled turban. She is accompanied by her regular crony, Battling Brenda Lee. The latter is sporting an impressive black eye, but that's not unusual. Brenda so far seems in an amiable mood; though I am aware that she is unpredictable after a few drinks, and just hope no-one says anything that might set her off.

Tommy and I are still sharing a chair—we are determined not to give it up, so take turns going for drinks or to the toilet in order not to lose our place. At this particular point, he is sitting on my knee, which he seems to find perfectly agreeable. And even though he is heavy, I am finding this change of position and the proximity of the gorgeous bottom uncomfortably stimulating.

Elaine is perched on one side of our chair, Little Joe standing next to her, his arm on her shoulder. Angie and Kay Kendall are over by the door chatting to Margot and Brenda. Behind them, Dorothy Provine is deep in conversation with a man who bears an uncanny resemblance to Acker Bilk, the jazz clarinettist. A new beau? Possibly. I certainly don't think I've ever seen him before.

Wilma holds court in her corner. Although one of the shoulder seams of her dress has given up the uneven struggle and gapes slightly, she appears completely unaware of this, and as I watch, she stands up and takes the floor for a dance with Nicky. The latter is his usual handsome, debonair self.

My interest in Nicky in *that* way has completely disappeared since I met Tommy. He is now, as he has always been, just my very good friend.

Music blares from the record-player, and the hits of the day pour out one after the other. Brian Poole and the Tremeloes ask *Do You Love Me?,* and like an antiphon, the Beatles remind them that, indeed, *She Loves You. Be My Baby,* beg the Ronettes, and Gerry and the Pacemakers assure them that *You'll Never Walk Alone.*

Ah yes, every one a gem.

I am sitting in my chair—Tommy has gone to the toilet, so I am making the most of the space. Elaine is still perched on the arm, while Joe has headed off to replenish our drinks.

"Thanks for looking after Joe on Thursday night, Audrey. Ah still don't know what it was we fell out about, Ah was that pissed. But when I sobered up I was worried sick in case he had got lifted or something."

"That's OK, Elaine. Joe was off his face when I ran into him, he could hardly walk straight. I had no idea where you might have got to, so I thought the best thing I could do was take him home with me and keep an eye on him."

She raises her eyebrows.

"Oh? Hope that's all you kept on him, Audrey. Ah mean, knowin' what a trollop you are. You didn't mistake my Joe for the gas man, I hope?"

I draw in a sharp breath. "Elaine!"

No-one else can hear us, but even so.

"Remember," I go on, "Careless Talk Costs Lives. You must promise me you'll never mention that business to anyone. Not even to your Joe."

"Come on, Miss Hepburn, as if I would. Just having a laugh. Of course I won't, I'd never do that. No, not even to Joe."

"What was that about Joe?" says the man himself, coming over with our drinks.

"Nothing, Joe," Elaine says. "Audrey was asking me about the dramas last night, what was going on. Ah said you'd give her the details."

Joe laughs as he squats down on the floor at Elaine's feet.

"Oh aye, Audrey, where do Ah start? What a night, all sorts, shame you missed it. Brenda Lee arrested for fighting wi' the polis—look, ye can still see she's got a bit of a shiner… Jackie Kennedy in full mourning gear for her husband… Then Pat Calhoun and Susan trying to find a taker for the Priest…"

He proceeds to give me a blow by blow account of the happenings of the previous evening.

"... and best of all," he winds up, "Maggie Wilde flyin' off intae the night wi' some wee guy she's picked up, like a dog wi' a bone, feart somebody might take him off her if she hung aroon' too long."

"Maggie?" I scoff. "She was lucky to find somebody brave enough."

"Aye, or drunk enough," puts in Elaine.

"Well, the wee lad was certainly pissed," says Joe.

"Just hope he had plenty of fags on him," laughs Elaine.

"Ow," I exclaim, as Tommy returns from the toilet and plops himself down heavily on my lap.

Inevitable, I suppose. A party in Glasgow without at least one punch-up is not considered to have been a success.

Kay Kendall, I learn later, has committed a minor act of *lèse-majesté* by making a critical comment about Dame Margot's appearance, and even dared to poke her on the shoulder to emphasise her point. A terrible miscalculation, for directly behind Margot is her bodyguard and protector, the fatal Brenda Lee. And Brenda is not one to allow such temerity to pass unpunished.

Quick as thought, Brenda pulls Margot to one side, and prepares to lay into Kay. She draws back her fist and lets fly.

Kay, obviously no stranger herself to contact sports, ducks at precisely the right moment, and the punch goes over her head and connects solidly with the jaw of Dorothy's gentleman friend, Mr Acker Bilk, who hits the deck, out cold.

"How *uncamp*," intones Angie from the side-lines, glancing over. Next to her, Vicky Lester starts to sob.

"Oh *really*, Brenda," says Dorothy, looking down. "You're such an oaf, look what you've done to the poor man. And Clive and I were just discussing possible dates for our Mediterranean cruise."

"Aw, screw the nut, Dorothy," growls Brenda, moving back to join Margot.

Dorothy raises an eyebrow. "Screw the nut? Really, Brenda, I don't even know what that *means*!"

Brenda is too busy nursing her bruised hand to enlighten us. Margot leads her off towards the bathroom, presumably to administer some kind of first-aid. I wonder briefly if there is something tootsie-ish going on between these two? They seem to be always together, though they are, to say the least, an improbable combination.

Kay Kendall wisely decides to absent herself temporarily from the company and wanders off in the direction of the kitchen. Dorothy tuts and looks down, more irritated than sympathetic, to where Mr Bilk lies unconscious at her feet.

Connie pushes her way through the crowd, Wilma behind her.

"Aw, come on, fer fuck's sake, it's supposed tae be a party, this, no' a rammy."

"Who is he, anyway?" says Wilma.

Connie shakes her head. "Never seen him before."

She puts her hands on her hips and surveys the damage. "Here, Dorothy, gie's a haun' tae get yer fella tae his feet, will ye."

"Me? As if..." Dorothy shrugs and turns away.

"Wilma?"

Wilma obliges, getting a meaty hand under one of the gentleman's armpits. The zip of her dress strains alarmingly. Connie bends down and gets a grip round the other arm. The little knot of curious spectators gradually disperses. Connie and Wilma between them manage to heave the unconscious Clive to his feet, and then into a chair. His head slumps on his chest.

Together they look him over. He is very pale.

"Is he deid, Connie?" whispers Wilma, hand to her mouth.

"Naw, naw, don't be daft, Wilma," scoffs Connie, although her tone is uncertain.

"Dead?" Shirley joins them. "What the fuck's happened? Did Ah miss aw the fun?"

Wilma grabs Shirley's hand. "Oh Shirley—Brenda Lee thumped this fella, an' Ah think he might be deid."

But right at that moment Mr Bilk half sits up, shakes his head groggily and mutters, "Where am I?"

I hadn't realised people actually said that.

"Where's Mother? What happened?"

"Oh, nothin', nothin'," says Shirley, patting his shoulder. "You took a wee funny turn for a minute there. Just sit and rest, yil be fine."

"Whit does he mean, '*Where's Mother*'? His maw's no' here, surely?" whispers Connie to Shirley, looking round.

"Naw, naw," Shirley scoffs, "he's jist a bit confused, that's all. Here, Wilma, you see tae the guests, get Alec tae help ye. We'll deal wi' this, me an' Connie."

"OK, OK," says Wilma, relieved, backing away.

Connie has an idea.

"Shirley, should we maybe ask Vivien Leigh tae have a look at him?

She's a nurse, Vivien."

"Good thinking, Connie."

Shirley calls over her shoulder.

"Vivien, get ower here and have a look at this fella, will ye?"

Vivien trots over, bends down, and examines the patient. She peers into his eyes, checks his pulse, looks in his mouth.

"Well, he hasn't swallowed his tongue."

"Why would anybody want tae dae that?" wonders Shirley.

Vivien takes a penlight from her pocket and shines it into Mr Bilk's left ear.

"Mother?" the patient says, looking up.

Vivien smiles patiently and pats him on the wrist. "No, no, dear, I'm Sister Vivien."

She completes her examination and stands up.

"Aye, I think he's OK, Shirley. Maybe a wee bit concussed? Imagine, thinkin' Ah could be his mother. Ah mean, he's older than me."

Connie puts her hand on Vivien's arm. "He's an awfy funny colour, dae ye no' think?"

It's true that Clive's face is sheet white.

"Yes, he is," says Shirley, nodding agreement. "Do you think he'll be OK?"

Vivien hesitates. Asked for a firm diagnosis, she is reluctant to commit herself.

"Aye, probably. But—well, I wouldn't like to say for sure. Might be best if somebody took a wee look at him. A doctor, I mean."

She bends down again and examines the patient critically.

"See, his eyes are rolling a bit. He could just go off again."

"Jesus, Vivien, dae ye think so?" says Connie, horrified. "Christ, the last thing we need is tae be landed wi' a dead body."

She looks around. "Ah mean, there's few enough chairs as it is."

Shirley agrees. "And apart from the inconvenience, it'll spoil the sparkling party atmosphere."

"Aye," says Alec, joining them. "An' it might be a wee bit hard tae explain a corpse away at the end of the night, dae ye no' think?"

Connie nods. "Maybe somebody could take him tae the hospital. What do you think, Shirley?"

Shirley is deep in thought. "Aye, maybe. We need tae get him out of here, that's for sure."

She stands up, and turns to face the room.

"Sandra—turn the music off fer a minute."

Miss Dee hastens to obey.

Shirley clears her throat.

"Right, you lot, pay attention—who here's got a car?"

"Not me, Connie, sorry," says Vivien, "Kay and me came on the bus. If I did…"

There is no further response.

Shirley raises her eyebrows.

"Aw, come on, Ah know some of yiz came in cars. You, Ava, for one— you and Lana and Vicky Lester, you three came in a car."

"Well, aye, we did," says Ava, coming over. "In my car. But Ah've just had the damned thing cleaned. Ah don't want blood all over ma upholstery."

"The man's no' bleedin', Ava," Shirley explains patiently. "He's concussed, that's all. Go on, it'll no' take ye more than fifteen minutes, the Western Infirmary's just doon the road."

Ava looks down at the patient.

"No, no, Shirley, sorry an' aw' that, but Ah don't want tae get involved. Find some other mug—pit him in a taxi, if ye like. But leave me out of it."

"OK, I see," says Shirley. "So that's the way it is? Well, Ah expected better from you, Ava."

She is suddenly determined.

"OK—here's the deal. Either ye help me oot, an' take this guy tae the Western in yer car like Ah asked ye—drop him off at the Casualty department, jist say ye found him in the street, say whitever ye like…"

She takes a deep breath. "…or yiz can leave now. The three of you— you, Lana and Vicky. It's up tae you. If you'll no' help us out, you're no' welcome here."

Ava, exasperated, casts her eyes heavenwards. Vicky Lester says nothing, but chokes back a sob or two. She removes her glasses to wipe her eyes.

"Hang on, hang on," says Lana, limping over. "That's taking the piss Shirley. Why should Ava an' me put ourselves oot for this idiot?"

She turns to Miss Lester, irritated. "And stop yer racket, Vicky, for God's sake, you're getting oan ma nerves."

Vicky stifles another sob and puts her spectacles back on

Lana faces Shirley again.

"OK, Shirley, have it your own way. We're no' takin' him. So ye're tellin' us tae leave, 's that right?"

Shirley's mind is made up. "Aye, that's right. OK, Lana, it's your choice."

She pauses. "But if ye *do* leave, yil miss the cake…"

Ava scoffs, and picks up her bag.

"Really? Shirley, hen, Ah couldn't give a fuck aboot yer cake… It's probably as dry as a nun's cunt anyway. C'moan, Lana."

"… and the cabaret."

Ava and Lana stop short and look at each other. They hesitate, puzzled.

"Oh—there's tae be cabaret? Ye never said," says Lana.

"Oh aye," says Shirley, nodding. "Cabaret tae follow, later on."

"Ah thought we'd just had the cabaret?" interrupts the returning Kay Kendall with a snigger.

"Oh, an' Ah love a bit of cabaret," gulps Vicky.

Ava pauses.

"Cabaret, eh? Who is it?"

Shirley smiles smugly.

"It's… Naw, Ah cannae say, sorry, cannae give details. But a surprise artiste, big star, a rare treat fer all of us. Trust me, girls, ye don't want tae miss this."

Ava looks round and gives a theatrical sigh.

She gives in.

"Aw, go on then. But Connie an' you'll have tae take the fella doon the stairs tae the car. This suit's new, Ah don't want it aw creased; Lana's no' able tae help, no' wi' her leg; an' Vicky's goat her new bifocals on an' cannae see fuck-all."

"OK. Nae problem, Ava, Alec an' me can manage him. Connie has tae look after the guests."

Shirley turns her attention to the victim, speaking very slowly and distinctly.

"Now, son, just going tae take ye for a wee drive, just tae make sure yer OK, awright? And if they ask ye for details at the hospital, just say ye don't remember. Don't mention where yiv been, or how it happened. Or the next thing ye know, we'll have the polis at the door. OK?"

"Well, if you really think…" says Clive brightly, struggling to his feet, where he balances precariously between Shirley and Alec. "I do feel a wee bit wobbly."

He shakes Shirley's hand politely.

"Thank you for arranging the appointment, it's most considerate of you."

"Nae problem, pal, nae problem," sighs Shirley. "Just remember—no' a word about where yiv been, OK?"

Clive nods in agreement, and the unlikely trio moves off down the hallway.

"You coming an' all, Alan?" asks Ava, examining her immaculate hair in a handy mirror.

Lana shrugs. "Might as well, Ah suppose. But leave Miss Lester here, Ah cannae be daein' wi' that noise she's making."

She turns to Vicky, who is by now racked with chest-vibrating sobs, and has once again taken off her glasses to wipe her streaming eyes.

"See you, if ye don't stop that noise, Ah'll rattle yer jaw for ye, so Ah will, an' then Ah'll ram they specs doon yer throat. Gie ye something' tae greet aboot!"

Vicky sniffs and looks at Lana reproachfully.

"Mind you, Jim, ye should be charging Connie Stevens for the petrol," mutters Lana as Ava digs in her pocket for her car keys. "What does she think we're doing here, running a taxi service?"

After they leave, tragedy averted, gradually conversation returns to its previous pitch.

"Here—whit happened tae the music?" shouts Wilma. "Pit the record player back oan, Sandra—c'moan, Nicky, let's have another dance."

By eleven things are in full swing. Pat Calhoun and Susan Strasberg have arrived with Jackie Kennedy. The latter appears to have decided that one day of mourning is quite sufficient to indicate her grief at the loss of a husband, however noteworthy. This evening she is lovely in pale green slacks with a rose-coloured velvet jacket.

Ava and Lana are back after their emergency hospital dash, and we learn that Clive has been safely delivered into the hands of the medical authorities without any untoward problems.

Vicky Lester is not currently crying, and one or two new faces have appeared. I wave *hello* to Lena Horne and Gina Lollobrigida.

The drink continues to flow—the supply appears to be unending—and the atmosphere is lively and carefree. I am a little worried about the level of noise we are creating, but Shirley reassures me.

"No, it's fine, Audrey, there's always somebody havin' a party roon here, naebody bothers aboot a bit of noise, especially on a Saturday night. Ah'll be bringin' the cake oot soon, jist waiting till things quieten down a bit."

There seems to be little likelihood of that at the moment.

"And what about the cabaret you mentioned, Shirley? What time is that happening?"

"When she gets here, Ah suppose."

"When who gets here?"

"Agnes. Ye know her? Agnes of God?"

My former neighbour. I haven't set eyes on Agnes for months. But oh dear, I know very well that the Catholic religion and its trappings are one of her obsessions, and the other is a predilection for arraying herself in female attire. I remember, too, her ambition to appear in cabaret, *'done wi' a bit of fuckin' reverence.'*

"Agnes? Shirley, she's a bit weird. What's she going to do? Sing *Ave Maria*? Say mass? Hear confessions? All three?"

Shirley is collecting glasses.

"Ah've nae idea, Audrey, but she offered, said she had her act worked oot. God knows what it is she's planning."

"Yes, well He will if anyone does."

I wander back to my seat, while Shirley heads towards the kitchen with her tray.

A ring at the doorbell. It's the first for some time, and I had assumed that all those who were attending were already on board. This is obviously a late arrival. The 'cabaret' perhaps? Tommy and I are squeezed together side by side in our chair. Angie is perched on one arm, while Elaine and Joe sit on the floor by our feet. I look at my watch. It's nearly midnight.

Quite a few couples are dancing; Connie and Alec, Wilma and Nicky, Brenda Lee and Dame Margot. Billy Fury is singing *Jealousy*, and Julie London and Shirley Temple are giving us something that looks like a lesbian tango. I am not dancing at the moment, and I know Tommy won't, he hates dancing. Earlier, Angie and I had a jive together, me leading. It's by way of being our speciality. And Wilma has astonished everyone with her high energy version of the twist/locomotion/turkey-trot, which I've seen many times before, but never tire of.

"Who can that be at this time?" I say, yawning.

I am hoping that the famous cake will make its appearance soon, as Tommy and I have been squashed together for so long and in such close proximity that we are suffering both from uncomfortable cramp and equally uncomfortable unsatisfied physical urgency. I have promised myself I won't go before the presentation of the cake—Shirley and Connie would never forgive me—and I don't want to stand up and lose our seat either, but it's all getting a bit too much.

I wonder how soon we can decently leave? It's been fun, but there are altogether too many people crammed into this little flat.

"Have a look and see who that was at the door, Ange, go on."

Grumbling, she stands up and cranes her head to see who has just arrived.

"Oh, it's only Maggie Wilde with some fella. Don't know him."

Yes, I can see the blinding gleam of Maggie's legendary white raincoat through the press of bodies. No need to get excited, Maggie's presence is not likely to alter the paradigm significantly one way or the other.

"Oh, wait," says Angie thoughtfully. "Yes, I do."

"Do what, Ange?"

Still looking across the room, she weaves her head from side to side.

"I do know him. Yes, it's that young guy, the one who used to work at the fairground, can't think of his name."

She looks down at me. "You had a wee fling with him, oh, ages ago. A fine boy. You remember him? He disappeared, ended up in prison, I think you told me."

"Brian?"

"Yes, that's the one right enough, Brian."

Oh, shit!

She looks over again, by now standing on tiptoe to get a better view.

"I'd forgotten how good-looking he is, and..."

She drones on. I tune her out.

"Oh," says Tommy in my ear. "That'll be the *famous* Brian then, eh?"

I fake indifference. "I suppose so."

He nudges me.

"Well, well—let's have a look at him then. Shift yourself, Ah need to size up the competition, don't I?"

"It's not a competition, Tommy," I say as I stand up.

"Aye, Ah know. All the same, let's see what he looks like."

He gets up too and we both follow the direction of Angie's gaze.

And of course, it *is* Brian. With Maggie Wilde clutching him possessively by the arm.

Am I wrong, or is it obvious from his body language that he is simply tolerating this because it suits him? Or am I just seeing what I want to see? Am I actually, on some level, a little bit jealous? Am I slightly piqued at having been so painlessly replaced?

Tommy nods. "No' a bad-looking lad, like you said. Just a wee boy, though. Nice coat he's got on, mind."

Brian is indeed wearing a very smart grey tweed coat.

"Oh, that's hers, Maggie's, I've seen it before. It was the Queen Mother's, and—oh well, it's not important. I'm pretty sure Brian doesn't even own a coat."

"How old did you say he was, your friend?"

"Not sure, nineteen or thereabouts. Same age as me, near enough."

Maggie is presenting her new conquest rather in the manner of a proud pet owner.

'She'll have him doing tricks next thing you know,' I think, unkindly. *'Any minute now he'll give someone a paw, or die for the Queen.'*

The queens certainly seem to be dying for him.

He doesn't seem to object to Maggie's proprietary attitude, though, and is all smiles and charm. There's no question that he is making an impression. Doleful Kay Starr is practically salivating, Ava Gardner is primping and posing in his eye line, and even *blasé* Dorothy Provine is examining him with some interest.

And Brian is perfectly aware of the fluttering in the dovecote. It strikes me that he is only just beginning to be conscious of his power, and the effect that his undoubted masculinity and his impressive physique can have on a cluster of susceptible ladies.

I try to look at him objectively. Maybe he feels my scrutiny, I don't know, but he suddenly looks over and sees me. He raises his eyebrows, smiles, doffs an imaginary hat and gives a little inclination of his head in my direction.

"Come on, Tommy, let's sit down," I say, feigning indifference.

"OK," he smiles. "Feeling a wee bit put out, are we? Now he doesn't love us anymore?"

"Don't be silly," I say, "I don't want him."

I wind my arms round his neck. "Why would I? I've got you."

"Well, well," he says, raising his eyebrows, "I think maybe you're actually growing up at last, George. That's the right answer. Go to the top of the class."

We sit down together, me back on his lap. Angie is still standing by the side of our chair. She looks down at me, then away again.

"Oh Audrey," she breathes. "He's gorgeous, that Brian. I'd forgotten…"

She draws herself up. "I've *got* to have him."

"What?" says Tommy. "One of George's castoffs?"

He looks at me with a grin. "One of the many, by all accounts. Well, you do surprise me, Gordon."

Angie ignores this, and puts a hand on my shoulder. "Please, Audrey. You *know* him. Introduce me, help me."

What can I say?

"Help you? Help yourself, Angie, go for it. Brian will probably jump at the chance to bask in the love of a good woman, especially one who doesn't mind buying her own fags. Stake your claim before someone else does. But I warn you"—I lower my voice and beckon her to bend down—"he's maybe a wee bit common for you."

She straightens up, shaking her head.

"No problem, Audrey, no problem. It won't be easy, but if that's what it takes, I'll *learn* to be common."

She is completely serious. Once again her gaze fastens on the object of her desire.

She flushes and looks away. "Oh God, he's coming over."

And right on cue, here he is.

He pretends to see me for the first time, doing a silly and blatantly fake double-take.

"Well, well. Nice tae see ye again. How're things?"

I look up, ice cool. "Things are fine, Brian, thank you. And how are your things?"

Mistake. He looks down at his crotch, and grins lewdly.

"Oh, everything's in working order and ready for action. You remember that, Ah'm sure?"

But I ignore his crude innuendo, and carry on as if I hadn't understood.

"That's nice. By the way, Brian, you remember Angie, don't you? Gordon, that is?"

He turns to look at her. "Oh aye, sure Ah do—how could Ah forget that face?"

How, indeed?

"OK, Angie?"

She is torn between embarrassment and desire. She simpers sickeningly at him.

"Brian, how *lovely* to see you again—and it's been quite a while."

"Yes, it has," he says. "Ah wis away for a wee holiday. Ah don't suppose Audrey here mentioned it?"

Angie inclines her head. "Er—yes, actually, she did say something."

He turns towards me. "Oh, really? Well, it's nice tae know she noticed Ah wis gone. Ah wis wondering if she had, masel'."

There is a brief, uncomfortable silence.

"And you'll remember Elaine?" I say hastily, to fill the gap, pointing down to where she and Joe are sitting. "Elaine Stewart?"

Elaine looks up.

He grins. "Oh yes, sure do. How are you Elaine?"

She scrambles to her feet. "I'm fine thanks, Brian. Ah must say, you're looking well. And where did those muscles come from?"

He grins again and flexes an impressive biceps.

"Och, got intae the exercise habit while Ah wis in the nick, helped tae pass the time. An' take ma mind off other things."

He stares at me. Angie stares at him. I stare into space. I can't see whether Tommy is staring or not, since I am sitting on him. But I feel him stiffen, and not in the way I like.

As if he's just become aware of Tommy's presence, Brian leans to one side and looks down at him.

"Oh—an' you'll be the new man, Ah suppose?"

"Aye, that's me," says Tommy softly, easily.

"Well, Ah wish ye luck, pal, keep yer eye oan this one." His tone is joking, but his intent is serious. "Audrey here disnae hang around for long as a rule."

"His name is George," says Tommy.

Little Joe, sensing the onset of trouble, gets to his feet.

Brian smacks his head with his hand. "Oh aye, that's right, sorry. George, aye."

He stretches out his hand. "Fancy a wee dance, George?"

"No thanks. I'm fine where I am."

I wait, but he makes no other move.

Eventually I say, "Maybe you should be getting back? Maggie will be wondering where her coat is."

He shrugs and smiles. "Aw, fuck Maggie an' her coat, who gives a shit aboot her? And anyway"—he folds his arms across his chest—"like Ah said, Ah fancy a wee dance."

Oh dear, this is going to end badly.

But Tommy has heard enough.

"Get up, George," he says.

I do, and he also gets to his feet. He faces Brian. They are about the same height, though the latter is considerably wider.

"Look, pal, Ah know what this is about. Ah know ye were together for a while. But that's done with. Away back tae yer friend. You're no' wanted here. Ye get me?"

Brian backs away a step or two, raising his hands.

"OK, OK, nae problem, big man," he grins. "Calm down, Ah'm no' lookin' for trouble. Like Ah said, Ah jist fancied a wee dance wi' an old friend."

"OK," says Tommy, nodding slowly. "Why not have a dance with Angie here, eh?"

I know he must be on edge, he didn't call her *Gordon*.

His tone hardens and his chin goes up.

"Unless ye want tae dance wi' me?"

They stare into each other's eyes for a long moment. Eventually Brian drops his gaze.

"OK. Ah'm out of order, you're right. Sorry."

He looks at me. "Sorry, George."

He takes a deep breath and turns to Angie. "C'moan, hen, let's shake a leg, whit dae ye say?"

"Oh," breathes Angie, hands clasped under her chin, "I say '*yes*'."

She cocks an ear. "I do believe this is a quickstep, isn't it?"

"Quick or slow, its' aw one tae me." says Brian, taking her hand. "Ah jist fancy squeezin' yer arse tae music, if it's all the same tae you?"

Angie is pink with delight and embarrassment. "Oh yes—I *theenk* I can manage that…"

And they're gone.

Tommy and I look at each other.

"Let's go home," I say. I have found the last few minutes difficult.

"Go home?" says he. "Why? There's loads of booze left. And I thought you were having fun?"

"Well—I was. I am. It's just…"

"Your old friend, you mean?" He smiles. "Don't think we've anything to worry about there, do you? He's got the message."

He looks after Brian and Angie. "Anyway, it looks as if he's got his hands full."

I look over towards the knot of dancers. Sure enough, Brian has his arms round Angie, and she is clutching him like he's the last floating spar in a shipwreck.

"Christ," Tommy says, standing on tiptoe to get a better view. "He'd better watch out, the poor wee guy. She'll have him for breakfast. It's the spider and the fly."

I scoff. "No, Angie hates insects. She wouldn't touch a fly."

He grins. "Not unless she was unzipping it."

This comeback is so good that as one we all collapse in laughter.

Now the drama is over Tommy is in a high good humour. The music changes. Cliff Richard sings *It's All in the Game*.

He turns round. "Joe, Elaine—keep our seats warm, eh?"

He turns back and puts an arm round my shoulder. "Now—fancy a dance, Audrey?"

Later, must be about one in the morning, as I am passing the front door on my way back from the toilet, the doorbell rings. The party is still in full swing, in fact it is livelier than ever.

"Get that door, Audrey, will you? It's probably the entertainment," calls Shirley over the hubbub.

"Sure, Shirley," I say, and open it. I am expecting to see Agnes of God in a mitre and cope, ready to give us all a Story, a Hymn and a Prayer.

So I am more than a little surprised to see that the new arrival is an old face. It's Clive, Mr Acker Bilk.

I look at him. "Oh—hello again… Er—didn't you go off to hospital?"

He smiles happily, enthusiastically.

"Oh yes, I did, but they let me out. No serious damage, apparently."

"Glad to hear it. But—might it not be wiser to maybe go home—it's Clive, isn't it?—I mean, after your accident and all?"

He grins, rubbing his hands together. "Yes, it's Clive, that's right. But oh no, I'm fine now. And I just had to come back, I was having such a wonderful time. Had a wee bit of trouble finding the place again. But I just followed the noise. I could hear the racket from out in the street."

He looks at me enquiringly. "So—may I come in? Party not finished yet, I hope? Dorothy still here?"

I remember my manners. "Oh yes, sorry, Clive, come in."

He does, and I close the door behind him. "Party's still on. And I think Dorothy is around somewhere, yes."

"Good, thank you."

I follow him down the hallway.

He reaches the door to the main room, which is still thronged. He stops abruptly, and I almost cannon into him.

Someone turns round. "Clive, dear! You're back!"

It's Dorothy.

"Yes, yes, I'm fine, all sorted out—glad to see you waited for me."

"Oh, well, I could hardly leave without my escort, now, could I?" replies Dorothy coyly.

I am about to pass onward when she stops me.

"Oh Audrey, meant to mention… You *will* be at Beanie's New Year's Eve Party, won't you?"

I haven't really thought much about it. Nicky had mentioned it, but I was deliberately vague, as I doubt that Tommy would be interested in attending.

"I'm not sure. Maybe."

"Maybe? Maybe's not good enough. I need to know one way or the other, I'm depending on you. To play for me, I mean."

Her face assumes the wheedling and ingratiating expression that appears to work so infallibly on susceptible gentlemen.

"Oh—say you will, do."

I consider my options. It is quite likely that Tommy will be planning to spend Hogmanay with his family. And that opens the door to the possibility that I could find myself at a loose end on New Year's Eve, that special party night, the highlight of the Glasgow social year.

"OK, I'll say yes for now. But I'll have to have a word with Tommy, see what his plans are."

She realises that this is the best she is going to get for now.

"Yes, I understand. But do let me know for definite, won't you? Otherwise I'll have to ask Trevor to play for me, and he doesn't—well, how can I put it? He doesn't quite have your flair. Now, promise me you won't forget?"

"No, I won't," I say, as I head back to my seat.

And promptly forget.

"Seen anything of Angie?" I ask Tommy, as I settle down on his knee. I have been trying to locate my sister, but there is no sign either of her or of Brian. I had thought they might have retired to the bedroom for a little privacy—their antics on the dance floor had only just avoided breaching the bounds of propriety—but they were neither there, nor in the bathroom or the kitchen when I looked. I can only assume that they have left already.

"Nope," he says. "Not a hide nor a hair—she must have gone, I suppose."

"Oh? That's funny—it's not like Angie to leave without saying."

"Caught up in love's young dream, no doubt. With your gorgeous ex-boyfriend."

He grins in a silly way. "Jealous, are you?"

"Oh, fuck off, you idiot," I smile.

But a little later, there she is. And so is he. They wander in from the direction of the hallway, his arm round her, looking a little ruffled, but very pleased with themselves. His coat, or rather, Maggie's coat, is round Angie's shoulders. They find a corner together, she sitting on an upright chair, he standing next to her, his hand possessive on her shoulder. I am torn between wanting to find out the state of play, and a reluctance to approach them. Angie *amoureuse* can be a trying experience, and I don't want to give Brian the chance to make any more of his smart remarks.

I confine myself to a little wave. Angie inclines her head briefly in response, Brian turns round, smiles and blows me a kiss.

"*Hmph!*" I think.

When I see him head off in the direction of the toilet, I excuse myself to Tommy, and seize the opportunity for a quick word with Angie.

She sits there, a slightly dazed expression on her face.

"Congratulations, Ange," I say, "well done. You got what you wanted, didn't you?"

She looks up at me as if she is not entirely sure who I am.

"Oh sorry, Audrey, miles away."

She looks over in the direction of the door. "Yes. He's lovely, that Brian, isn't he?"

I make a sort of non-committal noise. The look on her face attains such a degree of cloying self-satisfaction that I have to resist the urge to give her a little well-deserved slap.

"Yes," she goes on. "a fine boy. And—well, you will know this already, but he's very well—that is, he's very well…"

Oh dear, she's about to become graphic.

"Yes," I interrupt hastily, "very well. Quite a handful, let's say."

"Exactly, exactly, Audrey, how tactfully you put it."

It takes me a moment to fully draw the conclusion.

"Wait a minute, Ange. You mean you've already…?"

She casts her eyes down, demure, virginal.

"Well—not *that*, Audrey, not All The Way, not the first time. But a little—well—trial run, shall we say?"

"Right, I get it. I was wondering where you two had got to. So where did it happen, this trial run? Outside on the stairs? In the back close?"

She raises her eyebrows. "No, no, *indeed*. As if I would lower myself to indulge in open air cavortings! No, we found a quiet little corner, Brian and I. There's this big cupboard in the hall, for coats and things."

She giggles girlishly.

"We hid ourselves in there, such fun, like naughty children, it was his idea. Pitch dark, it was, and freezing. He had to lend me this, I was shivering so much."

She smiles in happy reminiscence, pulling Maggie's best coat tightly around herself.

"Not that the cold seemed to put him off."

"I see. And—don't mind me asking, Angie, but how far did it go, this little—what was it? This little trial run of yours?"

She beckons me to bend down.

"Well," she whispers in my ear, "further than I really meant to permit. He wanted to—you know…"

Yes, I know.

"But," she goes on, "I said 'no'. I was quite firm, Audrey. you would have been proud of me. '*Not yet, Brian*', I said."

"Good girl, Ange, never drop them on the first date."

"But I *did* let him go—well, you know what I mean."

"No, I don't. You let him go…?"

She is close to inaudible. "Between my legs."

I chuckle. "Ah, I see. A dry ride."

Her lip curls and she shudders.

"Really, Audrey, what a disgusting expression! Do you have to cheapen everything?"

I'm not quite sure in what way naming it is cheaper than doing it in a cupboard, but decide to mollify her. I straighten up.

"Sorry, Ange. I believe the technical term is 'intercrural intercourse'."

"Yes, better, that sounds much nicer."

She changes the subject. "Anyway, we're leaving soon, Brian and I. You don't mind, do you?"

"No, of course not, Ange, a girl's got to do what a girl's got to do. Hope you have fun."

"Oh, I will."

Her voice becomes once more confiding. She giggles.

"Just hope he doesn't do some permanent damage with that chopper of his!"

"Oh, charmingly put, Ange," I guffaw. "Speaking of disgusting expressions."

Just before I move away I glance down to where she is sitting, and something catches my eye.

I have some difficulty keeping my face straight when I realise what it is.

"Oh, Ange, before you head off—you might want to take a little trip to the powder room. There's something dripping off the inside of your coat."

She raises an eyebrow, puzzled. "Something dripping? What is it?"

I bend down and have a closer look.

"Looks like—now, how can I put this without using a disgusting expression? Looks like a touch of the old—er—Maria Monk."

She frowns.

"Eh? What do you mean? Maria what?"

"Rhyming slang, Ange. I'm trying to be tactful. Maria *Monk*."

"Maria? Something that rhymes with Maria?"

"No, something that rhymes with Monk."

She twists round and glances down. The look of dawning horror on her face warms my heart.

"Oh my God!" She stands up. "I didn't realise that he'd…"

She struggles to alight on the appropriate word.

"…that he'd *soiled* me."

"Yes, looks like he did. And pretty thoroughly too."

"Oh God, oh God, the shame of it! I must go and—er—deal with things. Here, sit down, keep this seat for me, Audrey."

I look down at her chair. "Sit there? Er—no, I don't think I will, thanks."

As she turns round to head for the facilities, I notice something else.

"Hang on a minute, Angie—what's that on your back?"

"Eh?" She strains to look over her shoulder. "Oh *no*! What *now*?"

"There's something else on the back of your coat."

I look more closely. It's a piece of sponge covered in squidgy pink icing. In the middle of it nestles a little plastic flower.

I use my finger to scoop up a little. I sniff it.

"What is it?"

"Oh, it's nothing. Just a bit of cake."

"Cake? What?"

I put my finger in my mouth. "Mm, nice."

"Oh, for fuck's sake!" cries Angie. As she dashes off in the direction of the toilet screeching, "*Brian, Brian*", I notice that she is still leaking slightly from the hemline.

I call after her, "Well, look on the bright side Ange—at least it's not your coat!"

Angie's overhaul appears to be taking quite a while.

In the meantime, the music rolls on. Shirley and Connie dance together.

The Crests sing *Sixteen Candles*, an oldie still adored by many for the deathless line:

>'You're only sixteen,
>
>But you're my teenage queen.'

'*Sixteen candles, make a wish come true,*' croons Shirley along with the record.

Something strikes her. "Candles, oh my God!"

She shakes her partner by the shoulders.

"Connie—the cake! We nearly forgot aboot it!"
"Oh Christ, aye, the cake!"
"Get it, get it now, afore everybody disappears."
"Aye, Ah'll bring it in right away. There'll be enough for everybody now a few of them have left."

Connie heads off to the hall at a canter.

A moment later she returns carrying a large salver before her. Everyone 'oohs' and 'ahs' appropriately. There is a smattering of applause.

"Nice cake," says Wilma, coming over, "looks great."
"Aye," says Connie proudly. "Ma maw made it."

She examines it more closely.

"Mind you, one side's fallen in a bit. Wonder how that happened?"

I decide to be a tell-tale.

"That would have been Angie and Brian, I suppose, Connie. She told me they were in there earlier."

Connie looks at me. Her jaw drops.

"In there earlier? Eh? What the fuck were they doin' in the hall cupboard?"

Wilma sighs.

"Aw, c'mon Connie, fer Christ's sake. Whit dae ye think they were daein', the Hokey-Cokey?"

Connie draws in her breath sharply.

"Ye mean they were daein' *that*? On ma maw's cake?" She sniffs. "Some people have nae class. Dirty bastards!"

Just before she leaves, Angie comes over to me. Brian waits for her by the door.

"We're going, Audrey. And you can stop *lar-fing*, if you don't mind."
"Sorry Ange, sorry. But you must admit…"

She bestrides her high horse.

"I will admit nothing, deny nothing, explain nothing. I will keep my counsel to the end and die a legend."

Having made her point, she descends from the saddle.

"I was wondering—any chance I can have your keys? Brian has nowhere to go, I've missed my last train, and I thought maybe…"

I shake my head.

"No, no way, Angie. Sorry and all that, but my place is not a knocking shop. Or if it is, it's *my* knocking shop. No, speak to Shirley, she's got a wee place in Wellington Street, she won't mind."

Tommy interrupts. "Och, go on, George—let Gordon have the keys.

That place of Shirley's is a tip."

I look at him. He does his appealing face, little smile at the corners of his mouth. I look at Angie.

I shake my head. If it were anyone else but Brian… "No, sorry."

"Aw, come on," says Tommy, throwing his arm round me. "Have you forgotten what it feels like tae be young and in love?"

He whispers in my ear. "Like you an' me?"

At this, of course, I cave in.

"OK, Ange. But not in the bed, on the settee, it pulls out. Not that comfortable, but it'll have to do you. No mess. Remember—*not* the bed. We'll see you later. And don't you dare disappear before we get back, I've only the one set of keys. Or I'll strangle you myself, and that's a promise."

I hand her my keys.

"Thanks, Audrey, you're a star."

She turns to him. "And thank-you too, Tommy."

"Nae problem, Gordon. Have fun."

I notice she is now only wearing her own light and trendy jacket.

"God, Angie," I say. "You'll freeze outside. What happened to the tweed?"

"I had to give it back to Maggie. It's hers, apparently."

"Yes, I thought it was. Nice coat."

"Yes, very smart."

She glances across the room to where Miss Wilde stands alone, the coat draped over her arm. With an obvious insincerity, she says, "Poor Maggie. Took her man to a party, and lost him to a younger woman."

"Well, not entirely. She's still got a wee bit of him on the coat, hasn't she?"

Angie chortles, winks at me, smiles, turns and crosses the room. She takes her new love by the arm, and they leave together.

We should have gone with them. But we decided to stay for another hour. Apart from anything else, we wanted to give the star-crossed lovers the chance to get whatever it might be over and done with before we got back.

On such trivial hinges do revolutions turn.

8. Marry Me

> Let's have a gay time
> Pretend it's May time
> When blossoms bud in the apple tree
> And you will marry me.
> *Mike Preston, 1961*

It is no more than five minutes after Angie's departure that the doorbell rings once more.

'*Oh, she's back,*' I think. '*Brian probably legged it when he saw her in the light.*'

The party has thinned out somewhat, but the diehards are still dying hard, the music is blaring and loud and the 'dance floor' is crowded. Maybe thirty guests still remain, the hard core. The booze seems to be lasting well, and, although there has been no really heavy drinking, everyone has managed to sink a few. I am sitting chatting to Shirley.

When she hears the doorbell, she calls out over the din, "Get that, Connie, will ye? It'll be the entertainment at last. Hardly worth the trouble at this time, but…"

I presume Connie hears this, and I see her move off towards the hallway. And I see her return seconds later with the new arrivals. Two uniformed policemen.

I immediately signal Sandra Dee to turn down the volume of the music. I am assuming there has been some kind of complaint about the noise. But no, I am wrong.

One of the officers, older, grey-haired, fat belly, pompous manner, calls out, "OK—let's have the music off, please."

Sandra turns the record-player off. From nowhere, four more police appear behind the two already in the room.

"Right," says the guy who appears to be in charge. "Ah'm here tae tell ye that yiz is all under arrest. There has been a complaint that these premises are being run as a disorderly house, that conduct constituting a breach of the peace has been taking place here, and I will thank you all to accompany my officers to the police station quietly and in an orderly manner."

I turn and look at Tommy. He seems as surprised as me.

"Anybody resisting arrest, or causing any difficulties for my men will be dealt with appropriately. So let's all be sensible, eh?"

My recollection of subsequent events is hazy and consists of unrelated flashes.

Shirley Temple determinedly but unsuccessfully endeavours to flush a blond wig down the toilet.

Brenda Lee transits effortlessly into the blind-rage stage at the sight of so many police uniforms and pays the inevitable price of a mild kicking.

Wilma resists arrest in a womanly but forceful manner, causing the abused seams of her dress to split asunder here, there, and just about everywhere.

Tommy and I make our way out together, with Lana Turner sandwiched between us, each of us supporting her by an arm, as her gammy leg gives her some difficulty coping with stairs.

Behind us, Vicky Lester hesitates at the top, and looks around, as if confused. She glances down, does a little stagger, then a little trip. A second later, she takes a header down the entire flight, and lands in a heap at our feet.

"God," I say to Lana, as Tommy and I help Vicky to stand upright, "I hadn't realised she was that pissed."

Lana frowns. "Vicky? Oh no, she's no' pissed. Naw, she's breakin' in her new bifocals. She wis tellin' me earlier that she cannae look down. Every time she does, she sees the ground comin' up tae meet her. She must have forgot."

Dame Margot, cool as a cucumber, and having taken note of the Fall of the House of Lester, accepts the arm of a policeman to negotiate the descent—"Thank you, officer, these heels are very unforgiving."

Shirley Eaton chats cosily and privately with the lead officer, and is told, mysteriously, that she is free to leave.

Agnes of God, hair in a chignon and glamorous in a gold lamé evening jacket with full-length black velvet skirt, draws up in a taxi just as the rest of us are bundled into the back of the police wagons. She is carrying a guitar and a bulging shopping bag. She half-opens the taxi door, sets one sequinned size ten on the pavement and takes in the scene.

"Fer Christ's sake, drive on. Wrong fuckin' address," she shrieks, withdrawing the foot and slamming the door.

I simply cannot believe at first that this 'arrest' business is serious. What are we guilty of? Attending a party. We are, all twenty-eight of us, charged with committing a breach of the peace. Connie, as the official tenant of the flat, is also charged with the rather more serious offence of running a disorderly house. The wonderfully elastic 'breach of the peace' regulation apparently covers acts taking place both in public and in private. But in what way have we breached the peace, or done anything at all? OK, the music was loud and it was late. But surely a polite request to moderate the volume would have sufficed?

The 'disorderly house' thing is usually applied to brothels, I had always believed; but apparently it can be invoked for almost anything from mild rowdiness to genocide.

It becomes clear to me gradually, from the attitudes of the arresting officers, that the complaint that led to this wholesale capture, whatever its source, has more to do with the peculiar composition of the all-male guest-list than any specific misbehaviour.

We are herded *en masse* into two police wagons, fourteen of us in each one, and carted off to the local police station, where each of us is asked for our name and address.

I am far more concerned about Tommy than about myself. Should any details come out in court, my name is not a particularly uncommon one, and my address in Glasgow has no connection with my original Rutherglen origins. But Tommy's surname, Molony without the 'e', is quite unusual; I am relieved that he has the sense to say his name is 'Molloy', and to give my address instead of his own.

After the identification process, we are shepherded into two large cells. The police station only has three, it's not really designed for mass incarceration, and one of these cells is already occupied, it seems. So we are crammed in together, fourteen of us in each.

We are pretty much allowed to choose which one we favour—'*Aye, in there, you lot, sort yerselves oot*'—and Tommy and I manage to squeeze in with Connie, Alec, Wilma and most of our closest friends—Elaine and Joe, Dorothy Provine still attached to the hapless Clive, Dame Margot and Brenda, Sandra Dee, Nicky and Lena Horne.

In the other cell are Shirley Temple and Julie London, half-in and half-out of female attire, Ava Gardner with Lana Turner and Vicky Lester, who finally has something worth crying about. With them are Kay Kendall, Maggie Wilde (who is no doubt wishing she had avoided this party altogether—she has not only lost her man, she's lost her liberty, although she still has her coat), Pat Calhoun and Susan Strasberg, Vivien Lee along with Kay Starr, Jackie Kennedy, Vera-Ellen and her Bobby.

The general attitude of these quarantined queens to this sudden interruption in their jollifications is for the most part light-hearted. One or two of the more high-profile of those arrested, that is, those in regular and respectable employment, express a momentary concern as to the possible consequences. But even they, buoyed up by the others, eventually manage to convince themselves that, yes, this is just a storm in a teacup, just your average raid on a noisy party, and that once the tempest blows itself out everything will return to normal. Maybe a three pound fine, cheap at the price.

Lena Horne informs us that she is off on holiday on Monday, and that nothing at all is going to stop her.

"Ah don't leave till the afternoon, it'll all be done and dusted by then," she says.

I myself am not so certain. I sense that there is more to this affair than there appears to be on the surface. But since I am not likely to be affected personally to any great extent, I make a determined effort to put my worries aside and join in the fun.

It is Dame Margot Fonteyn who starts off the sing-song.

> '*We come from Roedean, good girls are we;*
> *We take a pride in our virginity.*
> *We take precautions, prevent abortions,*
> *We are the Roedean girls.*'

Why this particular anthem, a familiar standby of the rugby changing room, should have such an appeal to our particular set is a minor mystery. But your average queen would happily spend a productive hour or two in a rugby changing room. And it's a fact that many of us see ourselves as free spirits, unencumbered by conventional morality and always on the *qui vive* for sexual adventure, just like those 'Roedean girls'.

Tommy and I are seated side by side in a corner of the cell. And try as I may to hide it or ignore it, my nagging concern about our present situation must be evident.

"What's the matter?" he says. "Why the serious face?"

"Oh, I don't know really. Nothing, it's nothing. Only…" I hesitate.

"Only?"

"Well… What do you make of all this? Why are we here?"

The deathless lyrics continue to pour forth:

> '*We have a head girl, her name is Gwen;*
> *She only does it now and again.*
> *And again, and again, and again, and again.*
> *We are the Roedean girls.*'

"It's you I'm worried about more than anything," I go on. "I mean— what if someone who knows you hears about this? What if the truth comes out somehow? What if this stupid business makes the papers, eh?"

He is silent for quite a while. He is looking intently at the chorus of merry songstresses. Their recital continues, blithe and unabated. The Gay Chorale of Glasgow.

> '*Sports mistress Jane is one of the best,*
> *Teaches each girl to develop her chest.*
> *We wear tight sweaters and carry French letters*
> *We are the Roedean girls.*'

Still avoiding my gaze, he says, "Well—it had to come out sooner or later. Has to, I mean. I've always known it would one day. Since I met you, anyway."

I am astonished. Not by the fact that he has considered the possibility. But that he has considered it and accepted it.

He turns towards me and looks me full in the face, his expression utterly serious. He takes a deep breath.

"You've asked me often enough if I love you. Well, I do. And if that means that everything else goes to hell, then that's the way it is."

> '*Janitor Jim is a silly old fool.*
> *He's only got a teeny-weeny tool.*
> *Alright for keyholes, and small baby's pee-holes,*
> *But I am a Roedean girl.*'

He loves me. He said it. At last.

So what do I do? Naturally I shed a few tears. My speciality, apparently, at moments of heightened emotion.

"Hey," he says, concerned, "what's the matter? Come on—are you telling me you're surprised?"

I gulp. I take a breath. And another. I turn away slightly.

"Well, no. I'm just surprised to hear you actually *say* it."

"Yeah. About time, eh?"

I draw back and look at him.

"Yes, it certainly is. And you know that…"

I hesitate.

He nods. "That you love me? Yes. God knows, you've told me often enough."

"Bastard," I croak, somewhere between tears and laughter.

> '*When I go down to the beach for a swim,*
> *The boys all remark on the size of my quim.*
> *"Blimey," they holler, "it's like a horse's collar;*

She must be a Roedean girl."'

After a moment, "Let's get married," he says.

I think I've misheard him. "What?"

"I mean, let's make it official. Live together, you and me."

"Live together? You and me?" I repeat like a sorry idiot, as if it's not what I have been waiting to hear for months.

"Yes."

Once again he whispers in my ear. "We shouldn't be apart any longer. What do you say?"

> *'We come from Roedean, we're full of flash,*
> *We spread our legs and don't ask for cash.*
> *Try us sometime if you fancy a bash,*
> *We are the Roedean girls'.*

I feel the sharp bite of ancient guilt. But I choke it back.

"OK, yes I will. But on one condition. You have to ask me properly, here and now."

He is a little taken aback. "Properly?"

"Yes. In front of everybody."

"Here?"

"And now."

He interrogates my expression. I am immovable, implacable.

He sighs. "OK."

He stands up, then gets down on one knee.

> *'Up the school, up the school, up the school.*
> *Right—up—the school!'*

Into the sudden silence drops his question. "Will you marry me?"

Some little show of reluctance is surely called for? I hesitate in an appropriately maidenly manner.

Someone, Sandra Dee, I think, shouts out, "Well, if she won't, I will."

"Yes. Of course I will."

There is a moment of quiet; then the drab cell erupts into cheers. The general chorus is led by Lena Horne:

> *'Audrey and Tommy were lovers.*
> *He wanted to give her everything.*
> *Flowers, presents, but most of all,*
> *A wedding ring.*
> *Tell Audrey I love her, tell Audrey I miss her.*
> *Tell Audrey not to cry, my love for her will never die.'*

I am seriously moved, and shed a few more tears. These are my dear friends. And this is my dear lover. Despite our miserable surroundings, and our slightly ambivalent situation, it's a joyful moment.

I wonder how many marriage proposals have been made and accepted in the confines of a police cell?

After the first hubbub has died down, individuals come over to convey their congratulations.

"Good for you, Audrey," smiles Little Joe. "Glad he finally decided to make an honest woman of you."

"Yes," muses Elaine, a wicked twinkle in her eye, and giving me a meaningful look. "With all those good-looking gas men around, you wouldn't have thought such a thing was possible, would you?"

Early Sunday morning, eight o' clock, we are bailed out. Just four of us. Tommy and me, along with Wilma and Nicky. The others are left to vegetate until the general court appearance, scheduled for Monday afternoon. No doubt most of them could have arranged their own release, through friends or family, had they chosen to inform their nearest and dearest of their situation. But discretion, it appears, has overwhelmed the desire for freedom under these particular circumstances.

Tommy immediately heads off to his family in Maryhill, after arranging to meet me outside the court the following day. He is as baffled as me as to who our mysterious benefactor can be.

But as Nicky and I turn a corner together, we are greeted by a familiar face.

"Ah wid have got Connie oot too, Wilma, but they widnae have it," I hear Shirley say as we head towards her. "It's a serious charge, this disorderly house business."

She registers our arrival.

"Oh there you are, Audrey, Nicky. Ah was just tellin' Wilma... Nae problem with you lot, breach of the peace, that's nothing. But Inspector Spooner drew the line at Connie. *'No, Shirley,'* he said, *'that Connie's the one we were after. That's the one the complaint was made about. The rest wis just casualties.'* That was it, he widnae say any more."

She turns back to Wilma. "OK, hen, see ye later. Ah'll pop round tae the flat and gie ye a hand tidying up, say aboot two tae half-past?"

Wilma's dress is a ruin. Every seam, every ruched flounce, every tuck and gather, has reluctantly parted company with its neighbour.

But her towering beehive remains intact. And, game to the last, she is in the process of applying a fresh coat of lipstick and a light dusting of powder.

"Aye, OK, Shirley, that'll be a big help. And thanks fer gettin' us oot. See ye later."

Wilma saunters off. Shirley turns towards me with an ingratiating smile.

I have always suspected, despite our long acquaintance, that there is a devious side to Shirley. Although she has always been fine with me, she has a self-serving streak—I was aware of it from our first meeting. Time maybe for a little frankness.

"So tell me, Shirley," I say, "how did you come to walk away scot-free last night? The rest of us are dragged off screaming by Lily Law, but, as far as I can remember, you had a word with the inspector guy and strolled off into the night without a problem."

Nicky frowns. "Aye, that's right. How did ye pull that one off, eh, Shirley?"

She has the grace to look just the tiniest bit abashed.

"Well, you see, Audrey, Nicky, it's…"

She hesitates for a second. "Well, keep it tae yourselves, but Ah know him, the inspector. And he knows me. It's me that drops the hush money off tae him every week—for the brothel, so the polis turns a blind eye."

I understand. Perhaps I have rushed to judgement a little too hastily.

She takes a breath and leans towards us. "An' he's a regular there too, Inspector Spooner. Big Marion's punter, usually. So I made it clear that it might be in his best interests if he just let me go."

She seems to become suddenly aware that we are questioning her behaviour.

"An' if he hadn't—well, where would you be now? You and Tommy, Audrey? Still locked up, is that no' right? You too, Nicky?"

There's no arguing with that. I decide not to look this particular gift horse in the mouth any further.

To defuse the tension, I link my arm through hers.

"Yes, of course, we just wondered, that's all. And thanks, I appreciate it."

And I do. After all, she could have chosen to favour others over us, but she didn't. Perhaps, along with Wilma, Connie and Nicky, I am really the nearest thing she has to a close friend.

But that said, I have always known she bears watching, does Miss Eaton.

She smiles at each of us in turn.

"And, Miss Hepburn," she goes on, "I believe congratulations are in order? You and Tommy?"

I wonder briefly if she has a paid informer inside the police department.
"Yes, that's right. How did you know?"
"Oh, Wilma was tellin' me. So—when's the wedding?"
To be fair, maybe I have misjudged her, Shirley.
Then again, maybe not.

I have completely forgotten about Angie and Brian. It isn't until I have climbed the stairs and am standing outside my front door, digging in my pocket for my keys that I realise I haven't got them—Angie does. Or she did, at least. I ring the bell.

'*Oh hell,*' I think. '*Where might she have left the keys?*'

I have a look around, but there are no obvious hiding places. I rattle the letterbox impatiently. Maybe Geg or Colin is in and will answer the door. Maybe Angie left my keys with one of them.

Nothing.

I bang hard on the door with the flat of my hand. It was cold outside in the street, half sleeting, half raining, and I am looking forward to the warmth and comfort of my bed. There, I think to myself, I can go over the events of the previous evening in my head calmly. I can reflect on my triumph. I can hug to myself the incredible realisation that at last Tommy and I are going to be a real couple. I can congratulate myself on my patience—not one of my usual virtues—and my forbearance.

'*How right I was not to push him too hard,*' I think, '*and to allow him to come to his own conclusion.*'

Though I have dropped odd hints here and there, I have never actually suggested at any stage that we live together. Well, not in so many words. So this can be considered his idea alone. He can't live without me—isn't that what he said, more or less?

The niggling guilt of my recent extra-marital adventure has receded to a dull hum in the background. I am so gloriously happy, so giddy with delight, and so generally pleased with myself, and indeed with the world, that for a moment I want to just sit down on the doorstep and grin in satisfaction.

The other main event of the evening—my first ever brush with the law—has come to seem of little or no importance. OK, I will pay a small fine, and I will have a police record. So what? I am in love and am loved in return. What are crime and punishment compared to that? Irrelevancies; nothing, nothing at all.

But this sub-zero temperature is decidedly *not* nothing. I am actually shivering—I am dressed in party mode, after all, for glamour, not for comfort. Oh, surely someone must be in the damned place?

I decide to give it one final try. If there is no response I will head for a warm café and have something to eat and try to work out how I am going to lay hands on the miserable Angie, who has, it seems, had her fill of fun and fucked off merrily into the night with my keys. I batter the door hard, kick it, beat a tattoo on it with my fists.

So intent am I on making myself heard that I fail to register the approaching footsteps, and nearly fall through the door when it is finally flung wide.

Angie takes a step back. I don't recognise her for a moment. I eventually realise that is because she is swathed in not one, but three of my blankets. One round her waist, one round her bosom, and the other thrown over her head and shoulders. The love child of Nanook of the North and Eskimo Nell.

I step into the hall. The temperature there is only a degree or two higher than it was outside—these old houses are not well-insulated—and I quickly slam the door behind me.

"God, Angie, let's get into the room, it's *freezing* out here. Thank the Lord you waited till I got back. I was beginning to think I would have to spend the day on my own doorstep."

She is all solicitousness. "Oh, poor Audrey, yes, yes, come in. Yes, that's a very thin *blouson* and slacks you're wearing, smart but hardly practical, you must be perished. I was beginning to worry—why are you so late? What's the time."

She peers short-sightedly at where her watch ought to be. "Oh, it's by the bed, my watch. What time is it?"

"Just gone nine, Angie."

I push past her and head for my door.

"Nine? Nine in the morning? So what kept you so long? Must have been some party after I left. Not really my scene at all, mind you, rather common and low-class."

She rambles on. I wish she'd shut up.

"But there was no shortage of drink, I'll give Connie that."

She trails after me down the hall.

"Well, you should know, Ange, you certainly sank enough of it. But perhaps you shouldn't have laid into the cake with such enthusiasm," I say nastily. "*Onto* the cake, rather."

"Oh Audrey, don't be so *uncamp*…"

I push open the door of the room, which, thank God, is cosy and warm. But not empty.

Brian is sitting on the settee, rolling a cigarette and nursing a cup of something. He is in jeans, bare-chested and looks completely at home.

"George!" He smiles. "We wis wondering what happened to you, you and your—Tommy, is it? Gordon was gettin' worried. Whit kept ye?"

He may be a rather unwelcome sight, but no-one could say he was a disagreeable one.

"Well that's a long story," I start.

"Shut the door, Angie, there's a good girl," he interrupts, "Let poor George get warm—he must be frozen."

What's all this 'George' stuff suddenly? He has never called me anything but 'Audrey' before now.

"Come on, sweetheart, hurry it up."

Angie smiles at him in a nauseatingly 'my lord and master' kind of way, and closes the door.

Brian stands up. "Cup of tea? I bet ye need it, it's Baltic oot there. Milk and one sugar if Ah remember, right?"

I nod mutely, not sure what to make of all this domesticity.

"OK, two minutes."

He gives a broad smile and heads off to the kitchen, closing the door carefully behind him.

I take the opportunity to make a quick inventory.

Well, I have to give her credit, Angie has obeyed my instructions to the letter. The room is clean and tidy, and the settee is where they obviously spent the night, although it has been straightened up. There is no glaring evidence of an unnatural union having taken place.

My own bed is untouched, except that the blankets have been carefully removed, no doubt to provide Angie with her Scott of the Antarctic get-up.

I sink gratefully onto a chair by the fire.

"OK, Ange, you can shed the blankets now, it's roasting in here."

She looks at me. "Oh, Audrey, I *cawn't*. I'm *nay-kid* as a jaybird under these. Brian and I were just about to –"

"No more, no more," I interrupt her hastily. "Keep them on, the blankets."

A jaybird? No doubt a hangover from the days of Canadian Al.

Brian returns with my cup of tea. He sits down next to Angie and throws a muscular arm round her shoulder. She nestles, quite the little woman. My God, they look like a *couple*. Is it possible that the potentially disastrous clash of two rivals for my affections has ended up throwing out a positive result?

'*Oh dear*', I think, panicking. '*I bet she'll want to double-date.*'

When they ask again why I was so late getting home ('*And where is the lovely Thomas?*' asks Angie) I explain briefly the events of the night before.

Her mouth falls open unattractively.

"No, Audrey, surely not? Arrested—you? In prison—oh my stars, Audrey, the *shame* of it. Thank God we left when we did."

She looks genuinely shocked.

"I don't think," she goes on in a self-righteous tone, "I've ever even *met* someone who's been in jail before."

"Really, Angie? Well this must be your lucky day, because not only am I sat here next to you, but the gentleman on your other side is something of an old lag, and has been at liberty for less than a week."

"Oh, Brian. Well yes, but that's different."

She doesn't seem to be in any hurry to explain in what way Brian's case is different.

"Oh—and don't forget your uncle Ralph—you know, the one who was arrested for flashing in Bellahouston Park... You remember telling me about that?"

She rises to her feet, flustered, and changes the subject shamelessly. "Yes, well, I suppose I'd better get dressed, hadn't I?"

"Yes, Angie, I wish you would. I'm shattered, need to get to bed, and I don't do sleeping in public, despite the many requests. Put your clothes on and piss off. And take him with you, please."

She leans over Brian and kisses him on the forehead.

"You bet I'll take him with me. You don't think I'd leave my man on *your* territory, do you?" she giggles.

Oh. He's 'her man' now, apparently.

"*My* territory?" I sigh. "Angie, just in case it's slipped your mind, Brian has already discovered, explored and thoroughly mapped that particular landscape. I'm quite sure that your virgin *Terra Nova* is a far more alluring prospect at present. Now go away and get dressed."

"Go away? No—I'll get dressed here in the warm. If you two will just turn your backs for a moment..."

"Angie, I am not in the habit of turning my back in my own home."

"Oh?" she mutters with a sly grin. "What about Tommy? I bet you've turned your back there a few times, no?"

Brian sniggers appreciatively. OK. I'll have to give her that one. But not this one.

"Angie, let me put it this way. I have absolutely no urge to listen to the sound of you struggling into your over-tight clothes, forcing a quart into a pint pot. And the snapping of those rubber buttons I find extremely trying. Go into the bathroom and get dressed there."

I offer a crumb. "Put the heater on if you like."

Grumbling, she picks up her clothes from a chair and heads off to the bathroom.

The silence stretches out between Brian and me. I simply don't know what to say to him. I pick up a newspaper.

But I don't have to say anything. He has something on his mind.

"Why are you so nasty to Gordon? He's supposed tae be your best friend," he says eventually.

I look up.

"What? Who?"

"Angie."

"She *is* my best friend."

"Then why are you so unkind to him? It's not very nice."

What did he say?

"Unkind? Am I?"

He offers me a cigarette which I take.

"Aye, you are." He lights up his own and passes me his lighter. "You're always bitchin' at her, makin' clever remarks, puttin' her down."

He draws on his cigarette. "It's none of ma business, Ah suppose. But I just wonder why you do it."

This makes me think. In our circle a little light bitching is par for the course, everyone does it, usually in a humorous way. But in my interaction with Angie, do I go too far?

I'm not sure how to respond.

"Yes," I say after some reflection. "I suppose I am a bit hard on her sometimes. But it's for her own good. And I don't think I'm actually nasty."

"Ah do. And it looks bad on you, it's very unattractive. Ye come across as a gobby bitch."

Well, well. Say it as you see it, Brian.

He stretches himself comfortably on the settee.

"Funny thing is, you were never like that with me when we were— well, together, if you want to call it that. You were always lovely to me."

He yawns indelicately. "But Ah'm seeing another side of you now."

Is it worth explaining to him that there is all the difference in the world between how I conduct my relationship with Angie and my friends, and how I deal with lovers, potential or actual? No, probably not. And it's an area I don't want to go into with him, anyway.

He has more to say.

"Just thinkin', maybe you should be a wee bit nicer to her, you know? She thinks the sun shines out of yer arse. It's *'Audrey this'*, and *'Audrey that'.* Maybe ye should be a bit kinder, eh?"

A concession is due, perhaps.

"Maybe I do go too far sometimes. I'll try to mix a bit more honey with the vinegar in future."

He smiles. "OK. Ah think that might be a good idea. Hope Ah've no' offended you by mentioning it?"

The tension between us has somehow evaporated.

"No, not at all," I say.

Suddenly Angie is at the door.

"Audrey, do you have a *ray-zor* I can borrow? Look at me—the bearded lady is not in it. I simply *cawn't* be seen in the street looking like this."

"Sure, Ange, blades are in the cupboard. Use the big mirror, the little one's cracked."

She stares at me, eyebrows sky high.

"A mirror? No need, Audrey, I do it by touch. I *nay-ver* use a mirror. Can't *bear* to see a woman shaving."

And she is gone again.

And so are Brian and I, laughing comfortably and frankly together.

"Imagine," I manage to choke out. "Angie. Shaving by Braille."

"Aye," he comes back, "God, shave the queen!"

I convulse at this, and have to grab him to maintain my equilibrium.

After we have calmed down, I say, "So Brian. What are your plans? Big romance? Or here today and gone tomorrow?"

He purses his lips and gives a little half-smile.

"Oh, Ah think that's more your style than mine, would ye no' say?"

OK. Point to Brian. Well, half a point.

"The only reason I ask, Brian, is because I don't want her to get hurt. Don't want you breaking her heart. God knows, she's hard enough to cope with when she's happy. And she's had a rough time in that department recently. So don't mess her around, or you'll be answering to me, OK?"

He seems to find the prospect hilarious.

"Oh dear—will you be comin' around tae rough me up?"

"No," I say calmly. "I'll get Tommy to call in and smash your kneecaps."

"Ah see."

He pauses, and then goes on, sounding reflective.

"Aye—an' I bet he would, too, if you asked him to. Bit of a tough guy, that new fella of yours."

Tommy? Tough? He's the gentlest person in the world. Still, maybe it's no bad thing if others see him rather differently. He's certainly made an impression on Brian, it appears.

I mellow.

"But, joking aside—just be nice to Angie, please."

"Of course Ah will—what else would Ah be? I'm a nice guy."

He leans towards me, his tone suddenly serious.

"Look, Audrey…"

Audrey? What happened to George?

"… Ah really like Gordon, we get on well, he's good fun, but we've only just met. We're having a laugh, not an affair. Maybe in time, who knows? But I can promise you, I'll be straight with him, and we'll see how it goes. That alright with you?"

"Yes, that's fine, Brian."

With the recent upheavals I had forgotten how decent and straightforward he is at heart.

Nonetheless, there remains one point I have to clarify.

"There's just one other little thing I need to mention."

He looks up. "Oh? What's that?"

"Brian, Angie is exceedingly clothes conscious. I mean, her outfits are one of the most important things in her life."

He indicates agreement. "Sure, Ah know that. Smart, always, immaculate."

"Yes. So it might be a good idea—just in the interest of keeping her mellow—if you were to be a wee bit more careful."

"Careful? Meaning?"

I'm not sure I can say this without breaking up in the middle of it and ruining the effect. But I will try.

"In future, I suggest you try to avoid blowing your load up the inside of her clothes. She won't appreciate it."

I just manage to keep my face straight, and then have to collapse back into my chair, holding my stomach, howling with laughter.

Luckily Brian seems to find it as funny as I do, and for a moment or two neither of us is able to speak.

Eventually he calms down enough to say, "God, it's great being back on the outside. I've missed having a good laugh."

"Oh, don't worry, with Angie around, you'll be laughing from morning to night. When you're not crying."

He frowns slightly. "Hey, hang on, I thought you were going to be nicer to her?"

I feel the laughter rising again.

"I said I would be nicer *to* her. Didn't say anything about being nice *about* her."

"Fair enough," he says, joining in.

Gradually our mirth subsides.

After a moment he looks at me.

"I'm sorry," he says.

"I'm sorry too," I say. And I am, a little.

"Friends?"

He stands up, and I can hear Angie heading back down the hall.

"Friends," I say.

He glances towards the door, and lowers his voice.

"And she's a great tight ride, your pal," he says with a cheeky grin and a wink.

As Angie bustles into the room, all smiles, I consider his last remark.

Well, well, so another legend bites the dust.

If she was ever *Angie, The Conflicted Virgin*, it seems the conflict has finally been resolved.

At last they are ready to leave. I can't wait for them to go, I am exhausted. Angie insists Brian head down into the street to find a taxi.

"I simply *cawn't* be seen in public in this state."

Despite my weariness and my desperate need to be alone, I am still curious. I know he said she did, but I want to hear it from her. I seize my chance now we are alone.

"Don't mind me asking, Angie. But last night, here, with him—did you yield? Did you make the virgin sacrifice to Venus?"

Her mouth rounds into an 'O'. Or as near as it can, given its uncompromisingly triangular shape.

"Audrey," she says solemnly, "that is something I prefer not to talk about. Sorry, but there it is."

I yawn. "No problem, Angie, I understand. Some things are just too sacred to share."

She nods in satisfaction. "Yes, Audrey, you put it very well. Too sacred, yes, exactly."

I grin at her. "What an effing hypocrite you are!—he already told me he screwed you!"

She looks down and actually blushes.

But she is grinning too, almost imperceptibly.

"Oh dear, what a blabbermouth. Well, OK, OK, yes, he did." She looks up again. "Twice."

I can't resist playing the shocked puritan, a new rôle for me.

"Well, I'm surprised at you, Ange, indulging in that kind of behaviour with a new beau; you know, you being famous for your high moral standards."

"You're right, I know."

"I mean, he would probably have been happy with a blow-job. And, as everyone knows, Ange, you are also famous for your high *oral* standards."

The last goes right past her. She is pensive.

"Yes, you know me so well… What can I say? I don't know what got into me."

Oh no, I can't let that one pass.

"Remember, Ange, Brian and I have shared more than the odd cigarette in the past. So I know *exactly* what got into you."

She giggles delightedly. "Oh Audrey, *please*! Don't be…"

"…so *uncamp*," we say together.

As she heads off towards the stairs, I have a final piece of advice for her.

"Angie, do be a wee bit careful. I mean, he's not a bad guy, Brian. But… you *do* know that he is involved now and then in things that are—well—a wee bit shady, not quite on the right side of the law?"

I pause, and try to gauge the effect of this.

She looks at me. Her eyes are dewy, her lip trembles, she glows.

'*Oh dear,*' I think. '*She's in love.*'

"Yes, Audrey, you're right. But—I've never told anyone this, not even you."

She hesitates, as if it is difficult to continue.

"You see, in spite of my high-class aspirations and my ladylike manners, underneath I've always cherished a secret desire to be…"

Her voice drops. "… a gangster's moll."

I can barely manage to control the hysteria rising within me. Oh, Angie, I love you, there really is no-one like you anywhere. I somehow keep a straight face.

She looks at me, her expression utterly serious.

"Is that awful?"

"No, Angie," I say, shaking my head, and, God knows how, avoiding laughing out loud.

"It's not awful, not at all. It's fabulous!"

The day of judgement arrives. I remember my first visit to the Sheriff Court, long ago, when Wilma was the accused. Then, I was in the front stalls. Today I am onstage.

We are herded into the dock, before the judge, in sevens—seven fours are twenty-eight, neat and tidy. I call him 'the judge'—I think he is actually a magistrate, or possibly a sheriff, but if I am going to be up in court, I want to appear in front of a judge. Each of us is charged with Breach of the Peace; each of us pleads guilty; each of us is fined two pounds; each of us is released. A short and utterly meaningless little homily is delivered four times. It is all unutterably and disappointingly dull and pointless.

That said, there are one or two bright moments. While Wilma, having been released on bail, has been able to change her outfit into what passes for normal with her, both Shirley Temple and Julie London are forced to appear in the remains of their party finery, and draw rather more attention than do the rest of us. Dame Margot too is still *en femme*, but has somehow managed to remain as lovely and well-groomed as ever. Not even the hint of a five o'clock shadow mars her alabaster complexion. The judge is understandably a little confused.

"Well, Madam, how do you come to be…"

He turns to his clerk. "Is this lady up on the correct charge? It seems a little unlikely."

The clerk whispers in the Honourable ear. But his Honour is obviously somewhat hard of hearing, so the poor man has to repeat it rather more loudly.

"That is Mr Fountain, your Honour, in a state of—er—transvestism. It's on the charge sheet. She was at the same party as the others. He was."

The magistrate peers towards the dock over his glasses.

"Really? Well, I have to say that, transvestism or not, you look very lovely, Mr Fountain. But perhaps you should choose your company more carefully in the future?"

A mild hysteria engulfs the court and the rest of the accused.

There is one other moment of utter farce. Lena Horne has been unable to attend the court—instead she has unconcernedly set off for her holiday in the south of France. In her place she has sent her elderly mother, the famous Mabel the Miracle Maker, to plead guilty on her behalf. Mabel must be about seventy, wrinkled and petite, but smartly attired in a musquash coat and a Queen Mary toque. As she peers over the edge of the dock, flanked and towered over by Wilma, Kay Starr and myself, she inevitably draws the judge's eye.

He assumes a severe tone.

"Oh—another one in transvestism, I see. Dryesdale, I believe? And tell me, sir, what is a man of your years doing attending this sordid gathering? Really—you should be ashamed. Have you a wife at home, I'd like to know? Does she know of this peculiar and unnatural secret of yours?"

The clerk vainly attempts to intervene, but His Honour is in full flood.

"It pains me to have to say it, sir, but it is men of your age, the age of wisdom, who should be setting an example, and counselling these younger gentlemen on how to behave; not leading them on in lurid and perverse escapades, ensnaring them and tantalising them with your feminine wiles."

Luckily, it seems Mabel's hearing is no better than the judge's, as she remains silent.

"I'm somewhat inclined to make a particular example of you, sir. I consider it an affront to my own years that a man of your age—"

His clerk taps him on the shoulder. He turns.

"Yes, what is it?" he booms.

Someone finally manages to convey to the Honourable gentleman that he is in error. After a whispered debate, he turns back to the dock.

"I apologise, Madam. Really, this is a very confusing case altogether. It's your son, I believe, the accused, not yourself? Is that right? Well, I ask your pardon, and thank you for representing him here today, it's very decent of you, and shows a proper family feeling."

He pauses for a second. "And—er—you look very nice, Madam, very nice indeed. A smart hat, very stylish…"

At last the silly charade is over, and we are all set at liberty. Well, not quite all. The unfortunate Connie, as well as the standard breach of the peace we all faced, has been charged with running a disorderly house. And has, for some unfathomable reason, chosen to plead Guilty to the first charge and Not Guilty to the other. She is remanded in custody until she can appear at the Crown Court.

"What is he thinkin' of, that eedjit, Jim," says Alec, "pleadin' Not Guilty? He wid have got a fine, ten quid, and time tae pay. It wid huv been all over by now."

"Tell him tae ask for a bail hearing," says Tommy, obviously something of an expert in this area. "He'll get bail, no problem, surely? He's hardly a master criminal, after all, is he?"

"Naw. He's a master cunt, that's what he is." Alec shakes his head. "Why the fuck?..."

"And if it goes to Crown Court, surely he'll need a lawyer?" I put in.

"Well, he'll get Legal Aid," says Tommy. "Might even get away wi' it. Let's hope so, eh?"

The three of us are standing in the well of the court. A few of the others are also gathered round in small groups, re-hashing the whole affair.

I am curious.

"Who was that guy sitting scribbling away while it was all going on? Not in the public gallery, in the main part of the court? Not a reporter, I hope?"

"Didn't notice," says Tommy. "But I wouldn't think so, it's hardly the crime of the century, is it?"

"Och, it'll be nothing, Audrey," scoffs Alec. "Clerk of the Court or some such."

We head off together. Just before we leave the courtroom, I glance up to the public gallery. To my astonishment, I recognise the unmistakable ash-blond waves and the plump and motherly figure of Miss Olivia de Havilland seated there. With a little shake of the head, the wave of a pudgy hand, and a smile mingling satisfaction with a contrived sympathy, she leans forward in her chair to survey our exit.

As we descend the steps outside the court, I notice Sandra Dee chatting to a young man armed with a pad and a pencil. As we get closer, I can hear what she is saying.

"Oh yes, plenty of drink. No drugs that I know of, but all sorts of camp goings on. We all have names, of course; there's Judy Garland, Ava Gardner... And then there's me. I'm Sandra Dee..."

She gets no further. From behind her, my open hand cracks smartly across her ear and fells her to the ground. I bend down, grab her by the scruff of the neck and haul her to her feet.

As I carry her off, I call back over my shoulder, "Yes, Sandra Dee. Next to be seen in *Emergency Ward Ten*. Don't miss it, it may well be her final appearance anywhere."

"See," I say to Tommy grimly as we hurry off dragging the reluctant Miss Dee between us, "I told you the press were in, didn't I? Shit!"

Yes, the whole affair is all over the papers. And the fact that four of those arrested were clad in female attire adds some more joyous fuel to the flames. The press jump happily on the band-wagon.

'*Party Girls Turn Out To Be Boys*', trumpets one headline; '*The Party's Over For Twenty-Eight Men*', reads another; '*That's Why The Lady Is A Gent*', a third.

Which confirms me in my belief that someone's fine Italian hand has been busy on the dial of the telephone, intent on assuring that news of this police *coup* did not go unreported. Rowdy parties leading to police intervention are standard fare on a Saturday night in Glasgow, and generally attract no press coverage at all, so commonplace are they. And the few that do are generally the result of near riots, aggravated violence or murder; not simply from a couple of drinks and a dance or two.

So why on earth was every known organ of the Glasgow press present in court to witness and report at length on our *débâcle*?

I remember the plump blond figure in the public gallery.

Something Shirley said comes back to me, when she was quoting the police inspector. '*That Connie's the one we were after. That's the one the complaint was made about. The rest wis just casualties.*'

A score settled? Payback? The revenge of a woman scorned?

No. Surely no-one, not even Olivia, would go to those lengths?

Whether our own details ever were checked, I don't know. One newspaper viciously printed the names and addresses of all the accused. But we were amazingly fortunate, both of us. Thomas Molloy, and by an unexpected piece of good fortune, George *Hogan*, were described as living at thirty-nine Carnarvon Street, Glasgow.

But others were less favoured. The fallout from the ensuing scandal included four lost jobs, two departures from Glasgow for more tolerant southerly climes and one attempted suicide.

To everyone's relief, Connie's case is dismissed on her first appearance in the Crown Court. The Legal Aid man who defends her makes mincemeat of the prosecution's case, which is indeed tissue-paper thin. Connie is returned to the bosom of her friends and family no worse for wear, and with a nice new line in stories of her spell in custody.

We are wondering where we will live. On the surface, the question is straightforward. Does Tommy simply move into Carnarvon Street with me, or do we look for somewhere else to begin our married life?

After some discussion, we both agree that a complete change is the way to go. I make the point that my present room is very small. Which it is. But underneath there is another reason. It carries the secret but pervasive taint of my recent infidelity, and I don't want to have that miasma suffocating me every time I open my eyes.

Besides, far too many people know where I reside, and are inclined to drop in whenever they feel like it. When I was living alone, that was fine. But I know Tommy would not be comfortable with it. Oh, he won't object to the odd evening's drinking in company by prior arrangement, or the occasional visitor, but the open-house policy I have instituted in Carnarvon Street would give him the horrors.

Anyway, if we are together, I am envisioning a life of simple domestic bliss. Simple and private domestic bliss.

For his part, he has never been happy with my socialising with my neighbours since I discovered the truth about Geg's addiction. And my arrangement with Elsie the prostitute bothers him too. In spite of his somewhat chequered past, and his occasional minor clashes with the law, he is, I have discovered, a rather conventional and moral person. Something, I fear, that I am not.

We are having a bite to eat together, nothing fancy, the inevitable fish and chips.

"We'll manage OK for money," he says. "I'll have to gie ma maw a couple of quid a week, but between what's left and what you get with your grant and that, we'll be fine. Just have to look for somewhere no' too expensive. Maybe cut down on the going out, keep it tae the weekends."

"OK," I say, happy to allow him to take the initiative.

"Anyway," he adds, forking up a piece of fish, "what are you planning to do about University? You've not been near the place since I've known you, months now. Maybe you should just drop it altogether and get yourself a job? Two wages coming in, that would be great. What do you think?"

"Yes, maybe."

I can't hide my smile.

"What's funny?" he says.

"I'm just enjoying you taking charge of everything. Sounds as though you've got it all worked out."

He grins and blushes slightly. "Well, truth is, I've been thinking about it for a while. How we'd go about it, I mean."

I set down my knife and fork and look at him. "I wish you'd said something sooner, then. We could have done this ages ago."

And if he had, the Big Joe business would not have happened.

He is suddenly serious. "No, this was the right time, I think. Don't know why, but it suddenly hit me a couple of weeks ago that if I didn't say something soon, make up my mind, we might not last."

He looks up. "You'd meet someone else, someone a bit quicker on the uptake than me, maybe."

This gets my attention. Did he sense more than I had realised? That is a matter he will need to know about sooner or later. But not now. One thing at a time.

"About the University thing." I change the subject. "Let me think about it, OK?"

The thought of dashing the hopes of my parents completely and utterly is something I need to consider deeply before coming to a decision.

"Sure, George, sure—it's up to you. We can manage fine, anyway, like I said."

He passes me a cigarette. "So—when do we start looking?"

I light up. "No time like the present. What are we waiting for?"

It doesn't take us long to locate our new home. On my insistence we pass up a rather attractive room in a large house at St George's Cross. Tommy is allured by the fact that the place has a games room; dart board, snooker cues, table tennis…

"No," I say. "The only games you will be playing will be with me, and in private."

The last thing I want is weekends spent watching him shooting the breeze with a load of hairy-arsed pool players.

We find a large ground-floor front room in Buccleuch Street, only a step from where I have been living. It is nearly ideal. Not only is it spacious and comfortable, but it has its own little kitchen alcove with a small cooker and a sink. No private bathroom, unfortunately—we have to share one with the elderly lady who inhabits the other ground-floor room. But it's cheap, three pounds a week. And it is much better than the other places we have looked at.

Unfortunately, there is a landlady on the premises—so things will not be quite as free and easy as they were at my Carnarvon Street address—but she seems a nice woman, and since we are not contemplating any riotous parties, we decide it will suit very well.

We move in on the twentieth of November, a Saturday. He actually tries to carry me over the threshold. Then trips on the edge of the carpet, drops me on the floor, and falls on top of me.

9. Hats Off to Larry

> Once I had a pretty girl,
> Her name it doesn't matter.
> She went away with another guy;
> Now he won't even look at her.
> *Del Shannon, 1961*

December 1963.

It's a weird thing, but now that Tommy has finally come to the point of confessing his feelings for me, it seems he can't stop. "*Love you,*" he says at least once a day. In the street, on the bus, in the cinema, wherever we are. Oh, quietly, for my ears only, but constantly.

We are utterly happy together. He continues at his job. And I? I take on enthusiastically the role of the ideal housewife. No thought of ever returning to the course of study I am meant to be following. I seem to be achieving that ideal mental state, to completely ignore the future, to live entirely in the present. I clean, I shop, I wash and iron, and I cook. I actually begin to cook quite well. I no longer fear a piece of steak or a lamb chop.

Our intimate life remains as active, if not as urgent. Now we have all the time in the world, and we can pick our moments. He is sometimes a trifle tired when he comes home from work, but he is young, healthy and fit, and ever enthusiastic. And at last a certain—ahem!—flexibility has entered our conjugal arrangements, which adds a little more spice to the stew.

Is that a delicately concealed yawn I hear? Yes, lovers in love are the dullest people in the world, except to each other. You will no doubt be far more interested to find out what is happening with Angie, Elaine and the others.

We have a surprising new visitor now and then. My sister, Jennifer, now seventeen, has become an honorary member of our exclusive little *coterie*. I first introduced her to The Twilight Zone a few months ago, uncertain at first how she would react. I was already aware that she understood my own personal situation, and had done so since well before the Great Revelation. It was interesting and gratifying to see that she accepted everyone, and was accepted by all, painlessly, on her induction into our happy band.

It's a great bonus that she gets on well with Tommy, and that he likes her. She is training as a hairdresser, and is able to pop in now and then in her break or after she has finished for the day, as her place of work, *Pettigrew and Stephen*, is only five minutes away.

Occasionally Angie drops by, usually in her lunch hour, when Tommy is at work. Sometimes Brian is with her, though I discourage this—his presence can still make me feel a little uncomfortable now and then.

But suddenly he's not there, and for a most unexpected reason. He has a job.

Angie tells me the full story.

"You did what?" I say to her, after pouring her the inevitable drink. "You took him home? Brian? To meet your parents?"

She fixes me with an glacial stare.

"Yes, Audrey, don't look so surprised. Why shouldn't I? He doesn't have two heads or anything. They like him, actually, my people."

Yes, Angie's parents are her 'people'. And it would not be difficult to like Brian.

"He's not like your Tommy, you know, not old or anything. He's the same age as me."

"Actually, Angie, he's two years younger than you."

Angie will be twenty-one in May, and Brian will be nineteen in March. I fall between the two of them, I will be twenty in July, in seven or eight months.

"And Tommy's not old—he's twenty-seven."

Actually, he is just about to be twenty-eight, on the twelfth.

"OK—but Angie—how did you explain—well, you know—how you knew each other?"

She takes an experimental sip, then puts down her glass. "Lovely sherry, Audrey—Oloroso, is it? Nice, so Christmassy. Yes, well, I didn't really. Explain, that is. Not in detail. Just said I knew him from work, said he was a customer in the shop. Said there had been a dreadful fire at his house, parents burned to death, poor boy, such a tragedy; and that he was homeless and out of a job."

What?

"My God, Angie—and they believed you?"

She smiles a little smugly. "Oh yes, Audrey, they're very simple people, my people, very trusting, very down to earth, they believe pretty much what I tell them. So, anyway—any more sherry, Audrey? It was so nice."

I top up her glass.

"Thanks. Anyway, they said he could move into our spare room till his problems were sorted out."

Angie described her parents as 'simple people'. If they swallowed this load of crap they must be simple-minded.

She smiles again. "Mind you, it's a little tricky sometimes, finding an opportunity to be—well, together, if you know what I mean, but—what is it they say? Love will find a way."

I consider myself something of an expert in the field of manipulation, forcing inopportune circumstances and reluctant individuals to conform to my will. But Angie has outstripped me. In a single bound she has overleapt the conventions, defied fate and achieved her heart's desire. Assuming, of course, that that's what Brian is.

She digs around in her bag. She is never without a bag of one sort or another.

"Oh, by the way, Audrey, must show you the photo we had taken together, Brian and me."

She eventually finds what she is looking for, and passes it to me. I examine it.

"Mummy took it, just a little casual snap, in the lounge, after dinner."

Yes, Angie's 'people' are 'Mummy' and 'Daddy'.

Angie and Brian are seated side by side on dining chairs, grinning into the camera. Angie has something that might be a shawl round her shoulders.

He looks relaxed and comfortable. She looks like Whistler's Mother.

"Very nice, Ange," I say. "Love the wallpaper."

She takes a sip from her glass. "Oh, it's just a casual photo, as I said. Doesn't really do me justice."

I examine the photograph again.

"No, it doesn't. But then, it's not justice you need, Angie, it's mercy," I mutter to myself.

"What?"

"Oh nothing, nothing." I change the subject hastily. "And Brian's job? How did that come about?"

She finishes her drink. I don't offer another.

"Oh, that was Daddy. He got Brian a position in the bank—you know Daddy's a bank manager, of course, Audrey?"

I know her father works in a bank, she's told me, but I didn't know he was the manager. And I rather doubt that he is.

"Oh, just as a messenger at first, but it's a start. Who knows where Brian might end up?"

I think I know very well where he might end up.

Brian in a bank? Foxes and hen-houses come to mind.

Tommy has the curious notion that we wants to introduce me to his folks. I can't at first imagine what has put such an idea into his mind. Given his history of head-below-the-parapet, why, I wonder, would he invite the scrutiny, not just of his friends, but of his immediate family?

What am I supposed to be?

"Just a friend," he says. "You know—they'll be wondering who it is I'm living with. I could hardly tell them I was moving out just to set up house on my own."

He doesn't seem to understand my reluctance.

"They know all my pals, I want them to know you too."

I don't seem to be able to make him appreciate that he can't have many pals nearly ten years younger than he is, obviously from a very different background, and of a decidedly—well—dubious aspect. To put it no more strongly than that.

But he is completely dismissive of my concerns. "Stop worrying, it'll be fine."

"But," I say, "what if they work out the situation? What's going on between us, I mean?"

"Why should they?"

"Well—I suppose I'm kind of—well—obvious. Obviously gay, I mean."

He laughs. "No, you're not. You've changed a lot since we met. Just be yourself."

All very well—but which self am I supposed to be? I am fairly sure that Audrey is not wanted on this particular voyage. George, then, I suppose.

With some misgivings I finally agree to his idea.

"Great," he says. "We'll just roll up, maybe on a Saturday afternoon, stay an hour or two. High time you met your mother-in-law. Ah'm tellin' you, it'll be fine."

The day arrives, a Saturday. I am more than a little nervous, worried about somehow giving the game away and causing him embarrassment.

But I needn't have worried. We never actually get there.

Instead, one of the most bizarre afternoons of my life unrolls.

We decide to visit 'The Barrows' in the morning. 'The Barrows' is Glasgow's large outdoor market, selling knockers, knickers, knitwear, and just about everything in between. Always thronged on a Saturday, in fact heaving, the atmosphere is lively and friendly. Our ostensible purpose is to buy our

Christmas presents for each other, as we are already well into December.

In fact I have already bought Tommy's, but he is one of those awkward people who has a birthday in the same month, so I need to find something he will appreciate for the twelfth, when he will turn twenty-eight. I have absolutely no idea what to choose, but we agree to split up in order to maintain the surprise element.

The Christmas present I have already picked out for him is something I know he will appreciate and enjoy. We have been working together at extending his guitar repertoire a little way beyond the hillbilly sphere, and he has been trying conclusions with Gershwin, Cole Porter and Irving Berlin. The problem is that, although I can tell him the names of the chords he needs, I have absolutely no idea how to achieve them on the guitar. So *The Complete Book of Guitar Chords* will be just the thing—purchased from Caldwell's, my former employer. I didn't quite have the nerve to ask for a staff discount, although I considered the possibility.

For his birthday, I finally settle on an LP. *Connie Francis sings Country and Western*, apparently. I am a huge fan of Connie Francis, and Tommy of Country and probably of Western as well, so it's something we should both enjoy.

Shopping concluded, when we meet up he suggests we go for a drink or two before heading off to the old homestead. I am more than willing—I feel a little Dutch courage would be welcome before I have to come face to face with the Molony family *en masse*.

"Ever been to the 'Sarry Heid'?" he asks me.

"No, I haven't," I say.

I have passed the infamous *Saracen's Head* pub many times on bus journeys into and out of Glasgow, but have never considered going inside; the pub's reputation is a daunting one.

"Fancy it? Just for a change? It's a right dump, but it might be a laugh—full of the dregs, but some real characters, too. And it's not far."

"OK," I say, nodding, "why not?"

I never worry about going anywhere, however rough, when he is with me. And I definitely need a drink.

We hop on a bus to Bridgeton Cross, only a two minute ride away.

We arrive, get off the bus, and cross the busy street.

'A dump' isn't really an adequate term to describe the *Saracen's Head*. It is shabby and dim, pure spit and sawdust. By comparison, Betty's Bar down at the docks, rowdy and dangerous as it is, is a masterpiece of interior design. It is only just twelve o' clock, and the place is as yet fairly quiet. A couple of elderly men sit separately on stools at the bar nursing their pints of heavy; two rough-looking younger guys are at a table; a crowd of raucous and disreputable-looking middle-aged women occupies the far corner, next to the jukebox, which they feed regularly. Kathy Kirby is currently informing the world that her secret love's no secret any more. Unsurprising, considering the volume at which she shouts it from the highest hill and tells a golden daffodil.

"What do you want?" asks Tommy. "To drink, I mean," as we head towards the bar.

"Oh—I don't know. Maybe a gin and tonic?" My taste in drinks has moved to a rather more sophisticated level.

He looks at me. "It's not really a gin and tonic kind of place."

No, it's not. I am at a bit of a loss.

"Well..."

"Cider? You like cider."

I don't particularly. But it's harmless enough, surely? Sort of like lemonade, really.

"OK then."

"Pint?"

No, I never drink pints. Imagine Angie's reaction.

"Just a half for me," I say.

We find a table, and I light up a cigarette and start to relax. The cider is pleasant enough, but not as sweet as I had expected. Not like the cider I had drunk in Betty's Bar. But that was laced with wine, the sweet sherry-like stuff that is such a popular favourite in Glasgow, primarily because it is strong but cheap. I wonder if I should ask Tommy to get me a wine as well. But then, remembering the unfortunate effect the combination had on me the last time I sampled it, I decide not to push my luck too far.

As we sit and chat quietly, I look around. The pair of youths sitting at a nearby table particularly interests me. They are young and good-looking, if definitely a bit on the rough side—not that that has ever put me off in the past. As I watch, a third comes out of the toilets (which I will definitely not be patronising, the bar itself is dirty enough) and heads over to join his mates. It is a second or two before I recognise Nicky.

'What's Nicky...?'

Oh, of course, he lives somewhere round here, I'd forgotten.

He doesn't see me as he passes. But when he has sat down, I call over, "Alright, Nicky?", using what I consider to be a suitable and convincingly masculine tone.

But I needn't have attempted discretion. The next thing, he turns round in his chair, grins and greets us.

"Audrey—good tae see ye, hen, how's things? An' Tommy, too—how are you, big man? What are you two daein' here?"

"And try to remember to call me 'George', Nicky, will you? I think Tommy's family might be a bit surprised to know he was living with a man called 'Audrey', don't you?"

"Nae problem, George, Ah won't forget."

Tommy looks relieved. I have managed to persuade him to invite Nicky to come along with us.

"I won't feel quite so conspicuous if Nicky's there too. You understand? It would take the pressure off a bit."

He sighs. "Ah don't know what you're so worried about. But if Nicky wants to come along, that's fine."

He turns to Nicky. "But don't forget, Nicky—it's 'George', and nothing else, OK?"

Nicky laughs. "Come on, Tommy—Ah'm no' stupid."

And no, he's not.

"Ah can be Alec, if ye like—after all, that's ma real name."

I think I will stick with 'Nicky'. This afternoon is going to be tricky enough as things are.

We are waiting for the bus to Maryhill. It won't be a long journey from Bridgeton, maybe half an hour. Through the centre of town, up to St George's Cross then onto the Maryhill Road. Tommy's family live in Shawpark Street, near Maryhill Barracks. Beyond there, Maryhill Road leads to the edge of the city, then outwards into the countryside.

As we board our bus, Nicky greets the conductor. "Awright, Patrick? How's tricks?"

"No sae bad, Alec. How's yersel'? Goat a job yet?"

Nicky laughs. "Naw, naw, no' yet. Ah'm restin' between engagements, me."

Patrick, a tall, thin, gloomy-looking middle aged man with a moustache and a put-upon air, smiles dolefully and shakes his head.

"Aye, aye. It's awright fer some, Alec. Where ur yiz off tae the day, then?"

"Maryhill, is that it, Tommy?"

"Aye, Maryhill Road, Shawpark Street, just by the Barracks."

Nicky digs in his pocket. "So, that'll be three tae the Barracks."

Patrick holds up a hand. "Naw, nae need, Alec. If the inspector gets on, leave it tae me, Ah'll have a word wi' him, cannae have Corporation staff payin' for their tickets, can we? Not even ex-Corporation staff, 's that no' right?"

I have forgotten that Nicky used to be a bus driver.

"Aw, thanks, pal," says Nicky, clapping him on the shoulder, "yer a star."

And we move off to find a seat.

"So—who's yer driver the day?" he calls over his shoulder. "Anybody Ah know?"

"Naw," says Pat as he follows us up the aisle. "New lad, no' been wi' us long. Larry something, or Lawrence, no' sure o' his second name. Good driver, mind."

He drops his voice.

"Though Ah'm a wee bit worried aboot him the day, tae tell ye the truth, Alec. He's no' hisself. He wis tellin' me his wife jist dumped him, went off wi' another fella, left him wi' the two weans."

We find seats right at the front of the bus, directly behind the driver's cab.

Patrick gives a double ring on the bell and the bus starts into motion.

He lowers his voice to a whisper. "Aye, he's right doon in the mooth aboot it. Ah telt him he shouldnae have come into work the day wi' things the way they are, but he said he needed something tae take his mind off his problems. Maybe he's right, at that. But he's definitely no' very happy. An' his drivin's a bit off too—he's all over the place now and then. No' concentratin'."

The lugubrious Patrick sighs.

I look through the partition. All I can see is the back of the driver's head; a narrow head, with fine fair hair breaking on the collar of his uniform.

Pat knocks on the sliding window. "Awright in there, Larry?"

The head turns. I see a woebegone expression and two red-rimmed eyes. The nose is running, his top lip glistens.

"Aye, fine Pat, Ah'm fine," he shouts.

Patrick turns away. "Och well, he's fine, he says. Last run of the day for us, anyway, he can get off home then."

And he moves away to collect fares. "He'll be OK."

I am not so sure. As the driver turns back to face the road, I see his hand go down to his side, pick up a bottle and raise it to his lips. I see the

Adam's apple on the thin neck bob up and down as he swallows.

Tommy and Nicky are chatting away and paying little attention.

I reach across Tommy and shake Nicky's arm. "Nicky—he's got a bottle in there with him—the driver has."

"Eh? What?"

"A bottle of vodka, I think."

One or two of the other passengers have heard me.

"He's drinking in there, did you say? Vodka? The driver?" says a short stout gentleman seated behind Nicky, as he leans forward.

"Christ," says Tommy. "The idiot. He'll get the sack if he's caught."

"Pat!" calls Nicky over his shoulder, "back here a minute."

Patrick ambles up the aisle to where we are seated. "Whit is it, Alec?"

Nicky grabs his arm. "Yer driver's neckin' a bottle of vodka in there, Pat. Fer Christ's sake, have a word wi' him."

"Eh? Vodka? Yer no' serious, Alec! Christ, Ah know he had a couple of pints afore he started his shift, but vodka—are ye sure?"

"Aye, Ah'm tellin' ye. Audrey here saw him."

"George," I say quickly.

"Aye, George, Ah mean."

"Aw, fer fuck's sake," says Patrick, banging once more on the partition. "Larry! Lawrence! Open up!"

The driver reaches over his shoulder and this time opens the sliding window.

Before he can say anything, Pat reaches through and grabs him by the hair.

"Lawrence! Are you drinkin' in there? Ye'd better no' be, Ah'm warnin' ye!"

Once again the tragic face turns towards us.

"Fuck off, Pat. Ye hear me? Ye can fuck off, right now. An' get yer haun aff ma neck."

"Larry," says Pat, loosening his grip and adopting a conciliatory tone. "Pass that bottle back here. Or Ah'm warning you, Ah'll be reportin' this. Hand it over."

The driver's face breaks into a silly grin.

"If it's a drink yer after, Pat, get yer ain. Yer no' havin' mine."

All I can think is how much I wish he would look at the road instead of at us.

"Whit are ye thinkin' of, Larry," says Patrick, reasonable. "Come on fer fucks sake, ye'll get yersel' the sack at this rate."

Larry takes a quick glance in the direction of the road and pulls sharply to the left, narrowly avoiding the back of a tram.

He turns back.

"Och, don't you worry, Ah'll no' get the sack, Pat. Nae chance. An' ye know why?"

"Naw, Lawrence, tell me why?".

Larry's foolish, amiable grin reappears.

"Because Ah'm goin' tae kill masel'. Aye, that's right, Ah'm gonnae crash this bus an' kill masel'—an' Ah'll take you lot with me if yer no' careful. So piss the fuck off, unless ye want me tae go for it right now!"

And he turns back to the road and floors the accelerator, after slamming the partition shut.

There is no immediate sign of Larry pursuing his fatal intent. He proceeds along London Road towards the Trongate and Argyle Street at a sedate and steady pace. He pulls up at all the bus stops carefully and tidily. He waits patiently for his conductor to ring the bell before turning out into the traffic again. He appears to be a model bus driver, considerate both to his passengers and to the other road users.

Nevertheless, remembering his face, I am uneasy. "Maybe we should get off, wait for another bus," I say. "What do you think?"

Tommy says nothing, but shrugs. Nicky, on the other hand, is calm.

"Ah widnae worry, Aud—er—George. He wis just windin' Pat up tae get a rise out of him. Ye get bored in there on yer own."

But the vodka bottle is still in evidence, I notice; it is about half empty by now. And it is when we get to busy Argyle Street that the first signs of something being wrong start to appear. Although in a way that is more funny than anything else.

We have reached the bus stop just by the entrance to Lewis's Polytechnic, the large department store colloquially known as the 'Polly'. After the usual passenger exchange has taken place, and the conductor has rung the bell for take-off, instead of pulling away, Larry continues to sit there at the stop, his engine idling. When I look back towards the mounting platform, I see that a short and plump middle-aged lady with a large shopping bag is heading towards us at a trot, one hand raised, presumably to indicate that she wants to climb aboard.

Then, just as she gets to the back of the bus—indeed, her hand is outstretched to grasp the metal pole, and the conductor is reaching out to help her—Larry suddenly revs his engine and pulls away smartly from the stop. Only to draw up again about thirty yards further on, engine still thrumming.

'*Oh—he's seen her now,*' I think.

By now the three of us are looking back. The lady continues gamely in pursuit; then, just as she seems about to achieve her goal, the engine bursts into life and she is baulked once more.

"He's doing that on purpose," says Tommy. "Daft idiot."

Patrick, the conductor, is dinging his bell like a madman. Heads crane backwards to see what is going to happen next. The other passengers have become aware of the dangerous game the driver is playing.

If, indeed, that is what he is doing. Or are we all wrong, is it just a coincidence? Is it that Larry has simply not noticed the lady in question?

He is forced to pull up at the red light at the corner of Jamaica Street, and, as I look back again, it looks as if the desperate passenger will finally make it onto the bus. Patrick, furious, is holding onto the pole and stretching back to grab her hand, still outstretched beseechingly. This time he manages to snag her heavy shopping bag. He swings round, drops it in the space reserved for luggage, and then turns back, hand once more extended to assist. I can see Larry's face in his rear-view mirror, and I realise suddenly from his expression that he knows exactly what he is doing. And sure enough, once more, with immaculate timing, he pulls away again. But this time straight through the red light and directly into the busy junction.

Somehow he gets us across safely, amid blaring horns, the squeal of brakes, the screeches of my fellow-passengers, and a stream of original and inventive curses from the conductor. Then he carries on blithely under the Central railway bridge, and turns right into Hope Street.

Despite the dangerous situation, and the realisation that we are being driven by someone who is, to put it no more strongly, not in a fit state to be in charge of a vehicle, I have found the last few moments amusing. The expression of mingled bafflement and fury on the lady's red face, her puffing and panting, her unfathomable determination to board this particular bus at all costs, despite the obvious hazards; the conductor's rage and remarkably fluent swearing; the fact that we now have the lady's Saturday shop on board, but not its owner; and the sheep-like reactions of my fellow passengers. All these in combination suddenly strike me as excruciatingly funny, and I disintegrate into slightly hysterical laughter.

I look up at Tommy, and see that he is tight-lipped, his expression serious. Nicky, on the other hand, like me, is having difficulty controlling his mirth.

"Well, that certainly gave the wifey a nice wee work-out," he chokes.

"Yes. Wonder what's in the bag?" I giggle. "A nice leg of lamb, maybe?"

"Christ's sake, what are you laughing at, George?" says Tommy. "It's not funny. That lady could have been killed."

I try to pull myself together. "Yes, Tommy, I know, you're right. But…" And once again I am doubled over.

"Sometimes I worry about you, George," he says with a grimace.

As I look up, still smiling, I catch Larry's face reflected in his mirror. He sees me laughing. He grins and winks, and gives a thumbs-up gesture. Then reaches once more for his bottle.

Things quieten after that. We turn off into Bothwell Street, continue up Elmbank Street and onward into Sauchiehall Street without further incident.

"He seems to have calmed down now," I say to Tommy, still not quite able to stop sniggering. "Think he was just having a wee bit of fun."

Patrick, the conductor, has tried by various methods to attract his driver's attention—by banging on the sliding window, shouting, swearing, pressing his bell repeatedly. But to no avail. Larry completely ignores him, and continues to drive steadily and correctly all the way to St George's Cross. From time to time he catches me watching him in his mirror. He continues to grin and wink; indeed, if we were sitting in a bar, I would have thought he was trying to get off with me.

But the smile is superficial, a twitch of the mouth, nothing more. The tragic, red-rimmed eyes never change their expression.

We turn into Maryhill Road without incident. It isn't until we reach Queen's Cross and the busy junction with Garscube Road that everything starts to go wrong. Two or three passengers are on their feet, waiting to get off when the bus pulls into the next stop. But it doesn't. Instead it carries on, past the half-dozen people waiting there with their hands out. It gathers speed.

Maryhill Road is for the most part long and straight. There are only two or three sets of traffic lights. Not that they have any effect; our driver continues through them whether they are red or green.

The bus continues to accelerate—it must be doing about sixty by now—and the other passengers begin to panic. As we tear past Shakespeare Street and Ruchill Street they get to their feet in ones and twos, clutching the seat backs in front of them as the whole thing sways sickeningly from side to side. Fortunately there does not seem to be a huge amount of traffic around today, and our driver manages to manoeuvre round it without obvious difficulty.

"Make him stop, make him stop, son," an elderly lady cries out to the conductor. "Pull the emergency cord, in the name of God."

Patrick simply shrugs.

I am not sure what the top speed of a Corporation bus is, but I am pretty sure that by now we are close to it.

"Put the brakes on, fer fucks sake," shouts the lady's elderly companion, probably her husband.

"The brakes are in there wi' him, ya eedjit, no' oot here wi' me," says Patrick. "There's fuck-all Ah can dae, pal. He's havin' a breakdown. An' before ye ask, Ah mean a *mental* breakdown, no' a mechanical breakdown. Ah knew he wis no' right the day. He'll no' stop. We might as well prepare tae die, the lot of us."

As a general shriek erupts, two young men thunder down the stairs from the upper deck.

"Whit's gawn oan pal?"

"Don't ask me, son, ma driver's gone mental. End of the road for the lot of us. He'll no' stop till he's killed us all," replies the lugubrious Pat, with what sounds like a certain relish in his tone.

He sits down on the long seat nearest the exit and lights up a cigarette. "Might as well just make yerselves comfortable and wait for the end."

The two young lads seem to be in some confusion. They appear to consider whether it's worth trying to jump from the platform of the moving bus, and then obviously think better of it. They sit down opposite the conductor.

"Fuck's sake, Ah jist came oot fer a pie an' chips," says one. "Ye mean we're aw gawnae get killed?"

"Nae point worryin'," says the other. "Ah've missed ma dinner, so ma maw'll kill me anyway."

"Ah've still got a few chips left, John," says the first after a moment, taking a greaseproof paper bag out of his pocket. "Want some?"

"Aye, thanks, Ah'm starvin'."

We pass Garrioch Road. As we approach the next turning, Tommy says, rather sadly and regretfully, "That's where ma maw lives."

And the junction with Shawpark Street flashes by.

Patrick the conductor continues puffing on his cigarette, apparently resigned to death's approach. The short gentleman seated behind Nicky, a rather upper class business type, makes his way rather unsteadily down the aisle towards him.

"Here, conductor," he says, in a decidedly non-Glaswegian accent. "Put that out. You should know perfectly well that smoking is only allowed on the upper deck. Put it out at once."

Pat looks him up and down.

"Away and get fucked, pal. This is *ma* bus an' Ah'll smoke wherever Ah want tae. Away and mind yer ain business."

He draws expansively on his cigarette. "Jump off, if ye fancy yer chances. Or jist sit doon an' examine yer conscience."

As the man heads back to his seat, Pat mutters under his breath, "English cunt."

The passenger turns back. "I heard that. I'll be reporting you. And I'm not English. I'm from Edinburgh."

Pat looks up.

"Oh, is that right?" He turns and addresses the rest of the company. "Did ye hear that? The man's no' English, he's fae Edinburgh! Christ, that's fuckin' worse."

The passenger hesitates. Then, obviously unable to come up with anything suitably crushing, resumes his seat. He unfolds his newspaper, takes out a pipe and lights up.

The bus continues to weave crazily along the road at top speed. Ten minutes later we leave the city behind. We pass signs for Bearsden, then Maryhill Road becomes Milngavie Road. We head out into the countryside.

Towards where? I have no idea. Loch Lomond, perhaps. I know it's in this general direction.

As we rattle along, I take the opportunity to weigh up my fellow passengers. Including ourselves and the conductor there are fifteen of us. The two young lads have finished their chips and are smoking morosely, sunk in apathy. Two girls of around the same age, maybe sixteen or seventeen, typical Glasgow herries, are seated about halfway down the bus on the left hand side of the aisle. One blond, one brunette, they are entertaining themselves and the rest of us by screaming loudly and quite unnecessarily every time the bus gives even the slightest shudder.

Then there is the elderly couple who had imagined that the conductor was in some mysterious fashion empowered to apply some kind of brake to the runaway vehicle. They sit white-faced, holding hands, she with her shopping piled on her lap, down near the back of the bus, not far from where the conductor is enjoying what may well prove to be his final cigarette.

The gentleman from Edinburgh puffs on his pipe, and tries to read his newspaper. The combination of the rough country road and the speed of the careening bus makes this pretty difficult. Nonetheless, he persists in the attempt, endeavouring to look unconcerned.

At one point, he raises his head and announces to the world, "And someone's bound to have reported this, the police will have been informed, and it won't be long before they appear behind us. Then Stirling Moss up there will have to give it up and pull over."

I concede that, should the police appear, Larry may well decide to pull over; possibly over the edge of a cliff. Not that we are in a particularly mountainous area, but the delightfully varied scenery of Bonnie Scotland could easily produce a sheer drop round the next bend.

The Edinburgh gentleman nods to himself. "Yes, he'll probably get five years. I mean, it's a straight road, isn't it? They can hardly miss him."

As if alerted to the possibility by telepathy, the driver immediately swings a left so sharp that the bus tips alarmingly to the right. Everybody, including me, screams in terror. The wheels on the left leave the ground, and for a second I think it is going to go over. But they are solidly built, these Glasgow buses, and it rights itself after a few hair-raising seconds, and we tear off again down a quiet country lane heading for who knows where.

A nun in full regalia sits alone, eyes closed, clutching her beads, mouthing what I assume are prayers. Am I hallucinating? Is she wearing make-up? Maybe the rules have been relaxed recently. She had appeared from the upper deck just after the two youths joined us. I wonder if she was having a sneaky cigarette up there, hiding behind her breviary. I don't actually know any nuns, but I have a vague feeling I have seen this one before, somewhere.

A youngish couple are seated together, with a small child on the mother's lap. They seem remarkably calm, all things considered. They chat quietly to each other, and I see her hold the youngster up to the window so that he can benefit from the view of the ravishing and rapidly changing scenery.

There remain the three of us, still sitting at the front of the bus, behind the driver, plus Patrick the conductor.

Is there any solution?

We have discussed the matter, but come to the conclusion that all we can do is sit tight.

I am not laughing any more. I have begun to realise that this situation is really serious. We all may well end up dead, or at the least unpleasantly maimed. Maybe the three of us should head further back, towards the rear of the bus.

"Would that be any safer?" I ask Nicky.

He seems relatively unconcerned. "Nae need. He'll calm down and stop soon enough. Don't worry, the man's a brilliant driver."

I take a glance at our brilliant driver, I can still see his face in the mirror.

My heart leaps to my mouth. His eyes are no longer filled with tears. They are closed.

"Shit, Nicky," I yell. "He's *asleep!*"

"Eh? Did ye say he's asleep?" mutters Tommy, who has actually been nodding off himself.

"Yes. He's asleep," I shriek.

"Asleep? Aye, awright, that's no' sae good," says Nicky, as the three of us leap to our feet and bang as hard as we can on the hatch.

"Larry, Lawrence, wake up…" I shout.

"C'mon, man, for God's sake…" bawls Tommy.

This desperate emergency instantly communicates itself to the rest of the passengers, who rise to their feet as one. They shriek, they yell, they curse. The racket in the confined space of the bus is deafening.

And miraculously, it has an effect. One eye opens, then the other. They blink confusedly for a moment or two. Then Larry turns around (and how I wish he wouldn't do that!) and slides open the partition.

"Sorry, folks, sorry for that. Just had tae take a wee snooze there. Nae problem, nae problem, everything's fine. Jist sit back in yer seats and enjoy the Mystery Tour. Admire the scenery. Lovely spot, this, wherever it is."

In fact the country lane we are driving down is a nondescript grey corridor, leafless hedges on either side, about as dull and uninteresting as can be. But Larry obviously does not share my opinion. His attention turns back to the road.

*'Bonnie Scotland, Scotland aye sae braw,
My heart is back in Scotland though I am far awa'.'*

He sings happily as he reaches for his bottle. Finding it empty, he pushes open his side window and throws it out.

It's maybe half an hour later that our adventure comes to an end. And in the most undramatic and mundane way possible. The bus simply runs out of fuel. We are on something called the B837, heading towards somewhere called Balmaha, three miles distant says the sign, when the engine starts to miss and splutter. Then the bus coasts to a halt gracefully without the help of its brakes.

The driver, Larry, turns to the open hatch.

"End of the line, folks, tank's empty, Ah'm afraid. Enjoy your stay, all gratuities to your driver will be gratefully received. Ah'm off fer a wee drink, masel'—join me if ye wish."

Then he swings his door wide, falls out, and collapses apparently unconscious in a heap at the side of the road.

"Where's Balmaha?" I ask Tommy as we all pile out of the bus. "I mean, where are we?"

"Loch Lomond," says Tommy. "Balmaha's a wee village on Loch Lomondside. Been there camping a time or two; nice wee place."

"Loch Lomond?" I say. I remember how I had wondered if that was where we were headed for. Maybe I have the psychic gift?

"Well, it's only three miles away," I go on, "according to that sign. Maybe somebody could walk there, find a phone? Ring the Corporation and get someone out here in another bus to take us back to the city?"

"Waste of time…" Tommy starts to say, but I interrupt him.

"Maybe these two young lads?" I say, pointing. "We could ask them."

Tommy sighs. "Listen, will you? Look, Ah could walk there masel' in half an hour. So could you. But there'd be no point. It's a tiny wee place, Balmaha, just a camp site, a wee hotel and a couple of pubs. They'll all be shut up for the winter, the owners'll be off tae Spain or Morocco, soaking up the sun."

I look around at my fellow passengers who are by now shivering in the chilly December air. The bus had been warm and cosy, at least. I see that the two boys have teamed up with the two girls, and the four of them are laughing and flirting, apparently none the worse for their recent escapade. Similarly, the young couple with the child and the older couple have struck up a conversation. The nun has remained on the bus, and the Edinburgh gentleman maintains his isolation, standing apart from the rest of the company.

The last two aside, our communal brush with death seems to have engendered a camaraderie reminiscent of the reaction to a wartime bombing raid. We go over and join the group

The two young ladies are apparently Senga and Jessie, and the two boys Ronnie and John. Mr and Mrs Macready (Drew and Marilyn) present their two-year old, Hugh, and the elderly couple introduce themselves as Bill and Marion McGovern.

Gradually the conversation, initially animated, tails away.

"So what are we going to do?" I ask Tommy.

He shrugs. "Start walking back? Or maybe we can flag somebody down?"

We haven't seen another vehicle for miles.

I turn to Nicky. "Any ideas?"

"No, can't think of anything. If we could lay our hands on some diesel... We passed a sign for Drymen, I remember. Did anybody notice a garage on the road—further back, I mean?"

It appears not. Anyway, I doubt if anyone would be happy for Larry to resume his place behind the wheel.

I look over to where Patrick, the conductor is endeavouring to revive his colleague. With nothing else to do, the three of us head towards them.

Our driver is once more conscious, it seems. Patrick, surprisingly solicitous, has an arm round his shoulder, and has produced a thermos flask from somewhere. He is endeavouring to pour something steaming from it into his driver—Bovril, by the delicious smell of it. My stomach rumbles.

Larry looks utterly woebegone. I hadn't realised just how young he is. No sooner does he see us than he starts apologising.

"Look, Ah'm sorry, Ah'm sorry. For aw this, Ah mean. Ah don't know what got into me. Jist went aff ma heid there fer a while. Hope Ah didnae scare ye? Ah wid never huv done whit Ah said, aboot crashin' the bus an' that. Ah wis jist depressed an' pissed off. Sorry."

Somehow I am able to ignore the fact that, however harmless his fundamental intentions may have been, he could easily have been the death of us all through an accident. After all, he was, and is still, seriously drunk. And he actually fell asleep at the wheel at one point. But he looks so utterly contrite and pathetic that I don't have the heart to have a go at him. Tommy and Nicky obviously feel the same. We shuffle our feet and say that it's fine, no problem, could happen to anyone, and other meaningless mumblings.

"Aye," says Patrick, standing up. "End of the day, we're aw still here and in one piece. It'll be somethin' tae tell the grand-children aboot."

I seriously doubt that any of us three will be relating the story to our descendants, but take his point.

By this time the rest of the group has gathered round. Immediately the recriminations burst forth. Drew, the father of the child starts it off.

"Ya stupit bastard, whit did ye think ye were daein' back there? Could huv got us aw killed. Ma wean's only two year old."

"Aye, man—ur ye mental or whit?" This from one of the young lads, the one who had the bag of chips, Ronnie, I think.

"You need lockin' up, so ye do," the elderly lady, Marion, contributes.

"Oh, he will be locked up, I'll see to that. I shall be making a full report of this to the police."

This from Mr Edinburgh, who has joined the enquiry.

"Aye, ya eedjit, an' Ah hope ye get life," says Senga.

Poor Larry, completely overwhelmed, bursts into tears, and covers his face with his hands.

Patrick steps forward, palms outstretched.

"Now, hang on a minute, you lot. Ah understand that yiz are annoyed, upset, stressed, and Ah get it, Ah don't blame ye. But go easy oan the laddie, eh? He's been havin a rough time, so he has, wan way an' another. Wife jist left him, ran off wi' the milkman…"

"It wis the bread man." Larry's sobs break out afresh.

"…and left him wi' two young weans, three year old an' six months. He's been at his wits' ends tryin' tae get things sorted oot, finding someone tae look after the kiddies, havin' tae keep workin' tae earn some money… Nae wonder it aw goat too much for him."

He pauses, and looks around the lynch mob.

"Aw, come on now, people, have a heart."

We Glaswegians (or Weegies) are a volatile lot. We have easily fired tempers, short fuses, we react badly to people taking the piss, we can be abusive and even aggressive when roused. But we also have, like most Celts, a strong sentimental streak.

There is a brief pause while everyone considers Patrick's words. Then, by some mysterious alchemy, the unfortunate Larry is transformed from villain of the piece—mental case, mass murderer, piss-head, maybe anarchist—into victim, and the object of everyone's compassion.

"Aw, the poor laddie," says Mrs McGovern, placing a hand on his head gently; though two minutes earlier she would happily have helped to string Larry up with that same work-worn hand.

"Tough break, man, tough," says young John, nodding sympathetically, man of the world, and clapping Larry on the shoulder.

"Dae ye need a baby-sitter? Ah love weans, so Ah do," says Jessie hopefully, crouching down beside him and taking his hand.

The atmosphere of sympathetic understanding is all-pervasive. Or nearly so.

There is but one dissenting voice in the general chorale of forgiveness.

The gentleman from Edinburgh is not going to plunge into this deluge of benevolence quite so readily.

"Are you all mad? This man is a criminal!"

It appears that the milk of human kindness does not flow quite as freely in the lofty Scottish capital as it does in lowly Glasgow.

"Look here," he goes on, "you could all have been killed. You said so yourselves. He's a psychopath, this fellow. He needs treatment, not sympathy. He should be locked away."

Larry's tears have gradually ceased. He looks up.

There is a brief silence.

Then one of the girls says, "But if he is… What'll happen tae his weans?"

"Aye, she's right, the lassie," says the elderly gent, Bill, I think he said his name was. "Taken intae care, nae doot. Ah widnae wish that on them masel'. Or on him. Poor bloke's goat enough on his plate as it is. Ah mean, will ye look at the state of him?"

Larry gives one more well-timed sob.

"Och, c'moan man, it wisnae his fault," adds Ronnie, a little illogically.

"Not his fault?" Mr Edinburgh is understandably confused. "Not his fault? Then who's fault was it, may I ask? Yours? Mine?"

There is no reply for a moment. Then Patrick, the conductor, gets to his feet.

"Well, what could he dae? Ah mean, if his brakes failed, what mair could he dae?"

Mr Edinburgh is for a moment speechless.

"His brakes?" he croaks. "If his brakes failed? His brakes never failed—he quite deliberately…"

"Yes, it was his brakes—I heard him say so myself," I put in, catching on.

"Aye, that's right, definitely," says Nicky. "We both heard him, didn't we?"

"Aye, me too," says Tommy.

Mr Edinburgh is barely able to force out, "But—he was drinking. In his cab. Drinking vodka."

He turns to us, a beseeching look in his eyes. "You saw him, didn't you, you three? It was you who told the conductor. For the love of God, tell them, this lot!"

I shake my head. "I saw him drinking some lemonade, that's all."

"I tell you, it was vodka! Come on, I heard you say so!"

There is a short silence.

He is desperate, but determined. "He was taking it straight from the bottle. Vodka."

Another much longer pause.

"Naw, naw, he wisnae," says John, folding his arms.

"No way," says Marilyn, after a second, shaking her head.

"Lemonade!" shrieks baby Hugh, waving his rattle in the air.

Mr Edinburgh is not quite beaten. He turns to Larry.

"And what have you got to say to this tissue of lies, you reprobate?"

Larry looks up, but says nothing.

Patrick intervenes.

"Tell him, Lawrence. Tell him it was the brakes."

"Yes, tell us, Lawrence—if you've got the nerve," Mr Edinburgh sneers.

Larry takes his time. He opens his mouth, but nothing comes out. He tries again, still with no success. Finally, he manages to get out one word.

"No."

Mr Edinburgh turns to the rest of us and smiles in satisfaction. "There, you see?"

"No," Larry goes on, "it wasn't the brakes…"

Nemesis nods. "No, indeed it wasn't."

"… it was the accelerator. It jammed."

"What?"

"The accelerator. Ah floored it, an' it jammed."

Mr Edinburgh is about to interrupt, but Larry, now that he has got his mouth in gear, is not going to be interrupted.

"Aye," he says, reaching into his pocket and taking out a packet of cigarettes, "Ah noticed it wis a wee bit spongy when Ah took the bus oot this morning. Then it seemed tae right itself."

He takes out a cigarette. "Ah wisnae worried, happens now an' again."

He pauses.

"Then in Argyle Street, it started stickin' a bit—Ah kept tryin' tae coax it back. That's why thon lady couldnae get on—Ah didnae dare stay stopped in case it failed again."

He puts his cigarette in his mouth. "Goat a light, Pat?"

Patrick hands him his lighter.

"Then at Queen's Cross, that was it. Jammed doon, an' Ah didnae dare apply the brakes, ye cannae if that happens, it wid jist burn them oot, so Ah thought…"

Larry continues on for a good minute or two with incomprehensible technical details. When he eventually finishes his explanation, Patrick nods as if he has understood every word.

"So there ye have it folks. A simple accident. Could happen tae anyone. Lucky this lad's such a good driver—otherwise who knows what might have happened?"

Larry grins. "Aye, well, Ah realised Ah jist had tae keep on until the tank wis empty. Ah'm sorry if Ah panicked you a bit, but there wis nothin' Ah could dae except steer an' pray."

Patrick smiles. "Aye, ye did well son."

He turns to the rest of us. "A round of applause for Larry, eh?"

We oblige, naturally.

Mr Edinburgh has finally managed to regain the power of speech.

"I never heard such a load..."

He surveys the group. "You mean to tell me you're all going to go along with this nonsense?"

Unanimous, we nod, yes.

"Well I for one will not. I shall be telling the authorities exactly what took place—the drinking, the falling asleep, the language, the smoking on the lower deck..."

The girl called Senga turns to face him.

"An' Ah'll be tellin' them aw aboot you."

Eyebrows arched, Mr Edinburgh looks at her.

"Oh? Telling them what?"

She raises her chin. "Aboot you touchin' me."

"Eh? I touched you? Where exactly did this happen?"

She indicates the area of her bosom. "Here. On the upper deck."

She turns to the rest of us. "Imagine, the dirty bastard—an' me jist fourteen!"

Mr Edinburgh has moved off and sits on a milestone ('Balmaha 3') puffing on his pipe, with a baffled and angry expression on his face. Sister whoever-she-may-be is still on the bus. The rest of us cluster round the seated Larry and the standing Patrick.

"What are we going to do now?" I ask. "Any ideas?"

"Well, the first thing we need to do is have a look at that faulty accelerator, see if we can do anything about it," says Nicky.

I laugh. "But it's not—"

"Ah mean, we're goin' tae need tae explain how it got put right. Later on, Ah mean," he interrupts, giving me a meaningful look. "When we get back tae the real world."

"Oh. Yes." I catch on.

As does Larry. "Aye, yer right, pal, Ah'll take a look at it now. Then Ah can fill her up, an' we can get back on the road."

"Fill her up?" says Tommy. "Ah thought ye'd run out of diesel?"

"Och aye," says Larry, standing up. "The tank's empty right enough. But there's a spare can in the back of the bus. No' supposed tae carry it, but Ah like tae be prepared—ye never know how yer trip's gonnae turn oot, dae ye?"

There is no denying that, certainly.

"But first things first," says Larry. "Have a look at thon pedal."

He wanders towards the bus, weaving very slightly from side to side.

"Here, Ah'll give ye a hand, pal," says Nicky with a wink at me. "Ah wis a bus driver masel' for a while, Ah know they engines inside out."

In no time at all, we are homeward bound. Through the driver's partition Tommy and I can see the back of Nicky's head. Larry snores in the seat across the aisle from us. The consensus of opinion reached was that he was far too shaken up (read 'far too drunk') to attempt the return journey, and after some little protest—'*Naw, naw, Ah'm fine now, really*'—he has agreed that Nicky (who is, after all, a fully qualified bus driver) can take the wheel as we head back towards civilisation. The latter drives carefully and expertly, and everyone has begun to relax. Indeed, the atmosphere is positively festive.

I turn and look back, in time to see the Edinburgh gentleman approach the nun, who continues to sit alone in her original seat, gazing out of the window. He bends down to speak to her, no doubt endeavouring to drum up some support for his version of events.

I am unable to hear what he says. Whatever it was, it doesn't elicit the response he was hoping for. She looks up at him, indicates her mouth, then shakes her head from side to side, and spreads two surprisingly large hands, waving them back and forth in a gesture of denial.

'*Oh*,' I think. '*Must be a silent order. That's a bit of luck.*'

But on reflection, that seems unlikely. Cloistered nuns are not a common sight on public transport. How would she ask for a ticket? Hold up a sign, maybe?

'*Perhaps she's deaf and dumb?*'

Mr Edinburgh heads back to his seat, baffled and baulked.

Only to rise again moments later and ding the bell furiously.

"Stop the bus, stop the bus."

He leans to one side, and points to the middle of the road ahead.

"There's the vodka bottle, the one he was drinking from, the one he threw out. There'll be his fingerprints on it. That's evidence, that is."

He continues to press the bell ceaselessly as Nicky drives straight over the incriminating bottle.

Sure enough, as we turn back onto the Milngavie road, there they are. Two police cars, sirens blaring and lights flashing, escort our bus all the way back to Maryhill garage.

As we draw up in the forecourt, I hear the thunder of footsteps, as a large lady I've never seen before tears down the stairs from the upper deck. Arrived on the mounting platform, she glares at our conductor, hands on hips.

"See you, Pat, ya eedjit! Ye know tae wake me up at Queens Cross! An' now look whit yiv done. Ah've missed ma stop. Now Ah'm gawnae huv tae walk aw the way back!"

Patrick looks at her. "Oh, it's you, Phyllis… Sorry an' that, but Ah've had other things on ma mind, whit wi' wan thing an' another. Yiv missed mair than yer stop, as it happens."

He takes her arm and helps her off. "Anyway, ye can get a bus back frae here. Or ye could walk—it's only fifteen minutes—the exercise'll dae ye good."

She grins up at him. "Ya cheeky swine! Now don't you forget next time. Ye know Ah need ma wee forty winks on the way home. See ye Monday, Pat, OK?"

As she turns to leave, Pat calls after her. "Aye, see ye Monday, Phyllis, enjoy yer weekend."

Ignoring the police officers who are getting out of their cars, indeed, unaware of them, she pushes her way through the crowd that is gathering round our vehicle and disappears.

Immediately behind her, I notice the mysterious Sister of Mercy leap off the bus with a surprising athleticism and follow her. As she does so, the hem of her black habit flies up slightly, and I am surprised to see what looks like the edge of a pair of trousers underneath.

Interesting—I've always been a bit curious about the underwear of the religious.

The rest of us passengers are rounded up by the police, and questioned in detail about our ordeal. With one obvious exception we all trot out the prepared story—that as far as we are aware, there was some mechanical problem, the bus went out of control, and that it was only due to the driver's skill that there were no fatal consequences, etc., etc.

Larry himself is rushed off in an ambulance for the state of his health to be checked; I just hope the hospital doesn't have the means or the interest to check his alcohol level.

Inevitably, the Edinburgh gentleman has a different version of events from the rest of us; and in reality, his is accurate in every detail. The police note his account down along with everyone else's, and we are all allowed to go after leaving our names and addresses.

As Tommy, Nicky and I are heading for the town centre and a pub—all thought of continuing on to visit the Molony family has been abandoned, I've had enough stress for one day—I am gratified to overhear an exchange between the two officers.

"Whit dae ye make of that one, Jamesie, the wee posh guy? Ah mean, his story disnae match up wi' the rest. Is he a wee bit mental, maybe?" says the first one.

The other simply shakes his head. "Och, jist ignore him, Bernie—whit wid he know anyway? He's frae Edinburgh."

A couple of days later, we are amused to see the newspaper headline: 'Fourteen saved by hero bus driver.'

I do finally get to meet my in-laws; on New Year's Eve, a family gathering inevitably. And true to Tommy's prediction, no-one seems to turn a hair, or find anything remarkable about me. I keep pretty quiet—well, what passes as quiet for me—and anyway, we're not there very long. It must be about eleven o'clock when there is a ring at the doorbell. Tommy's brother, Charlie—who looks like a taller, younger and more handsome version of my beloved—goes to answer it. After a moment he comes back into the room.

"It's for you, George—a lassie tae see ye. She widnae come in, she's waitin' at the door."

A girl? To see me? Here? Who on earth?...

I head off into the hallway.

"Oh, there you are, Audrey, took me *ages* to find the right place."

It's Dorothy. In her flapper costume.

"Now, got a taxi downstairs, we need to get straight over to Beanie's, the party will be in full swing. Are you ready?"

Oh God, I had completely forgotten. Beanie's party. The cabaret. My promise.

Ten minutes later we are speeding towards Queen's Park. Tommy has decided to come with us.

"Well, Ah wis a bit bored, to tell you the truth. One Hogmanay's much like another at ma maw's. And at least now you've met the family. Not as bad as you thought, was it?"

"No," I say, "it was fine."

I turn to Dorothy. "What I don't understand is how you managed to find the right house—it's not as if you know the address or anything."

"Well, I knew it was near the Barracks—heard you mention it. So I just knocked on a few doors and asked if anyone knew where the Molony family lived without an 'e'. Simple, really."

The composition of the party crowd is much the same as it was on previous occasions. And Dorothy's cabaret spot meets with, if anything, even greater success than it did on the previous occasion.

It is after she has finished, and the applause has died away, that our host takes to the floor.

"And now," Beanie says, "silence please, for a very special surprise. Direct from the Vatican, and to give you her tribute to The Singing Nun, will you please welcome… Sister Agnes…"

He takes a step backward, and extends an encouraging hand towards the door.

"… of God."

A small figure in full nun's habit enters from the doorway, clutching a guitar.

It seats itself on the piano stool I have just vacated and starts tuning up. This accomplished, it starts to sing:

> *'Dominique, nique, nique, all around the land he'd plod*
> *And sing a little song*
> *Never asking for reward, he just talks about the Lord*
> *He just talks about the Lord.'*

Something is familiar. It takes all of ten seconds for the penny to drop.

At the conclusion of her performance the nun leaves the floor to polite, if rather baffled, applause, and I follow her towards the bedroom, this evening doubling as the artistes' retiring room. Agnes is seated, adjusting her wimple, in front of Beanie's elaborate dressing table mirror.

"Well, Agnes, we meet again," I say, looking over her shoulder. "Last time I saw you was on a bus, if memory serves."

She looks up.

"Oh aye, Audrey, hen, recognised ye right away. Ah wid huv spoke, but…"

"But what?"

"Well," she says, half turning round, "imagine if Ah had—the shame,

Ah mean, the embarrassment. Whit wid folk huv thought, a holy Bride of Christ chattin' tae a screamin' queen like you?"

She is perfectly serious. And I understand that she is not trying to be deliberately offensive. She just says it as she sees it.

She is, I realise, completely mental.

She gives a little regretful smile, and turns back to the mirror.

"Sorry an' aw that, but Ah jist couldnae bring masel' tae talk tae ye."

I lean over her shoulder.

"I see. Well, you can keep it that way in future, Agnes, OK?"

I stand up and head for the door. "Oh, and by the way—Happy New Year."

"Thank you, Audrey."

"And fuck you too, Sister."

10. Down the Aisle

> Something old, something new
> Something borrowed, something blue
> I am yours to cherish and to hold
> With this little band of gold.
> *Patti LaBelle and the BlueBelles, 1963*

I can't now remember exactly where we met Charlie and Derek. Somewhere around the town, no doubt; in a bar perhaps, or through a mutual friend. And when? Certainly sometime after Tommy and I joined up, but well before we began to live together.

Wherever, whenever it happened, we became friends of a sort; though the 'why' eludes me as completely as the 'where' and the 'when'. I suppose it started because we were two couples in a sea of the unattached. It certainly wasn't because we had a great deal in common.

Tommy approves of them, not just because they are together, like us, but also because both of them are completely straight-looking, non-camp, not obviously gay. I don't really register it at the time, but, a little like Sandra Dee, with her 'up for anything' attitude, and her refusal to be tightly categorised, they are in a sense a marker, a straw in the wind, a harbinger of things to come. Gay society as a whole is on the verge of a deep-seated metamorphosis. Revolution is in the air. It will take some time before this sea-change reaches, penetrates and reforms Glasgow—Connies and Wilmas, Avas and Lanas, will continue to proliferate there for a few years to come. But oh yes, the times they are a-changing.

I don't, to be honest, care for Charlie very much. He is around forty, maybe a little younger. Ex-army, of all things, but currently not in employment; unimposing physically, medium height, glasses, wiry build and noticeably balding. Though in no obvious way effeminate, he has a peculiar mincing walk. I call him 'Charlotte the Harlot' in private, though not to his face, he would be most offended. Occasionally drily amusing, more often he is morose and silent.

And *mean*. Tight as arseholes, as they say; though I suspect his own is rather less so than most. Apologies for the vulgarity, but I don't say that lightly, or out of simple spite, as will become clear.

His boyfriend Derek is a complete contrast. Much younger, no more than eighteen or nineteen, Derek is tall and slim, and has the most remarkable mop of red hair. And when I say red, it is just that. Not ginger, not orange, not strawberry blonde. Not auburn, not chestnut, not copper. Red. A pure and brilliant red, vivid and beautiful.

I initially have as little time for him as for his friend—neither, I think, has much in the way of personality, neither brings a great deal to the table when we are out in a group. I occasionally wonder what on earth they do when they are alone, what they talk about, how they pass the time together, so devoid of character are they. Derek, at least, has the advantage of being decorative, which goes a long way, especially in our circle. But apart from that, he is about as interesting and original as the menu in the *El Guero*; that is to say, neither the one nor the other.

Appropriately it is in that very place that an incident takes place that causes me to revise my opinion of Derek somewhat. And that throws some light on the condition of Charlie's fundament.

January 1964.
Elaine and I bump into Derek one wet lunchtime, and bring our coffees over to his table. He is on his own, no Charlie. The two of us continue chatting busily in our habitual non-stop way, while Derek, as usual, contributes little or nothing.

Elaine has some news.

"No more *Pop* for us, me and Joe. We've managed to find a wee bedsit in Sauchiehall Street. The Charing Cross end, not far from the coffee stall. An' not far from you and Tommy either, just a couple of minutes' walk. Nice, eh?"

"That's great, Elaine, I'm really pleased for you."

"Oh, makes all the difference. Ah feel we're a proper couple now."

"How did you manage to afford it?"

I know Joe and Elaine live on next to nothing. And they are now having to find rent money instead of using the accommodation vouchers they get from the Labour Exchange.

"Well, it was a bit of luck. Joe's dole money was suddenly put up, no idea why. He gets ten or twelve quid a week now. Don't know how he managed it, but he's got a good line in patter, Joe has. Plays the poor wee boy, confused and bit backward, and they all feel sorry for him."

She leans back in her chair. "Unless he's lying to me, and he's sellin' his body on the quiet without lettin' on."

She smiles at the implausibility of this explanation.

I laugh too. Joe is a sweetheart; he's young, and not at all bad-looking; physically he is trim and neat. But the idea of simple Little Joe as *gigolo* is just too unlikely to consider.

When a brief lull arises in our conversation, Elaine changes the subject unexpectedly. She turns to Derek.

"Lovely hair you've got, Derek. Don't you think so, Audrey?"

I look at her, then at him.

"Oh yes. I've told him that before. Beautiful colour."

Derek looks up a little nervously and immediately turns red. He is rather shy, and blushes easily—in two seconds his face is about the same colour as his hair.

"Thanks," he mutters.

Elaine sips her lukewarm coffee, then looks up again. "What's it called?"

Derek frowns. "What do ye mean, what's it called?"

Elaine puts her cup down. "What does it say on the bottle?"

It takes Derek several seconds to catch up.

I am a bit surprised—it's unlike Elaine to be deliberately unkind. And poor Derek is hardly a fair target. He will be quite unable to deal with this, to come back with some equally pungent response.

But I have significantly underestimated him.

"Ye think ma hair's dyed?"

And he scrambles to his feet, positions himself directly in front of Elaine, unfastens his trousers, and pushes them down to his thighs. Oh dear—no underpants.

He pulls his shirt up to his navel.

"There, ya cheeky wee bastard!"

And indeed, as he implies, collar and cuffs are a perfect match.

"Seen enough?" he says to Elaine with a grin.

I imagine she has, as his cock is practically up her nose. For the very first time since I have known her, Miss Elaine Stewart is completely bereft of words.

The restaurant is not busy, but a good dozen lunchtime customers have been treated to the sight either of Derek's shapely backside or his flaming pubes, depending where they are sitting.

Elaine coughs, looks away, sips her coffee and tries unsuccessfully not to choke. Derek re-adjusts his clothing.

"Well, Miss Stewart," I say later, after he has left. "You certainly got your come-uppance there. And it served you right, winding him up like that. What were you thinking of?"

"Ah don't know. Ah mean—Ah *know* his hair's natural. Ah was just a bit bored, I suppose."

She looks at me, her brow wrinkled.

"Just imagine—the nerve of him, flashing the lot like that. And I always thought he was such a boring wee bugger."

"Yes—me too. Well, we got it wrong, it seems. More to Derek than meets the eye, obviously."

"Aye—much more. Ah mean—apart from the colour—did ye see the *size* of it?"

I'm pretty sure everyone did.

"Aye," says Elaine, as we get up to leave. "Who'd have thought it? No wonder Charlie's got that funny walk."

It is only a few days after this incident that we get some news. Charlie and Derek come round for a drink one evening, and they are not alone. With them is a pretty girl, no more than eighteen or nineteen. She is introduced as 'Vikki'; with two K's, it is made clear. What is not made clear is her position *vis-à-vis* Charlie and Derek. Not until she has left, that is.

Charlie looks at his watch. "Time ye were getting' off to work, Vikki, it's gone seven. Ten past, in fact."

Vikki, who has not said one word after the opening pleasantries, obediently rises and gets her coat.

"Careful now, hen, keep yer eyes open, Ah'll come down an' pick ye up about eleven, OK?"

"OK, Charlie. Bye, everybody."

With a bright smile, she leaves us.

"Nice girl," says Tommy after she has gone. "Pretty, too."

"Yes, very," I agree.

Then add, after a moment, "Where does she work—in a pub?"

"Yes, that's right," says Charlie.

Simultaneously, "No, she's a hoor," says Derek.

It turns out that Vikki is indeed a whore. And Charlie's 'girl-friend'.

"Oh?" says Tommy with a smile. "I thought Derek was your girl-friend?"

Derek blushes predictably, while Charlie says didactically and with perfect seriousness, "No, Derek's my *boy*-friend."

"Aye, an' Charlie's *my* girl-friend," sniggers Derek, having recovered his composure somewhat.

My suspicions as to the what-goes-where with these two are confirmed.

"That's a bit too complicated for me," I shrug. Shades of drug-addicted Geg, boy-friend Colin and girl-friend Valerie—also, as it happens a sometime lady of the streets. Is there a current fashionable trend here that I am missing?

It is eventually explained to us that there is nothing actually 'going on' between Charlie and Vikki.

"We just look after her," clarifies Derek.

'*Yes, and she looks after you. Financially,*' I think to myself.

No sooner have I considered this than, "Yes—and she looks after us, if you follow me," says Charlie.

As I had surmised.

"She takes her punters back to the flat. That's why me and him are always out in the evening."

Another familiar situation. Truly there is nothing new under the sun. Still, I console myself, I did it first.

I feel a bit sorry for Vikki—if she has to have a pimp, there have to be better options than mean and miserable Charlie.

I pour more drinks.

"Well, Charlie, you'd better be a wee bit careful. You don't want to be done for living off her immoral earnings, do you?"

He draws in his breath sharply.

"No, certainly not. But that's in hand. We're planning to get married, me and Vikki. In a week or two. Registry office."

I'm fairly sure that husbands can be charged with poncing just as anyone else can.

But Charlie has more to say.

"And we were wondering, Derek and me, if you and Tommy would be our witnesses?"

Over the next week I get to know Vikki rather better, and find out that she is not at all the unfortunate victim I had initially imagined she might be. She is sensible, practical, and down-to-earth. She has been working at her chosen profession since she was sixteen, apparently; and I am surprised to learn that she is actually twenty-three, not a teenager, as I had at first supposed. We become friends of a sort, and I get into the habit of going round to the flat she shares with her unlovely duo of kept men, to arrange her hair before she goes out on the late shift. Not that I am by any means expert, but she has long, thick hair, and I soon become skilled at styling it for her in 'the onion'—that is, piled up on top of the head, wide, with a smaller knot on top.

After we have discussed the matter, Tommy and I agree to act as witnesses for the wedding; but I have one condition. This is going to be a rather unusual affair. Consider the cast list: the bride is a streetwalker, the groom her pimp, and the best man his boyfriend. In addition, the witnesses are a couple of poofs, and the matron of honour is a colleague of Vikki's, a much older mistress of the pavements called Claire. So I tell Charlie that Tommy and I will be happy to oblige; but only if they agree to allow Wilma to act as bridesmaid.

Charlie is initially reluctant, indeed, a little indignant.

"Wilma? Aw, come on, George, you're treating this wedding as a joke."

I refrain from stating the obvious. But decide that proposing Dame Margot as flower girl might be a step too far.

We gather outside the registry office on the day of the ceremony, shivering in the morning chill—it is January and there is snow on the ground. It has to be said that, despite the unusual composition of the wedding party, each of us has made an effort. Indeed, with the possible exception of Wilma, we probably don't look much different from any other group gathered to celebrate the union of two loving hearts.

Suits are the order of the day for the men. Tommy and I have had ours made for the occasion—three-piece, double-breasted, same colour, donkey brown, eight pounds a head. Vikki is in white, which is something of an irony, all things considered, although she contrives to look appropriately virginal, and I have taken particular care with her hair for her special day. Claire, forty-something, is in a very fetching mother-of-the-bride outfit in tangerine, with matching hat. Wilma is also featuring a hat, complete with a discrete veil, perched on top of her inevitable beehive, and is in a two-piece in an eyeball-burning electric blue.

The ceremony goes off smoothly enough. At the '*Do you take this man...*' moment, I catch Tommy's eye, and mouth, along with Vikki, '*I do*'. He grins, and does the same thing in his turn.

"Right," he says to me with a smile as we are signing the register, "I guess we're married now, eh?"

"Well, as married as we're ever going to be," I reply.

There is, sadly, no photographer.

The wedding breakfast is held in the rather insalubrious surroundings of the buffet and bar in Queen's Street station, where we are treated to pork pies and half-pints of lager. Typical of Charlie, who is, as I have mentioned, one of the meanest people on earth. He wouldn't give you, as the delightful Glasgow expression has it, the pickings from his nose.

Consequently, it gives me inordinate pleasure when I notice him drop a five pound note on the floor, and manage to get my foot on it before he realises what he has done. When I contrive to pick it up surreptitiously a little later, I catch Derek's eye on me. As I smuggle the purloined note into my pocket he gives me a grin and a broad wink.

It is he, too, who, some time later, gives me the true story behind his relationship with Charlie. The latter has always given the impression that he left the army in the usual way, having completed his term of service; and that he teamed up with Derek somewhere subsequently.

But no. Charlie, it appears, is actually a deserter. Derek was, and is, the son of a former army colleague. The two of them simply disappeared together from the barracks one night a few months ago and have been lying low ever since.

And Derek is not eighteen. In fact he has just turned fifteen. Technically, I suppose, they are on the run.

When I discuss this with Tommy, we decide it is probably best if we cool off our acquaintance with this unusual couple. We've already run afoul of the authorities once. These two are obviously heading for trouble, and we think it wiser not to risk being a part of it.

Disaster! My poor friends!
Really, if it weren't so sad it would be funny.
It is a Sunday afternoon in late January when they call around to pass on the news. Tommy and I haven't been up long—we tend to stay in bed as long as possible on a winter Sunday. It saves on heating, for one thing, and there are other benefits.

But we have had some breakfast. Still in my dressing gown, I am reading, and Tommy, fully dressed, is strumming on his guitar, getting to grips with diminished and augmented chords. Then the doorbell rings, and I go to see who it can be.

"Oh look," I say to Tommy as we come back into the room together. "It's Michael and Gordon. Isn't that nice?"

I am only being slightly ironic, I am actually quite happy to see them. Tommy won't be delighted to have our weekend interrupted, but he is too polite to make his feelings obvious.

"All right Michael? Gordon?" he says, putting down his guitar. "Cup of tea?"

Elaine's eyes are red. Angie, with a tragic face, sits down on the edge of the bed—we only have a couple of chairs, and are currently occupying them.

"No," she says. "Not alright at all, Thomas. Very far from it."

She turns to the other. "Tell them, Elaine."

Elaine starts to speak, but then gulps, and is unable to continue. She seems genuinely upset. Angie, on the other hand, appears more angry than anything else. She tuts.

"Really Elaine, pull yourself together please. This is not helping."

But Elaine appears to be incapable of obliging.

Angie sighs, perhaps a little theatrically. "Oh, very well, I suppose I'll have to do it."

I get up to put on the kettle.

"Here, Elaine, sit down, you look worn out," I say, indicating my seat. "OK, Gordon, spill. What's the matter?"

I arrange cups and so on. I know who has what in the milk and sugar line, no need to ask.

"It's our husbands. Hers and mine. Brian and Joe."

I put some tea into the pot and look up.

"Oh? What about them? Have they run off together and left you two widowed?"

Highly unlikely, but not, I suppose, entirely impossible.

Angie takes out a cigarette. "No. But it might be better if they had."

Elaine seems to have recovered somewhat. She sits down in the seat I have vacated. "Give us a fag, Ange, Ah'm gasping."

Angie obliges somewhat reluctantly.

The kettle boils and I prepare the tea.

"Oh well, come on, don't keep us in suspenders—what is it?"

Angie takes a huge breath and adopts a tone of high drama.

"They're in jail. Both of them."

"What?" and "In jail?" Tommy and I say simultaneously.

"Exactly," says Angie, with an air almost of satisfaction; she is probably congratulating herself on having thoroughly punctured our somnolent Sunday afternoon complacency.

"Well!" I say. "Look, just let me finish with this tea and you can tell us everything."

Angie lights up. I hand out the cups of tea, and we all make ourselves comfortable.

Elaine sips. "You tell them, Angie, go on."

Angie raises her head and takes a draw on her cigarette.

"Well…"

It's a complicated business, but I eventually manage to understand at least roughly what has happened. Little Joe and Brian have been arrested for a swindle they have been operating through the bank where Brian is employed—the bank where Angie's father is, according to her, the manager. I'm not sure that I fully grasp all the details, but it goes something like this.

It seems that one of Brian's duties has been to post out new cheque books to the branch's clients when their current one was nearly used up. Before committing the book to the post, he would look at the branch's records to ascertain the credit on the account, and the pattern of withdrawals by cheque. If he considered this particular account suitable, he would remove a cheque and it's counterfoil carefully from near the back of the book, fill it in, date it, sign it, copying as well as he could the specimen signature held in the branch's files, and pass it on to Joe.

It was then Joe's job to go to another large branch of the same bank, preferably one fairly distant, and present it to one of the tellers, saying that he worked nearby, and had an arrangement at that branch to cash cheques. A not uncommon situation, apparently.

The cashier is supposed to ensure that this arrangement is on record, but Brian had realised, from watching the goings-on at his own place of employment, that very often no check is made, and the teller simply hands over the cash. Particularly when the branch is busy, perhaps at lunchtime, or on a Friday; and especially if the figure is relatively small. Joe was instructed to make himself scarce immediately if there appeared to be any suspicion or difficulty, and they were careful to make out the cheques for comparatively low amounts, maybe five or ten pounds at a time, no more. Their expectation was that affluent customers would be unlikely to notice these small withdrawals, and it's easy to overlook the missing cheque in the book.

All had gone smoothly for a time. Joe only occasionally had to leg it from a branch when it appeared that the clerk was taking an undue interest in his credentials, and between them they had managed to scam a couple of hundred pounds which they split between them.

Now I understand how Joe and Elaine come to be living in a comfortable bedsit at Charing Cross instead of at the Popular Hotel for the last few weeks.

I can see myself that this scheme is over complex and full of possible pitfalls, and that it is the kind of thing that should only be worked for short periods at a time. If Brian had been smarter, I'm sure he could have found some safe method of getting his hands directly on cash without leaving a trail.

"So how did they come to get caught?" asks Tommy.

Angie shakes her head. "Don't know exactly, Thomas. Joe was the fall guy, he was the one that got his collar felt. The kite he was trying to cash led back to Brian's branch, and it didn't take much working out to finger Mister Big."

Wow! 'the fall guy'? 'his collar felt'? 'the kite'? 'finger Mr Big'?

"That'll be the same Mister Big who's been fingering you for the last couple of months, I imagine?"

Angie gives me a poisonous look. I pinch a cigarette from her pack.

"Well," I say as I light up, "you told me you always wanted to be a gangster's moll, Ange. And you certainly seem to have got the dialogue down pat."

She still says nothing.

"You'll be going up to visit, naturally?"

She is aghast. "I most certainly will *not*! Me, prison visiting? Who do you think I am, Elizabeth Fry? God, if I did, and it got about…"

Elaine interrupts. "Well, Ah'll be goin' up tae see Joe. They'll be on remand, the two of them—Ah can take him cigarettes an' stuff. Maybe you'll come with me, Audrey? If you don't mind, that is?"

"No, I don't mind at all, Elaine, glad to keep you company."

There is a pause. Tommy looks at Angie.

"I thought you said you loved him, Gordon. Brian, I mean."

She is slightly flustered. "Well, I do, Thomas. Or rather, I did. But come on, there are limits."

I can't help remembering how Brian served his last sentence without the benefit of visits—my fault, on that occasion. So it immediately becomes my goal to coerce Angie into playing the convict's faithful and devoted wife in spite of her delicate scruples.

It isn't too difficult to persuade her in the end. It's obvious she actually wants to see Brian, if only to have the opportunity to screech at him for his stupidity. And despite her reservations, I can tell she is curious to see what it's like to play this novel role. I too am quite interested to have the experience of actually being inside a prison. I have been in a police cell briefly, but I don't imagine it's the same thing at all.

The three of us arrange to meet up on the following Friday. Tommy will be working, and anyway, he has no interest in accompanying us.

"No thanks, seen enough of jails tae last me a lifetime. Enjoy yourselves, and give the boys my best. Have fun."

Angie warns me that she will be coming lightly disguised.

"Well, imagine if someone I know saw me there—I'd never be able to live it down. No, Audrey, I will have to give this some thought, try to change my look at least a little."

"Who do you imagine is going to see you? And even if they did, who's going to care?"

"It's all very well for you, Audrey, with your bohemian lifestyle, but some of us have a reputation to maintain. No, if I'm going to go—and I suppose I really should—I will have to find some way to alter my appearance."

"And your behaviour, too," I add.

I remember Billy's concern about unwelcome prison visits from scarlet queens.

She looks at me in some amazement.

"My *behaviour*? Really, Audrey, I can't think what you mean."

"Well, for a start, it might be better if you were to call me George instead of Audrey."

She raises her eyebrows. "Well, naturally I shall. And I shall call Elaine William, of course."

I look at her in disbelief. "Well, you can if you like. But his name is Michael."

She appears a little distracted; no doubt wondering what particular modifications to her image she should undertake.

"Hm, yes, Michael. That's what I meant."

I come to the conclusion that Angie has a point, and that I, too, ought to change my appearance to some extent, and adopt a rather more 'man in the street' image for this particular outing. So—it's hair in a side parting, no makeup, ordinary jeans and shirt, and a donkey jacket that belongs to Tommy.

When we rendezvous in the town centre, Angie examines me critically

Her face folds into a grimace. "My God, Audrey, what on earth… You look like an amiable lesbian. If there is such a thing."

I am too stunned by her own appearance to give this remark the withering retort it merits. OK, I was prepared to see her looking a bit different. Perhaps a little more quietly dressed than usual, perhaps some kind of headgear. So I am not surprised by the black-framed glasses.

It's the moustache that does it.

"Wow, Ange," I breathe. "Where on earth did that come from? The moustache, I mean?"

In a strange way, it rather suits her. Maybe because it covers a lot of her mouth.

"Off one of the shop window dummies. We display *artistes* have access to lots of useful bits and pieces."

She turns her head to one side and poses.

"Like it?"

I look at it again. One slight problem is that the moustache is uncompromisingly dark, whereas her hair is light brown. Even so…

"What do you think, Audrey? The truth, now."

She hesitates.

"Do I look ridiculous?"

I consider.

"No, not ridiculous. In fact, to be honest, it quite suits your face. Maybe you should think about growing a real one?"

She shudders.

"Oh, Audrey, come on. As if I would contemplate facial hair!"

The truth is that it transforms her. I suddenly see Angie as she would look as a manly man. And that is a sight I never expected to witness.

"How does it stay on?" I say, leaning forward. "I mean, how do you attach it?"

She touches it gingerly. "It has these two little things that go up your nose."

I look more closely, and see what she means. Two small prongs at the top fit inside her nostrils, and presumably grip. But you can only see them if you look extremely closely. The general effect is natural enough, if rather bushy.

"But isn't it uncomfortable? And is it secure?"

She sniffs and the fake moustache twitches slightly to one side.

"Well, it's a *leetle* prickly, but not too bad, you get used to it. And I've stuck it above my lip with some spirit gum too, just to be sure it stays in place."

She pauses and reaches up to check its siting.

"Are you sure it's OK?"

"Yes, Angie, really, it's very good."

I don't mention that the effect might have been better if she was not wearing quite so much mascara; and if she had found a pair of spectacles that actually had glass in them.

Just at that moment, Elaine trots round the corner. Her mouth drops open.

"Good God, Angie, who have you come as? Groucho Marx?"

I'm at a bit of a loose end. We have passed through the preliminaries, signed the appropriate papers, had our bags of goodies—mainly cigarettes and sweets—checked out for contraband, and are seated in the shabby visiting room. Painted in the familiar Institution Green, it has scarred wooden tables with hard metal chairs. Warning notices festoon the walls, and the whole place reeks of misery and despair.

There are about twenty tables in all for the visitors—couples, friends, families with children, both sexes, most races, all classes. Angie and Brian sit holding hands—obviously Brian now feels secure enough in these surroundings not to have to concern himself with any possible damage to his masculine image. At a separate table sit Elaine and Joe, whispering, heads together.

I move from one to the other. The visiting time allowed is an hour. I have read all the notices on the wall. I have eaten an apple—one Elaine had brought for Joe. I have smoked two cigarettes.

I am thoroughly bored. I wish I'd thought to bring a book.

I look at my watch. Still half an hour to go.

I head over to Elaine's table and sit down.

She looks up.

"Good news, George. Joe's just been telling me he might get bail. It seems his solicitor is trying to shift the responsibility onto Brian, sayin' it was all his scheme—which it *was*—sayin' Joe wis just conned into it, sayin' he didnae know what it was all about. What do you think?"

Honestly? I think not. But I haven't the heart to say what I really think.

"Let's hope so. But—would you be able to raise the money for bail?"

Joe nods. "Aye. Ah wis jist tellin' Michael that ma share of the cash is planked away—aboot a hundred pounds. Ah've telt him where it is. That'll be enough for bail. An' tae keep oor place on for a while. Maybe until Ah get oot?"

I try to look enthusiastic. "Good, Joe, good thinking. Fingers crossed, eh?"

I endeavour to sound light-hearted. But this sad optimism, in my view unwarranted, is depressing.

They are immediately engrossed in one another again. I look at my watch.

I get up.

"Fancy a cup of tea?"

In one corner is a little counter that sells tea and coffee, along with sweets and snacks.

"Aye, great, Audrey, thanks," says Joe. "Sorry, George, Ah mean."

I get five teas from the counter and take two of them over. I carry my own cardboard cup and the two others to the table where Angie and Brian are sitting.

"Thanks, George," says Brian.

"Oh—could I have coffee please, Audrey? George? One sugar."

'Typical,' I think. *'Fucking pest.'*

"OK."

I get Angie a coffee and carry it back to the table.

"There you are, *Gordon!*"

"Thanks, Audrey."

Oh, for Christ's sake!

She reaches out a hand and takes the steaming cup from me, then sets it down on the table.

I manage to contain my irritation, and sit down next to them.

It takes me a moment to realise that Angie has her other hand stretched under the table and is doing something I'd rather not think about too closely to Brian. Considering the width of the table and the length of her arms, it can't be much more than squeezing his knee. But I wish she wouldn't, all the same.

I look again at my watch. Still twenty minutes to go.

I yawn. Nothing of any interest is being said. Must find a topic for conversation.

"So—what do you think of the moustache, Brian?" I try gamely.

He looks across at me and grins.

"Well, Ah usually prefer ma ladies clean shaven, but… aye, quite suits him, Ah suppose."

Conversation falters again. I guess I am a bit of a gooseberry here, definitely *de trop*.

"Oh, George," says Brian. "Meant tae mention—Ah've got that photey in ma cell—remember, the one Ah pit up last time? The one of you an' me thegither?"

"Oh—right," I say.

"Ah feel Ah've got a bit of company wi' that there. Hope ye don't mind?"

"No, not at all." I look at my friend. "But Gordon might not be too happy about that."

Angie purses her lips. The moustache twitches a little.

She nods and it wobbles a bit.

"Exactly, Audrey, George," she says. "I'm glad to see you are not totally devoid of sensitivity."

She turns to Brian. "I will see that you get one of me to replace it with. I mean, I know that you and her were an item for a while, but things have changed. It's hardly appropriate."

A fair comment.

"So you will have my photo to drool over instead. I will attend to it."

"Without the moustache, I hope?" sniggers Brian.

"Well, *netcherlee*, Brian."

She permits herself a tight little smile, picks up her cup, and sips.

I look at her. And am fascinated to see that the steam from the hot coffee is having an unanticipated effect.

As I watch, the moustache slowly begins to slide down her upper lip. She seems unaware of this at first. Until it finally detaches itself completely, and with a soft 'plop', drops into her cup.

I hug myself with delight. And have to double over when, with an unladylike, '*Oh, fuck it*!', she fishes it out and pushes it, dripping, back into place.

Brian's reaction mirrors mine. Both of us lean forward clutching our stomachs. He has to bang his fist on the table in an effort to control his hilarity.

Which brings over one of the guards.

"Everything awright here?" he says.

"Yes, fine, pal, fine, just havin' a laugh, somethin' ma mate here wis sayin'," says Brian, still convulsed.

"Yes, thank you, officer," says Angie, one hand still holding the moustache in place, trying to reattach it.

"OK then. Just keep the noise doon a bit, eh?" says the guard.

"Yes, sorry," I say as he moves away.

"Fucking thing!" says Angie, still trying to poke the prongs up her nose.

Too far up, it appears; because the next thing, she lets out a huge, '*Ehtchoo!*', and the damned thing shoots off her face and lands in front of a lady sitting at the next table. The latter looks down at it curiously.

"Oh, fucking *bow-lox*!" says Angie, reaching over to retrieve it.

Brian collapses forward, his head in his hands. I get to my feet. I can feel the beginnings of a rising hysteria that I know I simply will not be able to quell. I fear I might actually wet myself.

Angie looks up. She is still fiddling with the moustache. I realise that she has now managed to poke the left-hand clip up her right nostril. That does it.

"I'm sorry," I force out, gritting my teeth. "I can't stay. Sorry, I've really got to go. Excuse me. See you outside, Gordon."

I need some fresh air. I turn and flee.

But getting out of Barlinnie is not as easy as getting in. After I leave the visiting room and enter the reception area, I have to wait to be released by one of the prison officers, and they appear to be in no hurry. Three of them, uniformed, lounge round a desk in the middle of the anteroom, chatting, reading newspapers, drinking tea and smoking. Just like normal people, more or less. I tap my foot on the floor, impatiently.

Eventually, one of them looks up and registers that I am waiting. He nudges a colleague.

"Somebody wantin' the gate, Alan. Let him oot, will ye, you've goat the keys, Ah think?"

The one addressed turns round in my direction. He gets up. He looks at me without seeing me.

But I see him.

Oh my God! Suddenly I am not in such a hurry to make my escape.

Instead I turn and head back in the direction of the visiting room.

"Oh, sorry—I think I forgot my cigarettes."

I pass him, muttering, "Love a man in uniform."

As I push open the door, he looks after me, frowning in puzzlement. He doesn't seem to have recognised me. My disguise must be more convincing than I realised.

I tear over to the table where Angie has finally managed to re-attach her peripatetic adornment to her upper lip.

I grab her arm.

"Quick, Angie, quick—you have to come with me now. Right now, no time to waste."

She looks up. "Right *now*? What do you mean, *George*?" She looks at her watch. "We've still got *ages*. Well, fifteen minutes. What's the matter?"

I crouch down beside her. I keep my voice low.

"Angie, trust me, this won't wait. You won't regret it, I promise. It'll only take a minute. You can come back in here afterwards if you want."

She gets to her feet, sighing, with some reluctance.

"*Really*, Audrey!"

"Angie, *now!*"

She glares at me.

"Oh God, you're so *uncamp*."

"*Please.*"

"OK, if you *insist*."

She turns back to the table. "Sorry Brian, but…"

"Yes, sorry, Brian," I say, pulling her after me, dragging her in the direction of the door.

As we pass Elaine, she looks up.

"You going, you two?"

"It's OK, Michael, I'll wait for you outside," I call, not stopping.

"Really, Audrey, this had better be worth it," grumbles Angie as we reach the door to the reception area.

"Oh, it will be, I promise you."

I turn the handle, pull the door wide, and we both hustle through.

The three guards are back round their table.

"Oh, two of you now, is it?" says the one who had spoken to me earlier. "Mr Fraser, let these two oot, if ye don't mind."

The one in charge of the keys gets up again and heads in out direction. As he passes, he glances at us, and indicates the gate with a twitch of his head.

I elbow Angie in the ribs.

She doesn't react. I tread on her foot.

"Ow, Audrey, do you mind?"

God, she's so *slow*. I'm going to have to do this myself,

"How are you, Mr Fraser?" I say. "How are things with you, Al?"

Angie turns to me, her mouth dropping open like an oven door on its hinge.

She turns back. There is a pause. 'Pregnant' doesn't do it justice.

"*Ell*?" she squeaks. "Is that you?"

There is no question. The uniform alters his appearance somewhat. But there is no mistaking those pudgy features and no concealing that prominent spare tire, however belted in it may be. Angie ups the volume.

"*Ell*!" she screeches.

At this, the other two officers look over, no doubt wondering what is going on.

I will, I decide, leave this one to Angie.

But Mr Fraser is not, it appears, prepared to go down without a fight. He grins agreeably at us, in that oh-so-familiar way.

"Sorry—dae Ah know ye?"

The 'Canadian' accent is now pure Glasgow.

Angie's mouth snaps shut. Then opens again. She leans towards him.

"Do you *what*? Do you *know* me?" Her voice drips acid.

She reaches up, grips the moustache, and rips it from her face. It makes the same sound as a firmly attached Elastoplast.

She gives a little shriek. She looks up at him.

"There. Know me *now*, do you?"

Of course, he does. His eyes dart everywhere.

But I have to give him credit, he is pretty good.

After a moment, he shakes his head, "Sorry pal, never seen ye before. Least, Ah don't think Ah have."

The officer I take to be the boss gets to his feet.

"Some problem over there?"

I turn round and smile, shaking my head.

"No, officer, everything's fine. Just a little question of identity."

I grab Angie's arm. I look back at Al.

"We'll be going now, thanks."

Al nods. "OK. Sorry again."

He shrugs. "Ah suppose Ah must have a double."

He's a cool customer; but the relief in his voice is palpable.

He takes out a bunch of keys and proceeds to unlock the massive gate.

"But Audrey…" croaks Angie in my ear.

"Say nothing," I whisper. "Nothing."

The portal swings wide.

"We'll be in touch, Al. Soon," I murmur over my shoulder, as I drag my friend through the gate.

It slams shut behind us, and we can hear multiple locks being re-engaged.

Angie has a frustrated and baffled expression on her face.

"But Audrey… Why…? I mean, I was ready to *cleanse* him in front of his—well, his friends, his colleagues. Why did you stop me?"

I link my arm through hers.

"Because that way it would all be over too quickly. Maybe a little embarrassing for him at the time. But you know how devious he is, he'd manage to laugh it off, say you were just a nutter, something like that, talk his way out of it. No, that won't do. He needs to be made to suffer long-term."

"Hmm… Yes…" says Angie doubtfully.

"And he will. He won't have a moment's peace from now on. He'll be permanently unsure; he'll worry himself sick about when the blow is going to fall. A letter, a phone call… He won't know what to expect or when to expect it. Think, Angie. It's perfect this way, much better than yelling at him."

She frowns. Then gradually a grin breaks over her face.

"Yes, of course. Clever of you, Audrey."

I can see it all taking shape, the plan, the punishment, nemesis following hubris.

"Then we leave it for a while, say, a month. Just time for him to start relaxing again, to think that he's got away with it, that there's going to be no come-back. That's when we write or phone—a letter would be my choice, but it's up to you"

"A letter, yes, brilliant, a letter to his boss from the victim of his deceit. To the prison governor," breathes Angie, nodding, "the highest authority."

"And in the meantime—just to keep things bubbling—we'll tell Brian and Joe all about it. They will spread the word round the jail. His life in there will be hell. His reputation will be ruined. As he deserves."

She nods again. "Yes, just as you say. Yes, great."

She pauses. "He's a *bastard*!"

"Yes, he is, a total bastard."

Elaine re-joins us; visiting time is over, it appears. The other friends and relatives pile out of the heavy barred gate and disperse. As the three of us walk towards the bus stop, I give Elaine the lowdown on recent events.

"No!" she says. "Imagine that! Thon Al's a screw?"

"Well, as to his sexual habits, you'd have to ask Angie."

The latter tuts. "A *screw*, Audrey. A prison guard. A warder."

"Oh, right, I see. A screw, eh?"

I quite like thinking of Al as a 'screw'. It's his turn. *The Turn of the Screw*, in fact.

Elaine grins and nods. "Aye, poor bugger. Once the word gets about in the jail…"

She draws in a breath and shakes her head. "He'll have to apply for a transfer tae another nick. When the cons find out about his little games—an' Ah'll make sure Joe knows the whole story, tell him tae put it aboot—his life won't be worth living in there."

"A transfer? Where could he go?"

"Aberdeen, Inverness, Edinburgh—who knows?" Elaine smiles smugly. "But it disnae matter where he goes. Cons always end up back inside, one jail or another. Sooner or later somebody who knows him from in here will turn up and spread the word."

How gratifying. "Good. That's just what he deserves. Someone putting it about."

"Aye," Elaine smiles. "It might even be me."

Angie has not been taking part in this exchange. Something is occupying her mind. Must be something small, there's not a lot of room in there.

"And did you notice, Audrey, his accent? Pure Glasgow. What happened to the Canadian? He must have been putting that on the whole time."

She is astonishingly obtuse sometimes.

"Well, yes, Angie, *obviously* he was!"

I reflect for a moment. "You know, you'll say it's hindsight and all that, but he always *did* sound a bit phony, a bit exaggerated. Canadian? Remember my Johnny? He *was* Canadian. But Al's accent had more than a hint of 'Miz Scawlett' about it."

Angie laughs. "Yes, now you mention it. '*Ah* lurve *Edin-borrow, honey*'. Yes, you're right, Audrey. You might describe him as '*Con with the Wind*'."

Angie does come up with some marvellously funny lines now and then. This one gets just the rousing reaction it deserves.

Later, when we are waiting at the bus stop, she looks down at her hand. "Now, to change the subject—what do I do with this?"

'This' is the fake moustache, by now somewhat the worse for wear.

I shrug. "Stick it in your pocket. Stick it up your nose."

Elaine chimes in. "Or stick it up… "

"Oh, Elaine, don't be so *uncamp*!"

The residents at 43 Buccleuch Street are not nearly as fascinating a bunch as were my fellow tenants at 39 Carnarvon Street. The landlady has the second floor. On the first floor, room one, are a pair of university bods, dull, studious types, and, room two, a couple of girls, friends who work in the city, one a secretary, the other a hairdresser. An elderly lady, a widow with two cats, is in the other room near us, on the ground floor. Occasionally one or other of the cats pops in to say 'hello' and enjoy a saucer of something. That's fine, I like cats.

The only mildly interesting neighbours we have are in the basement. It is rented by two American sailors who are only occasionally in residence. They turn up every second or third weekend, get thoroughly sloshed, and roll home around midnight, usually with a couple of screeching and giggling girls in tow. They are both tall and good-looking young men, early twenties maybe, and unmistakably American in their style and dress. We only see them now and then; when we do they are perfectly pleasant. Indeed, by comparison with most other people we know, unfailingly polite and well-mannered.

It's a Friday evening, and I am preparing dinner, waiting for Tommy to get in from work. Steak and chips—yes, by this stage I can cope with chips. When he arrives home, just after six, he is carrying something.

"What's that?" I say, looking at the bag he is holding. It looks like an over-sized brief case in black leather. I think it's actually what they call a 'Gladstone Bag'. Obviously expensive, the leather is not shiny, but dull, matte, and oozes quality. It has a large and intimidating lock and a soft carrying handle; and tooled initials on the front.

"Found it," he says.

"You found it? Where?"

He sets it down on the table.

"Nice, isn't it?" he says, stepping back to allow me a better view.

I look at it. "Yes, it's lovely. Must be worth a bit. But where did you find it?"

He looks away. "Oh, on the doorstep."

"On our doorstep? Here, I mean? Our house?"

"Yes. It was just sitting there. At the street door."

I hesitate. He starts fiddling with the lock.

"It must belong to someone."

He looks up. "Of course it does. It belongs to us. Now."

"But… We can't just *keep* it, Tommy. Someone will be looking for it."

He continues poking around at the lock.

"We'll just have to make sure they don't find it then, won't we?"

I am not sure about this. I am no stranger to dishonesty, indeed, no stranger to petty crime. But this seems to me to be a bit—well, blatant.

He finally manages to force the lock open. He pulls the two sides of the top apart and we look inside.

Treasure trove!

Two one litre bottles of drink, one Bacardi and one vodka; two cartons of cigarettes, two hundred in each; some papers and a passport; and forty pounds in cash.

I draw in my breath.

"Tommy, we can't keep this…"

There is a knock at the door of our room.

Immediately Tommy snaps the sides of the bag together, picks it up and pushes it under our bed. Then he goes over and opens the door.

It is one of the American guys, tall, blond, and worried.

"Hey, sorry to disturb you, man, but have you seen a handbag? Black one? Left it on the doorstep while I went to pay my cab. Came back two minutes later and it's gone."

It's the word 'handbag' that nearly has me in nervous stitches. But Tommy doesn't react to it.

He scratches his head and shakes it from side to side.

"Naw, sorry, pal. Ah've just come in from work, an' there was nothing on the step when I arrived."

He turns to me. "You see anything, George?"

I shake my head dumbly, 'no'.

"Shit man, got all my papers in it, other stuff too."

He turns to go. "Thanks anyway. Guess some bastard in the street must have taken it. Teach me, eh?"

"Erm—you should ask the landlady—sorry, don't know your name?" I say, moving towards the door.

"It's Todd," he says, turning back. "Yes, I'll do that."

"She might have seen something, you never know. Or maybe one of the other tenants might have brought it in. For safety?"

"Yes, you're right."

"Good luck, pal," says Tommy. "Hope you find it."

He reaches for the door handle.

"Thanks," says Todd. "Once again, sorry to have bothered you."

"No problem, pal, any time," says Tommy, closing the door.

Within a fortnight the booze is drunk, the cigarettes smoked and the cash spent.

Remains the bag. I suggest to Tommy he gets rid of it, dumps it somewhere.

"No, no, it's real good quality gear. Might be able to sell it."

"Well, at least get it out of here," I say. "Take it to your mum's, or into work, or somewhere."

"Yes, good idea. I'll do that."

He puts it back under the bed. And we both forget about it completely.

February 1964

Joe's bail is refused, which doesn't surprise me. Elaine tells me this the next time she comes round. And a trial date has been set. Joe and Brian will appear in court in ten days' time.

"Ah'm hopin' he'll only get a light sentence, Audrey. Ah would like to think it might be only a fine. But of course, it's not his first offence, so Ah suppose Ah'm kiddin' myself."

I feel desperately sorry for Elaine. Due to the ill-gotten gains Joe has left her, she has been able to keep on their bedsit. But that money won't last forever. I resolve that when it does run out, I will help her if I can. I've still got some of the proceeds of my own criminal past left. She has managed to better her life a bit, and I would hate to see her slide back to the dubious comforts of *The Popular Hotel*.

"Aye, maybe just six months or so with any luck. The other one, Brian, he's got a record as long as your arm, he'll probably get a couple of years. But Joe—well, whatever he gets, I'll wait for him, so Ah will."

Poor Elaine. So decent, so loyal, so honest.

"Good for you, Elaine. Look, I'll pop round to your place later tonight and we can have a chat, OK? Have the kettle on."

"Thanks, Audrey, I'd appreciate the company."

Angie, on the other hand, seems quite ready to forget Brian altogether. When I next see her I have to tease her.

"You'll be going up to see him again, Ange? At least, I hope you will."

"Oh yes, Audrey, certainly. Not sure when I can manage it, though. I'll wait and see how much time he gets—maybe they'll just smack his wrist, what do you think?"

"You can forget that, Angie. Elaine thinks he might get a couple of years."

Her mouth drops open. "A couple of *years*?"

"Naturally, you'll wait for him?"

She doesn't know what to say. "Well—a couple of *years*, you said?"

Her face assumes a thoughtful expression. "Do you think I should? Wait, I mean?"

In truth, I don't think she should at all. Brian is obviously headed for a full-time career in criminality in the future. Nice guy in many ways, funny, sexy, good-looking, kind, and not, in a day-to-day sort of way, a bad person.

But there is no future with him for Angie. She has enough problems as it is.

"No, Angie, I don't think you should."

She lets out a sigh, maybe of relief. "Oh, good, Audrey. I was hoping you'd say that."

"But I think it's only fair that you should tell him so. Go up and see him again, explain. After he's been sentenced."

"Could I not just send him a rubber johnnie?"

I smile. "You mean a 'Dear John', Angie; a goodbye letter."

"Yes," she says, "that's right, a 'Dear John'. Trust you to know the prison slang, Audrey. Maybe that'll do, eh?"

I shake my head. "No. He would hate that. There's nothing else for it, Ange, you'll have to go and see him, tell him."

She nods a little reluctantly. "Yes, OK, I'll do that. You'll come with me, won't you?"

I remember the last prison visit.

"No," I say. "You're on your own this time."

Her face drops. "Oh Audrey—and you used to be such a *fun* person! Oh, say you will!"

I am deaf to her pleas.

"No. And when you do go, Angie, I have a suggestion. Lose the moustache."

Elaine's predictions turn out to be spot on. Brian gets two years and Joe six months.

"He'll only serve four, Joe, wi' time off for good behaviour. He'll be out for the summer."

"And you'll wait? Ever faithful?"

There seems no doubt in her mind.

"Oh yes."

I ring the bell.

It is late, maybe eleven. Tommy and I have been out to the cinema, and I have called round to see Elaine on my way home. He has work the next day and has decided to have an early night.

"You don't mind if I look in and say 'hello' to Elaine, do you?" I say.

"No, not at all," he replies. "Just be as quiet as you can coming in, OK? Try not to wake me up."

He grins. "Well, unless you feel you need something."

Elaine welcomes me, and we mount the three flights of stairs to her room, which is on the top floor, hard under the eaves.

I am surprised to see that she is not alone. There's someone in her bed, someone who is snoring softly.

"Who's that?" I say, looking over. "In the bed?"

She follows my gaze.

"Oh, it's that Big Robert. You know him? Landscape gardener, only in the town now and then. Seen him before?"

I approach the bed.

Yes, I know Robert. He's the guy who battered Brenda Lee when she threw a pint of beer over him. A big husky guy, maybe thirty, not bad-looking, very masculine, but gentle and polite. He has actually chatted me up a time or two, but never when I happened to be free.

I am a little surprised to see him in Elaine's bed after her protestations of eternal fidelity. But not too surprised. I am perfectly familiar with queenly frailty.

"Oh?" I raise my eyebrows. "I thought you were going to wait for Joe?"

"I am, I am. Robert here was just drunk and couldn't get home, asked me if Ah could put him up."

"Oh, really?" I say, with a grin.

"Yes, *really*!"

"Hm."

She fixes me with a gimlet stare.

"Don't judge me by your own standards, please, Audrey."

She is completely in the right. I look down. There is a moment's silence.

"Sorry, Audrey, I shouldn't have said that, forgive me."

I say nothing.

"Cup of tea?"

I have to smile. "Yes please, Elaine, thanks. And I'm sorry for doubting you."

We settle down companionably to our tea.

"Mind you, Elaine, I've heard that he's—well—how can I put this?—that he's remarkably well-endowed, that Robert."

She grins slyly.

"Oh aye, he is."

I look up. "What? How do you know? I thought you just said—"

"I did. But, like I said, he was drunk, and Ah had tae help him get undressed. And, well, ye can't help noticing."

"No, I suppose you can't."

I am bursting with curiosity, but don't want to be obvious.

"And—were you impressed?"

Elaine roars with laughter. "Ah certainly was."

She looks at me. She nods.

"You want to see for yourself, don't you?"

I shake my head, '*No*', and make a dismissive gesture. But Elaine is not fooled.

She laughs again. "Oh, come on, Miss Hepburn, admit it, yer dying tae have a look—anyway, he's unconscious, he'll never know that you've learned the secret of his success."

She gets up and walks over to the bed. Slightly embarrassed, I follow her.

Robert is certainly deeply asleep. He snores gently and lies there on his back, one arm flung over the covers, the other tucked under them.

Elaine pulls the bedclothes aside carefully and reverently, as if she were about to reveal the Holy Grail to a crowd of devoted worshippers.

He is naked. She tuts.

"Oh, damn," she says. "He's got his hand over it!"

I look down. I snigger.

"Yes. And his hand's not really big enough."

Elaine carefully takes the offending hand and moves it gently to one side. And poor, insensible Robert's private charms are fully exposed to the vulgar gaze.

I can't help but notice that he is heavily muscled all over—no doubt due to all that landscape gardening. But it is the specific part in question that holds my attention.

"My God," I say after a moment. "The dick of death."

"Yes, it is, isn't it? I could never—well, you know what I mean. I don't think anyone could. Ah mean—could you?"

"Eh? Me? No—no way."

With an equal veneration, Elaine re-veils the prodigy, and we return to our seats.

Pensive, we sip our tea.

"Ah mean, Joe's no' short in that department, but, all the same…"

"Yes."

I have seen Joe naked on a few occasions, and despite his weedy physique, it is true that he has no reason to feel short-changed in that particular area.

"But that thing, Audrey. Imagine what it's like when it's—you know—up. Ah mean, the size of it—what could you do?"

I shake my head.

"No idea—throw your arms round it and cry?"

I meet up with Elaine again the next day.

"Your guest gone, then?" I say.

"Oh yes, he was up and off first thing this morning," she says brightly. "Had to go to work. A bit hung over, he was, but I gave him a cup of tea, some toast and a fag, and he was fine."

"That all you gave him?" I say.

Elaine, unlike me, is essentially honest.

"OK, Audrey. So Ah gave him a wee wank in the morning, so what? Just couldn't refuse."

I raise my eyebrows. "Oh? A hand-job? That's all? Nothing more?"

She hesitates for a moment.

"Oh, all right, Miss Hepburn, yes. Yes, lips *were* applied. But that was it."

She looks at me, suddenly worried.

"But promise me you'll never tell Joe, Audrey, please."

I laugh. "I promise—your secret's safe with me. As I know mine is with you."

"Oh yes, it is. And the truth is, Audrey, at the end of the day, we're all size queens and slags."

She looks so seriously concerned, I hasten to reassure her.

"Don't worry, Elaine. It's not as if you… I mean, a blow-job, that's not *real* infidelity."

Yes, show me a nit and I can pick it; show me a hair and I can split it.

"Aye," says Elaine. "Trouble is, Ah should have been a bit less enthusiastic."

She moves her chin experimentally from side to side.

"Ah think Ah might have dislocated ma jaw."

11. We Gotta Get Out of This Place

> We gotta get out of this place
> If it's the last thing we ever do.
> We gotta get out of this place;
> Girl, there's a better life for me and you.
> *The Animals, 1965*

I haven't been able to stop thinking about it.

What had I said to Elaine?

'*Your secret's safe with me. As I know mine is with you.*'

Tommy and I are having our dinner. He is talking about work and his boss.

"He seems in a funny mood these days, Conrad. All smiles the one minute, grouchy as hell the next. Looks terrible too, bags under his eyes, smokin' like a chimney all the time. Maybe we should have a wee word wi' Nicky, make sure he's all right?"

My thoughts are elsewhere. Tommy carries on eating

"Sometimes I wonder if maybe he's got a drug problem, Conrad. Ah know he takes them now and then, pep pills, is it Purple Hearts they call them?"

He chews steadily. "These things can get out of hand. But Ah don't like tae ask in case Ah get ma head bitten off. Nicky's still goin' out with him, I take it?"

"Yes."

I am not really listening to him. I am hearing him, but there is a great lump in my throat. And it is trying desperately to get out. I can't swallow.

I have to tell. I put my knife and fork down with a clatter.

"You OK? What's the matter?" he says, looking up, concerned.

I just blurt it out. "I need to tell you something. I slept with somebody else. Months ago, Carnarvon Street. Not long before we moved in together. It was just the once."

Well, technically, it was just one encounter, if a rather protracted one. There. I've done it.

'*Now he'll leave. Maybe I will be able to get him back. Maybe I won't. But at least I know now where he lives, where he works, how to get hold of him, so I'll damned well try.*'

I can already hear in my mind the scrape of his chair as he stands up to go.

He looks at me.

"Yes, I know," he says calmly.

This is the last thing I expected to hear.

"What do you mean, you know? I mean, what do you know?"

Surely Elaine didn't tell him?

He continues to eat his food methodically. "Well, Ah don't know anythin' really. Not in detail. But I knew you'd been up to something. The way you were behaving. November time this was, I think, just before Wilma's party?"

I remember how I had been sure he would notice a difference in my behaviour. And then had congratulated myself that he hadn't.

I think back to when it was. November?

"Yes."

"You were on edge, nervous, not yourself."

He takes a sip of his tea. "But it wasn't until Ah saw the love-bite on the back of your neck that Ah was sure."

I push my plate away, puzzled. No, he's wrong there. Both Big Joe and I had agreed that there should be no physical record of our intimacy, for both our sakes. So what is he talking about?

"But—I didn't have a love-bite on my neck, Tommy. I'm sure I didn't."

He smiles.

"But you did. I know what a love bit looks like."

And suddenly the reality hits me. No, not Big Joe. Silly Sandra Dee climbing into my bed, a day or two before the Joe business happened. Yes, I remember how she had fastened herself to me like a limpet, and the trouble I had shaking her off.

But I decide not to explain. He knows the truth. The details are irrelevant. Oh, I am not out of the woods yet, I know, but for the moment he seems to be treating the situation as a kind of joke.

Is it possible he doesn't care? He *must* care. He must care, but also understand. A tall order, I know.

"Don't you care?" I say baldly.

He stares at me for a while and says nothing.

When he does speak his voice is low.

"Care? Ah was crazy with anger. Mad. More angry than Ah think I've ever been in ma life. I kind of wanted tae kill you. Ah'd half decided Ah was out of there, and not coming back. Ah was hurt as much as anything. All I could see was that you'd lied to me, in spite of all your '*I love you*' nonsense."

Some instinct tells me that this is a very good time to say nothing at all. I am astonished as much as anything to learn that he was suffering; and that I had been completely unaware. He had hidden it very well, but all the same, insensitive doesn't begin to cover it.

He has finished eating. He lights a cigarette.

"Then, later, after Ah'd left, I kept thinking about it. And bit by bit Ah began to wonder if it was maybe partly my own fault."

He stares at me intently.

"I knew how you felt about me. Or how you said you felt about me. And Ah knew you were waiting for me to tell you that I felt the same way about you. Which Ah did, and do. But I wouldn't say it."

I can feel my eyes pricking. Yes, the tears will be here right on cue any minute.

"So Ah made my mind up. I didn't want us to break up, not if there was some way round it. I waited for the right time, and made ma move. I hoped you'd tell me the truth one day, that you would be honest with me. It took you long enough. But in the end you did, you have. And Ah'm glad. So that's it settled, as far as I'm concerned."

"Settled? You mean, you forgive me?"

"Yes, I forgive you."

"Well, it was just..."

He stops me. "Ssh. I don't want details, we won't mention it again."

He puts out his cigarette, half-smoked.

"Just one thing. Ah'm hoping it wasn't that Brian guy."

Relief floods through me.

"No. No, it wasn't Brian, God, no. He was still in prison then, Brian."

I am so overcome, so amazed at the goodness and the good sense of this man I have been fortunate enough to capture that I am not paying very close attention to what I am saying.

"It was just a ship that docked, discharged its cargo, and sailed away."

"Eh?" He nearly chokes. "God, George, you certainly have a way with words!"

But he is smiling. I manage a watery smile too.

Are you thinking, '*There we are*'? The harvest is safely gathered in? Little Audrey, Happy At Last? True love, despite the obstacles, has finally found its reward?

This story is about many small things. But primarily it's an account of growing up, undergoing a rite of passage, like a hundred other stories. Starting lost and confused; gradually making a corner in the world and gaining confidence; passing from childhood to a kind of maturity; acting sometimes wisely, more often foolishly, but hopefully learning a few lessons along the way; making a few good friends and one or two good enemies, and not always being able to tell the difference between the two; and finally finding love and fulfilment, as we all hope to do.

This is at heart a love story. But it is perhaps not the love story you imagine it to be. It's my love story, but it's not Tommy's. Oh, his story forms a part of it, an important part. But we are dealing with a larger issue. It's the story of my love affair with the city of Glasgow. The gallus old whore who took me in when I saw myself as orphaned and alone, nurtured me in her generous bosom, held my hand while I took my first uncertain steps towards independence, and taught me by her own example how to carve out a niche for myself in a society which had appeared to have no place for me.

No love lasts forever. And my love affair with Glasgow will come to an end. But I'm afraid that you will have to bear with Audrey just a little longer, gentle reader, if you want to see that rupture finally take place.

March 1964

Who the hell is ringing our bell at one in the morning? Oh, we are not asleep, not even in bed. We were out for a drink Saturday night with Alec and Connie, got home around eleven. Just having a nightcap before turning in, music on the record player, not by any means pissed, but mildly merry.

Ring-ring.

Tommy stands up.

"Oh, just leave it, Tommy, probably some drunk on the way home from the pub, entertaining himself by disturbing decent, honest folk."

I yawn.

Long ring.

"I'd better see who it is, might be an emergency, somebody in trouble, you never know."

He heads towards the door.

"OK, but I bet it's just some idiot—maybe somebody who forgot their keys. Go and see, then."

But it is not some idiot. It is Elaine.

She is sheet white, trembling. Tommy has his arm round her shoulders as they come in.

She can barely speak. "Oh, Audrey, Tommy, thank God you're in. Ah don't know what Ah'd have done. Didn't know where to go, what to do."

I stand up. "For God's sake, Elaine, sit down, here, take my chair."

I turn to Tommy. "Get Michael a drink, there's some whisky in the cupboard."

He gets a glass.

"What's happened? What's the matter?"

I am thinking, '*She's had bad news. Something's happened to Joe, something bad, in prison.*'

Elaine sits with her face in her hands. Tommy pours her a whisky and passes it to her. She can barely hold it, her hands are shaking.

"Come on, Elaine, tell us what's wrong. Is it Joe, something to do with Joe?"

She looks up. "No, no, nothin' at all, went up tae see him yesterday, Joe. He's fine."

"So what is it? Did somebody die?"

She nods. "Yes. Nearly. Somebody nearly died. Me!"

I lean forward.

"Good God, Elaine, what happened? Did somebody attack you in the street or something? A gang of roughs maybe?"

"No, no."

I am becoming exasperated.

"So *tell* us! Tell us what happened."

Tommy glares at me. "Don't shout at him, George. Can you not see the state he's in?"

"Sorry, sorry," I say hastily. "Sorry, Michael. Whenever you're ready."

"Just let me finish this wee whisky, Audrey, OK?"

"Oh yes, go on."

We wait. It takes a second glass, but eventually Elaine calms down enough to give us the story.

"Just sittin' in ma room, reading the paper, still dressed, but thinkin' about going to bed—oh, did ye know, Brendan Behan died? The Irish playwright? Wrote that thing, *The Hostage*, remember, wi' a couple of queens in it?"

I shake my head impatiently.

"Aye, Rio Rita and Princess Grace they're called, saw it in London."

"Elaine!…"

"Sorry, sorry. OK, just sittin' there, and all of a sudden there's this bang, bang, bangin' at the door of the room, an' this voice shouts out, '*Famie, ya slag, open this fuckin' door or Ah'm warnin' you, ye'll be sorry.*'

"So Ah'm thinking, '*It's just yon head-banger from next door, pissed again, makin' an arse of himself. Got the wrong door.*' So Ah just decide tae ignore it. '*He'll go away in a minute*', Ah tell myself."

She takes another sip of her drink.

"But no, he keeps thumping the door wi' his fist. '*Euphemia, Ah'm tellin' ye, open this fuckin' door or yer deid.*' So Ah go over to the door and shout through it, '*You've got the wrong door, Craig, the wrong door, OK?*'

"But he pays no attention, doesn't understand. Next thing, it's, '*Ah hear ye, ya dirty bitch, Famie, yiv got a man in there, haven't ye? Aye, Ah can hear his voice. Well just you wait, Ah'll be back, sort the baith of yiz oot.*' An' Ah hear him walk away. I think, '*Well that's the end of that, bloody loony.*' So I go back to my paper.

"Two minutes later he's back. '*Aye, well, ye were warned, Euphemia, dinnae say ye weren't.*' An' the next thing, whit comes through ma door but the head of an axe! Now, thae doors are like plywood, silly wee things, an' the axe splinters the left hand panel tae bits. An' then he draws it back again, and cowps it on the other side, same thing, bits of wood flyin' in every direction. Now by this time, Ah'm shittin' masel'."

I can imagine.

"Ah don't know whit tae dae at first. Then he hits the door again wi' the axe, an' Ah realise Ah've got tae get out of there, he's mental, this Craig, he's going tae kill me if he gets through the door."

"Christ, Michael! So what did you do?" says Tommy.

"Ah pull the table over, you know, ma dining table, the Sheraton, lovely piece of furniture that, and get it under the skylight."

I remember that Elaine lives on the top floor of a four-storey house. And recognise that she must be feeling a little better if she can joke about Sheraton tables.

She mimes her gestures.

"Ah reach up and try tae push open the skylight—Ah'm thinkin', '*Bet it's stuck, painted shut.*' But no, luckily it opens easily enough. That'll be nice in the summer, won't it, a bit of fresh air?"

"Elaine!"

"Sorry. Anyway, Ah somehow manage—don't ask me how Ah did it, Audrey, Ah'll never know—Ah manage tae howk masel' up an' through it onto the roof. Just as I see his hand come through the splintered panel an' reach for the door handle."

She puts down her glass. "Any chance of another wee drink, Tommy."

"A *small* one," I say, as Tommy reaches for the bottle. "And you'd better give me one too, my nerves are shattered listening to this."

"Aye, it's quite a story," says Tommy, as he pours.

"I hope it's the *truth*, and not just a story. Not just a way of getting a few free drinks, you?"

"Audrey!"

"OK. Sorry, sorry."

"So there Ah am," she goes on. "Picture it, a Hollywood actress fleeing for her life, marooned on a roof. An' as Ah look back down into the room, Ah see that the door's burst open wide and he's in the room, wavin' this hatchet about. He must have seen ma feet disappearing through the skylight, for the next thing Ah know, he's on the table an' reachin' up tryin' tae grab ma ankle."

"Oh, Jesus!"

"Well, luckily, he's a great big guy, this Craig, an' the table won't take his weight. As he stretches up to grab the skylight frame, it collapses under him—an' Ah loved that table so Ah did, it was a family heirloom—and he crashes onto the floor. So, what can Ah do? Ah take tae ma heels."

"Over the *roof*?" says Tommy, as incredulous as I.

"Aye," says Elaine, sipping. "over the roof—over the *roofs*. Ah have tae jump from one building to another at one point, fifty feet above Sauchiehall Street. Ah'm desperately lookin' for another window, one wi' a light on. So Ah can get back down an' out intae the street."

"And—did you find one?" I realise how stupid this is as soon as I've said it. "Well, you must have, I suppose—otherwise you wouldn't be here."

There is more than a hint of sarcasm in Elaine's tone. "No, Audrey, Ah wouldn't be here, Ah'd be deid, wouldn't I?"

She relaxes back into her chair. "Aye, Ah found one eventually, nice young couple wi' a baby. Ah managed to explain whit had happened, an' they let me get out that way. An' well—here Ah am."

We are all three silent for a moment.

"We'd better phone the police," I say eventually. "You can't go back there with that madman around."

"The polis is there already. Somebody else must have called them. Saw them pull up, two cars, just as I was leaving."

I frown. "So why didn't you stop and tell them? Explain what had happened?"

Elaine smiles disparagingly.

"No, no, not me. I stay away from the polis as much as possible. I've got a bit of a history there, as you know, Audrey. Best leave them to it. I'll go back tomorrow when everything has calmed down."

She settles herself. "And Ah was wondering—any chance you two can put me up, just for the night?"

Tommy says, "Sure we can. I'll make up the settee for you, OK?

Elaine smiles. "Aw, thanks, Tommy, you're a darling. Thanks, Audrey."

"No problem, Elaine."

As we fuss around getting her bed ready, she is plumping a pillow when she says, "You know, Audrey, while I was up there on the roof, in spite of the panic, funny things were goin' through my head. I suddenly started thinkin' about Anna. Anna Neagle, I mean. You remember when we met her, you and me?"

"Yes," I say, tucking in a sheet, "I remember. What about it?"

She puts down the pillow and smiles in reminiscence.

"Well, do you remember that wee pair of wings she had on her jacket, on the lapel? The one that was given to her by the Canadian Air Force?"

"Yes." I recall the little brooch Miss Neagle wore, and her pride in it.

"Well, don't you think they should award me one too? After my exploits on the rooftops of Glasgow? After all, I bet I was a lot higher up than Anna ever was!"

Only Elaine.

I laugh in appreciation of her wit. And naturally, she takes advantage of my temporary distraction.

"Any chance of another wee whisky, Tommy? Just tae help me get off to sleep?"

One Friday, around five o' clock, when Tommy and I return from a visit to his folks (where I am by now, it seems, accepted pretty much as a part of the family, though my exact position in it is unclear) we find the police waiting for us.

It's that damned bag! The one Tommy 'found' on the doorstep. The one, full of fags and booze, belonging to our American neighbour. The one I had asked Tommy to get rid of, the one we subsequently both forgot about completely.

It has been under our bed for over a month. What prompted our landlady to look there I have no idea. She doesn't usually put herself out much when she is doing the weekly bedding change. But this time she did. She saw the bag, recognised it, and called the police.

We claim that we simply found the bag and had no idea who it belonged to. But the landlady knows very well that not only Todd, owner of the bag, but she herself, had asked us more than once if we had seen a sign of it anywhere. And we had replied that we had not.

I am quite drunk—oh, not falling over drunk, but Tommy and I have shared a bottle or two with his brother during the course of the afternoon. So when we are charged with theft, I am at first inclined to smile. However, when we are hustled off to the local police station, thrown into separate cells, and told we will be there until Monday morning—the courts do not sit on Saturdays—my smile fades away.

That first night in my cell alone, I start to think. There's nothing much else to do. I sleep for an hour or two, and wake up with, not exactly a hangover, but a bit of a head. The cell is just as you might imagine it. Hard rubber mattress-shaped thing on the floor, for which I have been given a couple of blankets; and a smelly toilet in the corner; that's it. Oh, and a harsh blazing light that seems to be on permanently.

When I was last in a cell, it was with a crowd of others. We laughed and joked at the ridiculous thought of a troupe of the brightest stars in the Glasgow firmament having to spend a night in confinement.

I am not laughing now. I am no longer in control.

Why am I suddenly so weak, such a coward? I didn't think I was. I thought I was tough, experienced and able to deal with anything; independent, hard-headed, in charge of my own life; settled with my man forever and ever, amen. OK, for the moment in limbo, career-wise, but with everything moving in the right direction.

It is quite an eye-opener to realise that, underneath the bluster, I am not the capable, self-reliant adult I thought I was. I am the same scared and confused child I was ten years ago.

But why am I giving in to this? I am letting the side down, am I not? Wilma or Elaine, Connie or Shirley, my friends, my peers, would no doubt simply put up with this situation as a minor inconvenience. After all, I will be in court on Monday, get a fine of some kind—I can't imagine that this fairly petty offence will attract any heavier punishment—and will be at liberty once more.

So what's the problem? Tommy and I will laugh about it together.

But after I have mentally stepped back, weighed matters up and done my bit of thinking, I am nearer to tears than to laughter.

How on earth did I end up here? Me, George Logan, nineteen years old, intelligent, literate, clever. Successful at school, top pupil, or nearly. University student, more than talented musician, fluent French speaker. Son of a loyal and understanding family. Product of a solid (until I broke it) and loving home.

How did I end up alone in this horrible place? And not like the last time, for a non-crime, a pardonable bit of bad luck, but for the undeniable offence of theft?

And what a pathetic offence! Not a grandiose scheme of embezzlement or fraud, or a bank hold-up, where the rewards might have made it worth the risk. The kind of exploit that might, from some peoples' point of view, have made my behaviour comprehensible, even admirable; Tommy and me a latter-day Bonnie and Clyde.

But for a picayune, utterly stupid piece of silliness. The theft of a sailor's—what was the word again?—yes, his 'handbag'. It would be funny if it weren't so utterly foolish.

How did this happen to me?

I know how. Instead of easing myself carefully, one step at a time into the world which appeared to hold the answer to all of the questions that troubled me, I jumped in feet first, eyes closed, heedless, gave up everything—yes everything and everyone—worthwhile in my previous life.

And to do what? To be *myself*, as I saw it. More realistically, to feed my utter self-absorption.

I castigate myself remorselessly for a while. I even shed an indulgent tear or two.

After a while I actually come to quite enjoy relishing my bitter self-reproach and recrimination.

Then I fall asleep.

When I wake up, I have no idea what time it is; they have taken my watch. But I can see through the barred window of my cell that it is now daylight. It's maybe eight o' clock.

I think back on the previous night. I conclude that the darkest hour was before the dawn, as it is said to be.

I consider my earlier wallow in guilt, try to think of it dispassionately. OK, there was a certain amount of truth in my reflections. More than a little, if I am to be honest. Yes, I have done some things that were completely stupid, and hurt people who had nothing but my best interests at heart.

But I am rallying, it appears. It isn't all negative, I tell myself. I have found a place in the world, I know who and what I am. I have made some of the best friends anyone ever could. And I have met someone special, someone decent, kind and considerate. I nearly said 'someone honest', though that might sit strangely alongside our current situation. But he *is* honest, in the larger sense. He is someone who loves me and cares about me profoundly. That's not nothing. And if someone feels like that about me, I can't be all that bad.

So I balance the books in my mind. I need to change, that is certain. I need to find the point of intersection between the two worlds. Oh, I've tried to before, then allowed myself to be carried away by what I saw as the primary and overriding importance of my own desires and wishes. But surely, surely a balance can be struck, surely that can't be impossible?

The important thing for now is to put this present hiccup behind us, then take another look at our life together, his and mine.

So I come to a kind of truce with myself. And decide that I will just sit it out, this temporary incarceration, just endure it.

But I wish I had a book. A good long book would make this situation just about tolerable.

Some time later, I hear someone at the door of my cell; whoever it is, he wants to know what I would like for breakfast. It seems I can just about have anything in the fried or boiled line. I ask for a bacon and egg sandwich and a cup of tea.

After half an hour he brings it to me. He is another policeman, not one of the two who arrested us, I haven't seen him before. His manner is pleasant and agreeable enough. It seems he wants to chat.

And I come to understand that our situation is far worse than I had thought.

"So—you're nineteen, George, is that right?"

"Yes," I say.

"And the other guy, your pal, Molony—he's what?—twenty-seven?"

"He's twenty-eight, actually," I say, munching and slurping, suspecting nothing.

"I see."

He scratches his head. He is maybe in his forties, fair, red-faced, a bit overweight, sing-song accent; a Highlander, perhaps from Aberdeen or Inverness.

"So—what is your relationship, you two."

It's the word 'relationship' that does it. I know what he is after.

For his own interest, private curiosity? No. There is something afoot here. He is just too nice, too friendly. He is, I sense, on a scouting mission.

"What do you mean?" I say.

He smiles and shrugs.

"Just wondered—with the age difference an' that. Just pals, are you?"
I should say nothing. Or 'no comment', perhaps.
"Yes, that's right," I say.
He shifts his weight and leans back against the open door of the cell.
"And you share a room, I believe?"
This time I *do* say nothing.
"And a bed as well, I'm told?"
I simply look at him.
"OK," he says, "Just wondering."
He grins, straightens up and makes to leave me.
"Here, eat up your breakfast before it gets cold."
He clangs the cell door closed, and I hear the grating of the key in the lock.

This is going to lead to trouble. I know perfectly well that we are criminals according to the law of the day, Tommy and me. Not for the silly theft, but for our very beings, our very natures. Or more accurately, for indulging them.

In all the time I have been around the scene, two and a half years now, I have never known of any male couple being arrested or charged for their private behaviour. I know one or two who have been nabbed for cavorting in semi-public places; toilets, parks, woodlands, car parks. They are apparently guilty of the crime of Gross Indecency, and it seems it is more the public nature of their behaviour rather than the acts themselves which is the issue.

But I recall my long-ago fling with the unfortunate Andy, and his story. Yes, that had happened well before I met him, in the nineteen-fifties, but nonetheless, I remember the outcome, and the dreadful effect it had on him. What if something like that were to happen to us?

We were told, when we were charged, that we had the right to make a telephone call, perhaps to arrange bail. Full of wine and bravado, I had declined the invitation. But now I have to take it up.

I summon the jailer by the simple expedient of yelling my head off. It is about ten minutes before someone arrives. It is not the policeman I spoke to earlier—perhaps that one is by now quoting my responses to his questions to a fascinated audience armed with blank notebooks and sharp pencils.

I explain my request, and this turnkey, small and insignificant-looking, not much older than me, takes me into the front office of the station. There is no-one else there but a desk sergeant dozing behind his counter.

I consider that I could probably make a break for it if I chose, but what would that achieve?

My escort shakes the sergeant's arm gently, and explains to him that I want to make my phone call. The latter yawns, gets to his feet and passes me a telephone, then settles back down in his chair with a sigh and a newspaper.

Angie, it will have to be her. Hers is one of the few numbers I have in my head; her work, not her home. Like all of us, Angie has always kept her family life separated from her private life. Except where Brian was concerned. Unwisely, as that turned out.

I dial, and ask to speak to Gordon Curran.

"Sorry, he's not in today, it's his Saturday off—can I give him a message? He'll be in on Monday."

Damn!

"No thanks, it's OK."

I put the phone down.

"Sorry," I say to the sergeant, "my friend's not there. Can I try someone else?"

He sighs. "Aye, OK, go on. As long as it's no' Australia yer callin'."

I dial Caldwell's. When the phone is answered, I ask for the record department.

I recognise the Olszyinski woman's voice.

"May I please speak to Rosemary," I say, putting on a bit of a cut-glass Angie accent, which causes the sergeant to look up from his *Tit-Bits* in slight surprise,

"Oh, I'm sorry," comes the voice. "Rosemary doesn't work here any longer—she left about a month ago. Can I help you, by any chance?"

I put the phone down without answering.

"One more, *please*."

"OK, but this is the last. You'll get me shot. Last one, OK?"

"OK."

With the heaviest of hearts I dial my old home number. Rutherglen one five five eight.

My wonderful father is there within half an hour, and we are granted bail. Not just me, Tommy too, after I have explained to my father that we were arrested together, that we *are* together. Our possessions are returned to us, and Tommy and I head thankfully down the station steps, while my father deals with the necessary paperwork.

The first thing Tommy says is, "Christ, Ah'm sorry, George. This is my fault, all this. You told me not to keep the damned bag, not to take it in the first place. Why did Ah no' listen?"

I take his arm and squeeze it, after checking we are not under observation.

"Forget it, that doesn't matter. The important thing is how we deal with it. What do we do now?"

"You better go home, George, wi' your Dad. I'll get off tae Maryhill. There's no way we can go back to Buccleuch Street today. The American lads'll be there, and Ah don't want to get into a fight, and end up on an assault charge on top of the one we've already got."

"But what about all our stuff? Our clothes, records, your guitar, all that?"

He lights up a cigarette and passes one to me.

"Don't worry. Ah've got a couple of mates with a van, me and Charlie can get hold of them, go round there maybe tomorrow and get all our gear. It's not as if there's that much. The guy'll no' start anything if I arrive mob-handed. Give me the keys, I'll need both sets. Have tae give them back."

I pass them to him, and look at my watch. It's eleven o' clock.

We wait. It's some little time before my father comes out of the door of the station. He is looking calm, but I can sense his concern underneath the casual attitude.

"Right, you two. A wee drink might not go amiss, what do you think?"

I am more than a little surprised. I had expected to be hustled away at the earliest opportunity.

"Yes, Dad, that would be great."

Tommy shakes my father's hand. "Thanks, Mr Logan."

He turns to me. "George, I'll call you at home tomorrow, Sunday, and let you know how things are going. I'll get off now."

I'm just about to say 'OK' but my father interrupts me.

"No, no, you come along too, Tommy. Come and have a drink."

Tommy acquiesces a little reluctantly.

"Good," says my father as we get into his car. "I need to speak to you both."

"It's like this. The head man in there had a word with me about this situation."

He lights up a cigarette. We are sitting in a little bar in Partick, not far from where my granny Rae lives.

"This is a bit difficult."

I know what's coming.

"You mean about Tommy and me living together. And..." I too am finding the conversation tricky. "... well—the *way* we live together. Our circumstances. As a couple."

"Yes. He explained to me that they have instructions from higher up not to proceed against people in your position, people in private, even though technically..."

I interrupt, trying to spare him as much embarrassment as I can. "Technically we are breaking the law."

He looks a little relieved. "Yes, exactly."

He is no more relieved than am I.

"So that's OK then?"

Tommy says nothing.

My father sighs. "No, it's not. Not in this case."

"Why?"

"You're not an adult. You're under twenty-one."

He holds up his hand to stop me interrupting. "No, hang on a minute, George, let me finish."

He puts out his cigarette.

"So, even though, legally, you are *both* breaking the law, because of your age it would be seen that Tommy here, as an adult, was the instigator, and you an innocent party."

I actually laugh. "Innocent? Me, the victim of a wicked seducer? Come on, Dad, you know me a bit better than that!"

He smiles a little. "Oh yes, I do."

He stops and looks at me. "Or I thought I did. I'm not sure I do know you, these days."

Tommy turns away.

"Maybe I should go?" he says. I sense his embarrassment

"No, stay," I say.

My father pauses again. "If I ever really knew you at all."

This is edging into dangerous territory. It's true that he was absent a lot during my growing up. Due to his work commitments, in part, but also due to his reluctance to totally abandon his independent bachelor life style. He only became a settled husband and father quite recently, after a battle with cancer and major surgery.

I decide to close off that avenue of discussion, to skate over that crack in the ice.

"Anyway—I understand. So—what do you suggest, Dad? What else did he say?"

"Another drink, anyone?" says Tommy, who, despite his slight embarrassment at this public airing of family linen, has been listening intently.

My father looks up. "Yes, thank you, Tommy. I'll have a Scotch and water—not too much water."

Tommy goes off to the bar. My father looks after him.

"Nice man. A decent man, I think. I'm glad to have met him."

"Yes, he is, Dad. All of that and more."

"Good. That makes it easier."

"So—go on," I say.

H hesitates again. "Yes. To get back to what we were talking about... The police have had to make a report on the situation. Oh, nothing official at the moment. But—you won't like this, George..."

"What?"

His tone is firm, "He says it's important that you come back home now. To live. For the moment."

He once again prevents me from interrupting. "Just for a while, till things calm down. Once you're twenty-one..."

Twenty-one?

"But that's more than a year away—I can't..."

I stop, I don't know what to say.

"No, I understand. But if you don't... Well, think about it, it's Tommy who will pay the price if anything comes of this, not you. If they ever *do* decide to follow it up any further, that is."

Tommy arrives back with our drinks and sits down.

"OK," I say. "I understand. I'll deal with it."

I stand up and move away. I need to think. I leave the two of them together.

God, this is positively operatic. To save the man I love, I am supposed to give him up. It makes no sense to me that I am considered to be a child, at nineteen, almost twenty. OK, I can't vote, but if I were a girl, Tommy and I could be married. I wouldn't even need my parents' permission. It's crazy.

But no, it's not. It's 'special circumstances'; where the law has the right to decide where adulthood starts and childhood stops. Quite arbitrarily.

Well, I won't accept this, I simply won't. I will find some way round it.

I look back over at the table I have just left. They are chatting away, if not quite like friends, at least comfortably and amicably.

That's something, I suppose.

I agree to move back home.

It's not too bad at first. My mother is delighted, though less than enthralled by the police involvement. But I get the impression that she thinks I have learned my lesson. You would think she would realise by now that I am a bit of a slow learner in some areas.

I don't know if my father has discussed Tommy with her—I suppose he must have. But she never mentions him. My sister Jennifer, on the other hand, refers to him regularly, my father now and then. It's only my mother who appears to be unaware of his existence.

It is she who accompanies me up to the University offices to see if anything can be salvaged from my educational situation. Yet again, the Powers That Be are quite astonishingly sympathetic and helpful. It is arranged that I will re-start in September, take my final year, and hopefully get my degree in 1965, a year later than originally planned.

I can't help but feel that I am fundamentally unworthy of such incredible consideration. But my parents are happy, and it is certainly the least I can do for them.

As far as our offence goes, Tommy and I each receive a fine, ten pounds in my case, fifteen in his. We both ask for time to pay, as he has advised me to do, and are told we can pay off our debt to society at a pound a week.

Tommy arranges the collection of our personal bits and pieces from our erstwhile love nest, and my share is delivered to my home. It's not much; my record-player, my precious records, and a few clothes—that's it.

I have made it quite clear to all and sundry that, although we will not be living together for the time being, I intend to keep seeing Tommy regularly. We meet up on Fridays and spent the night together at the same Bed and Breakfast we visited once before—the funny, tiny old red-headed lady with something of the air of a former tart about her welcomes us warmly.

We can afford this extravagance because I have found myself in employment. In fact I applied for the position without the least expectation of success. But no doubt my glowing and quite unmerited reference from Caldwell's helped.

I am working for a finance company. My job is to chase up those whose payments are late, make telephone calls, write to them if necessary. It's pretty boring, but it's interesting hearing the ingenious excuses the customers come up with to explain their difficulties, if nothing else.

It's a large office in the centre of Glasgow, and the rest of the staff are mostly girls, with whom I get along well. We spend a fair amount of the day laughing together, listening to the radio provided, and joining in the latest song of the Beatles when the supervisor is absent, as she often is. It's easy, uncomplicated work. The wages are nothing special, but they do enable Tommy and I to have some private time together.

On Saturdays, we sometimes manage to find a party of one sort or another to attend. It's not unusual for someone to offer to put us up. So on Saturdays we occasionally contrive another night of togetherness. If this doesn't happen, we have to make our way to George Square and get one of the all-night buses home. He to his and me to mine.

That is hellish torture. We seem to have stepped back in time to the period before I left home, when everything was difficult, when the best we could hope for was the occasional night spent together at Shirley's place. I have no fear, at least, that I will lose him, which is something. I know we are meant to be together, him and me.

But it's all just so damned trying and stressful. I want to be with him all the time, to wake up with him every morning, to sleep with him every night.

I have gradually come to believe that the worries and fears that beset me after my questioning by the police, the vague menaces and hints they delivered to my father concerning the dangers of our situation, may well be no more than groundless, idle threats.

After all, what are they going to do?—follow us everywhere we go to be sure we are not actually spending time together alone? And if it came to it, there is no direct evidence that our friendship, however unusual it may appear, is anything but an innocent one. We have never written letters to one another, and though everyone I know assumes that Tommy and I have a physical relationship, no-one can actually say they have seen evidence of it.

'*It was all bluff,*' I think to myself. '*Just a bluff, nothing else.*'

I convince myself that, as long as we avoid coming to the attention of the authorities, nothing at all is going to happen to us.

And so I begin to consider how this intolerable situation might be rectified.

Once in a while, I happen to encounter Barry Nelson, and he continues to be obliging with his flat—so that is another place where Tommy and I can be together now and then, however temporarily. I ask Barry if there is any chance he might consider letting the flat to me, or to us, on a permanent basis. Not to live in, it is too far from the town centre to be convenient; but to be able to use as a bolt-hole when it suits us. Barry, however explains that, although he is still involved with his current well-to-do *amour*, and spends most of his time with him, he likes to keep his flat on 'just in case'.

"Sorry and all that, but you never know how long these things will last, do you? Ah could find myself out on the street one of these days, last year's model. He might meet someone else. And Ah'm gettin' on in years."

He laughs. "Not as young as I was. Got to think of the future."

Barry's not more than twenty-four or twenty-five. I wish I was as sensible as he obviously is.

"But you're welcome to use the place whenever you like, as long as you see me first."

But it's laying hands on him at the right time that's the difficult bit.

I am having some lunch in the *Yellow Bird* cafeteria in Sauchiehall Street with a couple of the girls from work. As we get up to pay our bills, I notice a familiar face at a nearby table.

"Just going to say a quick 'hello' to a couple of people I know—you carry on, girls, I'll be along in a few minutes," I say to my colleagues.

After they leave, I head over to the table where Vikki, Charlie's girlfriend—no, Charlie's *wife*, I remember—is sitting with a friend.

"Vikki!—nice to see you, how have you been?"

She looks up from her lunch.

"Oh, George, hi, how are you—here, come and join us. You remember Claire, don't you?"

Claire? Yes, I recognise her—she's Vikki's friend, fellow prostitute and matron of honour at the wedding for which Tommy and I were the witnesses.

"Yes, yes, how are you, Claire?"

Claire is much older than Vikki, she is perhaps forty or even more. Well preserved, on the whole, but her treads are definitely a bit worn by comparison with pretty and youthful Vikki.

"Alright, George. Yourself?"

"OK, thanks."

Vikki moves along one place to let me join them.

"Thanks," I say, sitting down. "I've got ten minutes."

I turn to Vikki. "And Charlie? And Derek? How are they?"

Vikki raises her eyebrows. "Haven't you heard?—they left."

"Left? Left *you*, do you mean?"

"No—they left Glasgow. Couple of army guys were asking round about them, talking to the girls on the game. They must have heard something somewhere."

She pushes her plate to one side and pulls over a bowl and a spoon. "You know the story, I suppose? Theirs, I mean?"

"Yes, most of it."

"So they packed a case and moved on. Had to, God knows what would happen to Charlie if they got caught. They'd put him away for life, the age difference. Derek being underage an' all."

Where have I heard this before?

"And the truth is, even though Derek was only young, he was much more grown up than Charlie, in a way. It was him that made all the decisions, he was the one in charge."

Oh yes. The story is starting to ring a very familiar bell.

"Felt sorry for Charlie, really." She takes a spoonful of her ice-cream. "Helluva way to live, that, always looking over your shoulder. Wish I could figure out what the big attraction was—not a bad-looking boy, Derek, but no personality, never got anything to say for himself."

I don't think it quite appropriate to mention to ladies, however tarnished, that Derek's attractions do not lie in the field of conversation, but in rather lower regions.

We chat away some more, and it's not long before I mention my own current problems, and explain the difficult position Tommy and I find ourselves in.

"If we could just find somewhere we could be together now and then, it would help."

Claire looks up.

"Ah've got a wee flat Ah want tae sell—room and kitchen, up the Cross, George's Cross. Ah used tae use it for business, but Ah'm off in a week or two, givin' it up, the game."

She smiles. "Getting' too old."

"Oh?"

"Aye," she goes on. "Bought a wee hoose doon in Ayr, on the coast. Had a bit a' money put by."

She looks at her friend. "Tryin' tae persuade Vikki here tae move in wi' me, get a proper job, pack all this in. Easy find a wee job down there in the summer, she would, waitress or somethin'. Whit dae ye say, Vikki?"

"I'll think about it, Claire. Might not be a bad idea. Had about enough of the game anyway, especially since Charlie went on the missing list."

She pushes her ice-cream away only half-eaten.

"You have to be careful, there's some bad bastards about."

"Well, you're welcome, hen, any time. Gie it some thought, eh?" Claire stands up. "Anybody fancy a coffee?"

I should be getting back to work. But I need to ask Claire about this flat she is giving up. Maybe we can rent it from her?

It turns out that, no, she wants to sell it.

"Not interested in renting it out, George. Too many problems with a tenant. Ah want tae put this all behind me, forget all about Glasgow."

She puts a far-too-milky coffee in front of me and sits down.

"But ye can buy it if ye want. Sixty pounds, since you're a friend. Take ye up there tae have a look at it some time if ye like."

I have just about a hundred left over from my criminal past. I won't leave home and move in, I have promised my parents that I will change my ways, and that's a promise I intend to keep. But it means Tommy and I will always have a place to be together in private whenever we want, whenever the notion takes us. He can decorate and paint it, after all, he's a professional. Then when things have moved on, when I finish university and reach the age of twenty-one, I can sell it on, and we can find something better. It seems perfect.

But it is a disaster.

Not the place itself, which would be ideal, although it is small. We have moved a few bits and pieces into the flat. I have used the little money I had left over to buy a bed, a cooker, a small fridge and a few other items, trying to make the place a little homely. Tommy plans to start on the decorating soon, when he has some free time, at the weekends probably.

We arrive to spend our first night together in our new home.

The front door is hanging off its hinges, the lock broken. Nearly everything has been taken, even the bed. What hasn't been stolen has been smashed. Including the toilet.

I just sink to the floor and burst into tears. I can't believe it.

"Why is everything going wrong for us?"

Tommy crouches down and puts his arms around me.

"That's it. We need to get out of here."

"Yes," I say. "we do. I never want to see this place again."

He nuzzles my head with his chin.

"I didn't mean that. Not out of the flat. I meant out of here. Out of Glasgow. Start again somewhere else."

I look up.

"What? Leave Glasgow?"

To me this is unimaginable. "Where? Where could we go?"

"London," he says. "We'll go to London, start a new life there, put all this behind us."

He helps me to my feet.

"London?" I say.

"Aye."

He looks around at the shambles of the flat.

"Fuck this town, and all the rotten bastards that live in it."

12. The Carnival is Over

> High above, the dawn is waking
> And my tears are falling rain
> For the carnival is over
> We may never meet again
> *Tne New Seekers, 1965*

April 1964

"Ah'm off down tae London masel' the morra'. Nae problem, angel, just you get the train down whenever you like. Send me a wee post card tae let me know when yer arrivin'. Or phone, Ah'll give ye Harry's number. Ah'll come an' meet ye off the train at Euston. Or better, you and Tommy can get the tube from there tae Notting Hill Gate, only takes about half an hour, an' Ah'll meet ye in the *Champions*. That's a gay pub just along the road from the tube station."

It is Judy Garland who is giving me the instructions. She and I are not particularly close friends, though we have known each other for ages. She seems to have taken a notion to me, however, since I recently agreed to accompany her on a visit to the clap clinic after one of her late night adventures produced an uncomfortable and tingling result.

Judy has a regular boyfriend called Harry, who lives in London. I gather that Judy is a kind of on-again, off-again lover of this Harry, and that he has a flat in Notting Hill, an area of London I only know of by reputation from the race riots that took place there in 1958 or thereabouts.

As I have a huge interest in literature dealing with true crime, killings especially, the gorier and weirder the better, I also know that Notting Hill was the home territory and hunting ground of John Christie, renowned mass murderer of the '50s, later to be immortalised in the film *10 Rillington Place*.

And, according to the papers, this same suburb is playing host currently to what appears to be another series of murders—three ladies of the night have been found dead so far. Most recently the body of an Irene Lockwood was discovered on the eighth of this month.

'*Nice place*,' I think to myself.

"Oh, it's great, Notting Hill," enthuses Judy, unaware of my thoughts. "Full of students, artistic types, hippies—gays and straights, black and white, very mixed, everybody gets on. And two gay bars. Then just down the road is Earl's Court, there's a couple more bars there, the *Bolton's* and the *Coleherne*. Chelsea just a wee bit further on, King's

Road, all the boutiques and trendy types, good restaurants, couple of clubs there too, *The Place* and *The Gigolo*... An' then there's the West End, the *White Bear*, good place for a young girl tae make a few bob, lots of old punters around..."

Back and forth, back and forth, we have discussed it, Tommy and I. He has no qualms whatsoever. With his professional skills he is sure he will be able to find work easily.

"You too, you'll find a job—maybe in a record shop, just to start with? After all, you've got the experience, haven't you?"

"Yes," I say, warming to the idea, "I have. And I've got the reference too."

"Good, aye, of course you have. See? It'll be fine. And then if you want to, once we get settled, there's nothing to stop you going back to University down south—maybe take the music degree you really wanted, part-time job at the same time? Piece of cake for you, brain-box, eh?"

Gradually it all comes to seem possible, even desirable.

But there is just one massive obstacle in my way. My parents and I have finally, it seems, come to an accommodation. While it would not be true to say that they are ecstatically happy about my current situation, the knowledge that I am planning to finish my degree, given time, has made them more ready to accept the other side of things; and the fact that my father and my sister have met Tommy and like him, means that I am allowed reasonable freedom. Up to a point.

But that we are unable to be together permanently is a constant torment. We shared a home for nearly four months, our bond was growing strong and solid. To have it suddenly ripped apart like this is unendurable. It is going to be more than a year before we are able to take up our relationship properly again.

No. I will not wait that long.

I will pass over the difficult time that ensued. It is still painful to me to this day, particularly in the light of subsequent events. Had I known that within four years both my parents would be dead, would I have acted differently? I don't know.

And that's a question I would rather not contemplate too closely. Though I am certain that, had they lived long enough, they would both have derived pleasure and satisfaction from the professional success that was to ultimately be mine, I am sure that the future they imagined for me at the time of my departure was not a glowing one.

I truly believe that regrets for past actions are, of themselves, useless and serve no practical purpose. The most one can hope for is to learn from previous mistakes, and behave differently in the future.

I wish I could say, hand on heart, that that is what I have done. But I am not sure I managed to achieve even that much.

Tommy and I catch the night train to London. It leaves Glasgow around ten in the evening and will arrive at Euston station early in the morning. We are far too short of money to afford sleeper accommodation—indeed we have about twenty pounds between us after paying for our tickets.

Though we have told all our friends that we are leaving, I have specifically asked that no-one come to see us off. We stored our luggage early in the evening, and spent a couple of hours sharing a farewell drink or two with our nearest and dearest.

So we carry our cases into the third class accommodation and manage to find an almost empty compartment. We chat quietly for a while as the train pulls out; then, minutes later, he is asleep leaning against his suitcase. How I envy him his ready ability to nod off anywhere and everywhere without the slightest difficulty.

I look at him.

He shaved his beard off completely a week earlier; a new start, a new image. He looks more Italian or Spanish than ever, and, asleep, young and innocent. I feel a great surge of love for him. This is the person on whom I will be entirely dependent in the future. There is no-one else now. If things go awry for us, we will have to sort it out ourselves, he and I. And I have no doubts that we will. He will never let me down, of that I am sure.

He frowns slightly in his sleep. But his face is smooth, virtually unlined, he's suddenly a boy; he could be twenty or twenty-one.

As for me, I feel incredibly ancient, withered, old in sin and ravaged by experience.

Though I am exhausted, I hardly sleep at all throughout the trip. Instead, I think back over the journey that led me to this place.

Connie and Alec. Wilma, Nicky, Shirley. Elaine, Dorothy and Angie. These are my closest friends.

Can it really be just over two years since this all started? Is it possible that so many adventures, so many triumphs and so much laughter (and the occasional tear) were all crowded into such a brief span of time?

I smile as I remember the idiotic telephone disinfection incident. How ridiculous (and how long ago) that now seems. And what incredible nerve (or stupidity) led me to concoct such a mad scheme.

My first encounter with queens *en masse*, when I paid a visit to the cinema, hidden still behind my mask. My fascination with their interaction, and their outrageous behaviour. Baffling and intimidating, but alluring and wonderful.

My first timid steps on the road to stardom, my encounter with Nicky and the others, and my desperate passion for him. As unrequited now as it was then.

My visit to the theatre *en travesti* with Dorothy, and the disaster that nearly led to; and our subsequent surprising success performing as a duo.

My unique sister Angie, and the many escapades we shared; our scary visit to *Betty's Bar*, her tales of her trip to London, her disastrous affair with the unreliable Mr Al Fraser, her equally doomed *liaison* with Brian, and a hundred more incidents. Poor Angie, playing Snakes and Ladders with life; ever struggling just so far up the ladder, finding a precarious footing and steadying herself for another assault on the heights; then slipping and sliding down the sneaky snake that was lying in wait for her.

My truest friend and the finest person of the many I have come to know—Elaine Stewart, the inimitable, always down, but never out.

My own adventures in the Realms of Venus—tortured Andy, nice Canadian Bobby, and the Three Stooges, George, Brian and Billy.

And finally the man sitting opposite me, head back, mouth slightly agape.

Yes, it's been quite a journey, one way and another.

And I mustn't forget the most important player of all in this, the drama of my life so far. The city of Glasgow, the place where I feel at home, where I always have somewhere to go and someone to talk to; which began my life in many ways, and ended it in some others.

Will I ever come back?

Yes, I will.

But not for a while.

Because it is nineteen sixty-four, and the sixties, it appears, are swinging. And if they are swinging anywhere, they are swinging in London.

The story continues in

**ALL ABOUT AUDREY
BOOK 3**

'TURN AGAIN, AUDREY'

ISBN: 9798690623654

Soon available on Amazon

Printed in Great Britain
by Amazon